Contents

∞∞∞∞∞∞∞∞∞∞∞∞

Manufactured in the United States of America

4th Printing 1995

How To Start
Acting In Film And Television
Wherever You Are
In America

ISBN 0-9615288-4-2
Library of Congress Cataloging in Publication
Number 93-070044

OTHER ACTING WORLD BOOKS PUBLICATIONS

that may be odered from the publisher if not available at your bookstores

For All Actors

"THE FILM ACTOR'S COMPLETE CAREER GUIDE", by **Lawrence Parke**, who has been called "Hollywood's Foremost Career Maker" by Editor Hank Spalding, *Hollywood Talent News;* Coach and Teacher of many of today's top stars; former Film and Television Casting Director and respected Hollywood Talent Agency Head; noted author of several best-selling acting career guidance books. Details all the steps actors should take from the point of starting out in Hollywood all the way up to maintaining top stardom. What to do, how and when to do it for best results. Page after page of little-known, behind-closed-doors industry secrets that many actors never learn. ISBN 0-9615288-9-3. 304 p. $24.95 Pbk. To order direct, add $3. for shipping and handling.

"SINCE STANISLAVSKI AND VAKHTANGOV: The Method As A System For Today's Actor", by **Lawrence Parke**, Coach and Teacher of many of today's top stars. This book supplies the important "missing links" codified by Eugene Vakhtangov, Stanislavski's most important pupil and later his personal coach on Stanislavski's own roles, without which many thousands of actors have felt the Stanislavski System to be incomplete . . . and, *more important,* includes this noted teacher's adaptation of the combined Stanislavski/Vakhtangov Method, to better serve the decades later needs of today's actor for the unique demands of film and television acting as well as theatre. ISBN 0-9615288-8-5. 288 p. $12.95 Pbk. To order direct, add $2. for shipping and handling.

For The Actor Already in Hollywood or Preparing to Relocate There in the Near Future:

THE "SEMINARS TO GO" SERIES . . . consisting of six Acting Career Guidance Books of the following titles: **How To Get, Work With and Keep The Best Agent For You; Increasing Your Success Ratio in Interviews and Readings For Roles; The Film Job, Step By Step---Before, During, After; The Film Actor's Career Building Stepladder; Self Promotion, Self Publicizing, Self Advertising For The Actor** and **Audition Tapes, Audition Scenes And Showcasing**. $40. for the complete series if ordered direct from the publisher, plus $3. for postage and handling . . . or single titles may be ordered by direct mail from the publisher @ $10. plus $1. for postage and handling; two books may be ordered for $18. plus $1. for postage and handling; three for $25. plus $1.50 for postage and handling; four for $30. plus $2. for postage and handling; five for $35. plus $2.50 for postage and handling. **Note**: While much of the information in these books---that applies for actors not yet in Hollywood---is included in the book now in the reader's hand, each is far more thorough as to details involved. These books are more for the actor already in Hollywood.

'THE AGENCIES---What The Actor Needs To Know" . . . Hollywood's best-selling Update publication about all Hollywood agencies. Issued bimonthly, with interim month Updates. Listings of all Hollywood and Southern California talent agencies franchised by the Screen Actors Guild; agency staff names; client categories represented; appraisals regarding importance, longevity and quality of representation. Available in Hollywood and Greater Los Angeles Area bookstores, $10. Or may be ordered direct from the publisher for $10. plus $1. to share postage and handling costs. Full year subscriptions (6 bimonthly issues plus 6 interim month Updates) cost $40.

"THE HOLLYWOOD ACTING COACHES AND TEACHERS DIRECTORY" . . . issued quarterly, in Spring, Summer, Fall and Winter editions. Listings of most individuals and facilities offering Acting Study Programs; details of their programs and study approaches where available; backgrounds of the teachers and coaches; advice about Finding The Right Place To Study Acting; etc. Available in West Coast bookstores, $12.50, or may be ordered from the publisher for $12.50 plus $1. to share postage and handling costs.

Acknowledgements

So many industry people have contributed to this book's contents that it would be impossible to acknowledge all of them by name. But a few must be mentioned: In 1950 it was the noted playwright Ben Hecht who told the author (then a strictly "New York theatre" actor) that actors', writers' and directors' futures lay in _film and television_. In 1955 it was Chico Marx, during our summer theatre tour of "_The Fifth Season_", who said what Hollywood meant to him was "More work than anywhere else. More money than anywhere else." That same Fall, it was Sir Laurence Olivier who in a brief conversation confided that theatre was still his "happy holiday" but film was more and more his career. The next year, during our location filming of "_The Harbourmaster_" television series, it was Barry Sullivan who told me "I live in Hollywood so I can work all the time and live the way I want to . . I'd come east if I could _afford_ to do a play." And that Fall, when that series finished its Rockport, Mass., location filming, it was the late producer Jon Epstein and studio head Maurice Unger who persuaded me to leave New York and come to Hollywood, beginning some of the most productive and most exciting years of my life.

A few people and organizations do need to be thanked: Joan Meyer and Craig Uchida of the Agency Department of the Screen Actors Guild; the Film Commission Directors of all U.S. states; the Casting Society of America; Breakdown Services, Ltd.; and the Mayors' offices of major cities and their Economic Development Offices for helping with agency and casting listings when their State Film Commissions didn't have complete information.

And this unbelievably timetaking book couldn't have been written if it weren't for the patience and understanding of my loving wife, Virginia, when dinners got cold while I finished "one more page" and when pleasure trips had to be cancelled for expected telephone calls and FAXes.

About The Author

Lawrence Parke is one of the most uniquely qualified Hollywood film industry leaders for the laying out in this book's clear and concise terms, for new actors determined to pursue film and television acting careers, all the complicated do's and don'ts, career-starting musts, information about---and the ideal manners of the actor's relating with---people in early and later job-giving positions, and the wealth of behind-closed-doors and all the other information that actors who are puzzled as to how to take their first steps need and that Mr. Parke's years of experience in most aspects of the entertainment industry make it possible for him to pass on in this book.

Parke himself has appeared in over 200 film and television roles and three television series---as Mr. Jenkins in "Mama", Luke in "Harbourmaster" and Perkins the Mailman in "The Real McCoys"; has been a recognized and respected casting director of motion pictures, television series and their pilots, Movies of The Week and daytime dramas (soap operas); was a Screen Actors Guild and AFTRA talent agency head in Hollywood for several years; has been a recognized careermaker and unofficial personal manager for a number of today's leading actors during their early years; and for thirty years has been one of Hollywood's and other cities' leading acting coaches responsible for the training, career starts and later advances of a growing list of stars.

For twenty years he presented in Hollywood his *Professional Acting Career Seminars*, with guest panels of leading casting directors, agents, producers, managers, press agents, performing unions executives, etc., appearing before his audiences to provide actors with completely candid information that is impossible to obtain---at least in so full detail---anywhere else. He regularly presents weekend *Film Acting Career Seminars* and *Film And Television Acting Workshops* in other cities throughout the country.

While in reading this book it will be evident to the reader that Mr. Parke is extremely biased as to where actors must seek *meaningful and fulfilling* acting careers among today's entertainment mediums, it should be pointed out that he himself had many years of successful theatre experience as well---as a two time New York Theatre Awards winner, as director of New York and national touring theatre productions, as producer of his own summer theatre, as one of the organizers of New York's League of Off Broadway Theatres, as producer and director of the selected American entry at the French and German World Theatre Festivals in 1972, as founder and president of the League of Los Angeles Theatres, and as Executive Director of the 1975 Los Angeles World Theatre Festival. He simply advocates *film and television* acting careers as the primary avenues to *meaningful and enduring success* in the current entertainment world.

He authored the recently published 304 page book *"The Film Actor's Complete Career Guide"* which has become an immediate best-seller in actors' bookstores in Hollywood and New York. He is also currently the editor for Acting World Books of the bimonthly *"The Agencies---What The Actor Needs To Know"*, the quarterly *"The Hollywood Acting Coaches And Teachers Directory"* and the six-book *"Seminars To Go"* series of career guidance books for film actors, in addition to his celebrated book on acting techniques that fits the needs of both theatre and film actors, *"Since Stanislavski And Vakhtangov: The Method As A System For Today's Actors"*.

1

First Things First!

Is <u>Any Kind</u> Of Acting Career What You Really Want?

Before deciding whether you want a film and television acting career, you should really stop and consider the fact that *almost everyone else* has at some early moment entertained the thought that they could do just as well, perhaps better, what they've seen film and television stars do, and wondered if they shouldn't try for acting careers.

The acting performances they've watched on the big screen or on television looked <u>*so natural and so easy*</u>. There didn't appear to be any real talent involved...certainly no *"acting"* as the young observer understood the word to connote. It all looked so easy. And with tabloid newspapers' and magazines' reports of the multimillion dollar salaries being paid to those in top starring positions, why spend all those years of expensive study and hardship preparing for some other highly paying profession like doctor, lawyer or whatever when film and television acting creates so many millionaires *overnight*, brings so much public adulation and appears to require *no study or preparation*?

Those who took any steps at all toward finding out the logistics, laws of averages and developing profiles of film and television acting careers were soon discouraged as they learned that *a mere few* ever achieve the career positions that bring continuous employment, those wonderful salaries and all that ego-gratifying public acclaim; that many thousands of film and television actors---even thousands of those professionals who carry the acting unions' membership cards---must work at nine-to-five jobs ninety-nine percent of the time for survival; only rarely obtain acting roles; receive only minimal or slightly better salaries when they do work; and never receive even the slightest public recognition of their face or their name---the ego gratifications that in too many such cases were probably the main reasons they wanted to become film and television actors in the first place!

Most other professional careers, if prepared for with sufficient and dedicated study, offer at least a modicum of assurance of steady employment and implicit opportunities for upper mobility. Many professions even offer immediate openings for employment to college graduates who've specialized toward definite types of work. Abilities, degrees and internships are often rewarded with open doors ready to accept the more qualified newcomers. Not so, *any* kind of acting career!

Starting an acting career---even after study and developing of what talents the newcomer has---can be one of the loneliest, most self-doubting and most heartbreaking one man or one woman *business ventures* in the world. And that's exactly what it is---a <u>*busi-*</u>

1

ness venture, from the very first moments. And it often remains just that for what seems like an eternity before the actor lands even that first professional, paying role.

There's no "internship" or other "entry level position" offered the new actor that will pay even a penny of salary. About the only opportunities for young actors to "learn by doing" are in nearby community theatres and little theatres, but it's rare that those can pay even small salaries. And even if the actor manages to advance into leading roles in those venues each acting role must still be considered simply further study, experience and preparation. For most it will remain simply a *hobby* for as long as they involve with it. They may love it, may continue doing it, may be either fairly good actors or terrible "hams" without knowing it....but it's certainly not a profession.

Even those who later move to New York or some other large city to seek *stage* acting opportunities are usually doomed to years of futile seeking with little or no result, of still performing for little or no pay at all if a role is occasionally obtained, and along the way realizing that even to continue in *theatre acting as a hobby* there they must pay *theatre-oriented* acting teachers to study in their classes to be accepted and taken seriously by the local hierarchy of whatever theatre group they want to work with.

For those who decide to continue their formal education past high school and at least "minor" in Drama and Theatre Arts in colleges and universities there can be challenges to their talents in the universally requisite classics---certainly Shakespeare, probably Ibsen, etc., but what the serious actor must remember is that colleges and universities are generally worlds of academia, interested in educating but so often little connected with or concerned about acting as a livelihood-earning profession. The seriously intentioned actor will usually learn much theatre history, much about the playwrights of all times and probably the basics of stage design and stage lighting, and perhaps become a "college theatre star" as the favorite of the Head of the Department and be cast in many leading roles.

. But upon leaving the warm limelight of starring roles for the college or university Theatre Arts Department and---encouraged by successes on those college stages to think in terms of a *theatre* acting career---heading for New York, the mecca, the college stage star will find that the only venue open to him or her is the tiny, dingy Off Off Broadway theatre where, again, nobody in the cast is paid, few agents and casting people are likely to attend, current roles seldom lead to future rules, etc. Further, while involving with *theatre as a hobby*---yes, even in New York it's usually still that---living expenses of all kinds there are staggering!

And should some incredible strokes of luck bring the new theatre actor a Broadway role or two within just a few months or years of arriving in New York---which is almost beyond credibility---what that actor can look forward to over many years of remaining a *stage* actor is perhaps one role every five years or so, a barely living salary if even that, some long runs of spinning one's wheels doing the same roles seven or eight times each week, or perhaps Saturday night closings after just a few performances, with only unemployment and despair in the intervals between roles, while always being painfully aware that no one will ever know the actor's name or face. There have of course been some happy exceptions to this rule, but they are so few.

It should be obvious by this point that this author agrees with director John Huston, who long ago advised his daughter Angelica as she planned an acting career, *"Theatre is a hobby while you're waiting to be discovered."*

Those who aspire to professional acting careers and who opt to pursue *theatre* first, rather than film and television immediately, may be brought into film and television or simply decide to turn to those mediums in utter frustration at some later point, but so many will realize---after years of theatre, hoping it could lead to any kind of career---that they've been needlessly spinning their wheels, possibly developing theatre habits that must be shed for most work before film cameras, and wasting many precious years of their lives.

2

Those who finally turn to film and television may or may not become successful---but Hollywood (whether after New York or not) is the only place they *can*---may or may not work frequently---at least in film and television there's the possibility; may or may not become famous and wealthy--- but at least in film and television both of those possibilities can occur quickly for some; may or may not be one of the few who become top stars---but what the more observing actors eventually realize is that even after playing some important roles on Broadway for years there's no such thing as stardom or public recognition. In film and television just a few lucky breaks can create both!

In film and television you can be totally unknown in August and become a household name across America in September when a television series in which you have a starring role begins its network run. Or, also in *film and television only*, you can be a steadily working actor, earning increasingly large salaries and increasingly prominent billing by name, in increasingly large roles---even without any fabulous lucky breaks, constantly advancing from bit player to featured actor to co-starring, then perhaps starring, even guest starring, etc., on the strength of your talents and personality. Even in terms of available employment if nothing else, the comparison between the number of Broadway roles that are available each year and the number of roles available in Hollywood feature film and television is absolutely staggering!

But Your Talents Will Need Developing---Yes, For Film Too!

If you decide to aim for film and television from the start, you should be very selective as you start looking for the most productive place for learning how to act for film cameras.

If you're continuing your academic education---by all means including Liberal Arts, Communication and Media Arts of whatever kinds, Psychology and other personality studies, etc., simply recognize that you should look elsewhere for film acting coaching. Except for those few colleges and universities where a serious Film and Television Department exists in conjunction with some acting program, the focus is usually on developing *theatre* talents of all nature including *theatre acting*. Emphasis is usually placed upon *perfect speech and diction, voice projection from large prosceniums, classical grace of movement* and other items that are certainly of importance for actors aspiring to *stage* careers but potentially detrimental for actors wanting *film and television* careers. What actual acting *methodology* is taught in such academic institutions is too often simply textbook-based theory and practice under the tutelage of someone whose background doesn't include much if any acting experience in the professional mainstream. In almost none of the academic institutions---even those where Film and Television Programs of the mostly *technical* areas are offered---are there opportunities for student actors to work with experienced *film and television acting professionals*.

In some states' larger cities there are one or two acting workshops where the acting classes are personally conducted by experienced *film and television actors* who've simply relocated from Hollywood. If you can find one of those Hollywood-experienced actors whose résumé includes a goodly list of film and television work, that's where you should enrol to study. That Hollywood-experienced teacher, if sufficiently talented and techniqued that he or she has played all those roles in Hollywood film and television, knows what you'll need to learn---even if gifted with extraordinary talent still needing to learn about *acting for film cameras, behavior on film sets, auditioning for film and television roles, film set vocabulary, relating with talent agencies and casting people, etc.*

For serious preparation for a film and television acting career, you should be taught not only how to act but also the terms used on film sets and in film and television salary, role and billing matters, how to "hit your marks", "match" your actions in several different angles of the same sequences, the basic head, eyes, hands and body use that apply for on-camera acting, the "living presence" level of talking, how to keep film frames interesting without appearing to be conscious that you're doing it, etc.

3

It was also the legendary director John Huston, again advising his daughter Angelica, who said *"The things a film actor or actress needs to know would fill a book."* Those things are what this book is filled with.

Of Course Do Theatre Roles Too When You're Beginning If You Want To, But Be Careful!

There are always one or more community, civic or little theatre groups in most actors' home towns. Their quality varies, and therein lies the problem about which new actors just starting out should be warned.

Beware the director who keeps admonishing the cast to "Pick up your cues!" That's not only a misapprehension of how to breathe life into a theatrepiece; it's also a very bad habit for anyone to develop if they're planning a film and television career. Even in comedy, "picking up your cues" doesn't enhance comedy, in fact it overlooks that prime ingredient that is all comedy: "Takes" and reactions. These take a moment. Comedians know they're of first importance. Comedy, like farce, is most often "being done to". That's what "takes" and reactions are all about. And in film, *reacting* is even more important than *acting* (taking action). Actors auditioning for comic film roles who can't and don't automatically do "takes" are quickly dismissed and forgotten.

Depending upon the size of the theatre itself, the director may ask the actor to "Project!" The film and television actor will later have to learn to *not* project and become totally comfortable working on the "living presence" level. These are only two examples of the habits that can be formed in little theatre work and, if acquired there, will need to be shed later for working on-camera.

However you decide to proceed---for a while developing in theatre or directly aiming your preparation toward film and television from the start, there comes the moment when you feel you're ready to start.

2

Starting Can Be Easier
Than You Think!

...if you do it _before_ you head for Hollywood. Don't take off for Hollywood to _become_ an actor. Many who do are usually slowing their starts rather than beginning with any objectivity, because they've come with no credentials to attest to their talents. There are so few opportunities for _starting acting careers from scratch_ in Hollywood's always glutted talent market. There are _so many_ opportunities for obtaining first film and television roles _right in the new actor's back yard or a few miles down the road_. This book was written to explain the steps you can take to do just that.

These days, motion pictures and top television mini-series and movies of the week are filmed not only on Hollywood sound stages. They're filmed on location in the most remote and the most improbable back country and miles-from-nowhere small towns and empty desert sand dunes imaginable. At any time, now, in any state of the United States, there are probably one or two major film or television projects in production on location either within the state or right nextdoor. When a film script calls for a farm in Nebraska, a whistle-stop diner in the Everglades, a weather or forest ranger station atop a mountain in the Rockies or whatever, a team of "location scouts" usually consisting of the Executive Producer, the Line Producer, the director (if one has been signed), a Location Manager and one or two others go out to one or more states' Film Commissions and are whisked around to the various locations that those states have to offer.

Persuading film and television projects to come to their states are the main jobs of those Film Commissions. Hawking every possible encouragement---sales tax rebates enacted by their State Legislatures, low-cost use permits for very desirable scenic locations, facilities to serve as sound stages, experienced production crews for all departments, predictable weather, discounted hotel accommodations and everything else they can use to promote filming in their states, they advertise all of it at conventions once a year in Hollywood and, when an inquiry comes, place everything enticingly before the Hollywood company. Most states' Film Commissions publish handsome, thick, full color and handily indexed books about their states' many resources. Some medium-sized and smaller states' books even include sections devoted to categorized photos of available acting talents and brief lists of their professional credits as one type of assets the state can offer.

5

Because there is so much film and television location filming _everywhere in the country_ these days, there are also in every state a number of _talent agencies_ and in even some of the smallest states as many as five or six _"location casting directors"_ because some of those smallest states have precisely the kinds of locations many films and television projects need to find.

Like the bias expressed so clearly throughout this book, the talent agencies know that they aren't going to earn any sizeable commissions from their clients' theatre roles. They know that most of their commission income is going to come from obtaining _film and television_ roles for their people. While some of that film and television work for their actors is of course in local and regional commercials and perhaps at least occasionally a good "National Class A" commercial, modelling jobs and print jobs, the agencies are always eager to represent the kinds of acting talents that will most often be called for by location film and television projects. However, since it's impossible for any agency to anticipate _what kinds_ of location projects will be coming and _what kinds_ of acting talents and looks will be needed---contemporary, period, urban or rural color---most agencies across the country will consider "all ages, all types, union or non-union". Some will not even require that the actor have much talent. It's to the agencies' advantage to be able to supply _good_ actors for speaking roles and _people with special looks_ for "extra" jobs.

Although most roles of any size and importance in projects shooting on location are cast in Hollywood and brought to the distant location for the filming of their roles, there are usually quite a number of smaller "bit" roles reserved for local casting. And in location filming areas there are fewer actors vying for those roles than there would be in Hollywood. Also, those roles often being very minor---sometimes just one speech roles, they are cast more by "look" and "manner" than by outstanding talent. Therefore a new actor---even one with no prior film experience---has a far better chance to win some of these small roles with location projects near his or her home town or where he or she goes to school than the same new actor would have in the glutted Hollywood market of eager bit players hungry for even a single day's work.

In addition to a number of minor speaking roles reserved for local casting at location, there are almost always _many non-speaking "extra" jobs_---some for just one day, but often some needed for several weeks of work as the story-established people of small towns, as other inmates in a cellblock, as other patients in a hospital ward or as other neighbors to be seen raking leaves and mowing their lawns in sequences involving front yard exterior filming for the projects' principal casts.

New actors with no prior film experience who are eager to get onto film sets and learn film set procedures should certainly consider trying for those "extra" jobs for starters. They usually pay only about $50 or so per day, but sometimes, as mentioned above, that "extra" job turns into _several weeks_ of $50 days. Plus, you're learning a lot of the things you'll later need to know as a film actor that you might not be taught in any of your acting classes.

Also, you're gaining "credits" on your résumé. Pasted on the back of your professional photo should be a résumé that boasts that you've had some experience, even if it hasn't been important. Simply _working_ on a film set---whether in a role or as an "extra"---carries more weight with film and television directors than a bunch of decent roles in college and community theatres. They know you're familiar with film sets and how they function and that you won't need as much if any teaching of what to do.

Even if a new, location-cast actor's role has just one speech, that actor---whether new or not---is immediately eligible to join the Screen Actors Guild and have the SAG membership card that it would probably take many more years for the actor to earn in Hollywood. For such a "bit" role the salary isn't bad either. It's much more than the same actor would be making at MacDonald's or Burger King for three weeks' work.

And---again with regard to working as an "extra" in what some consider a lowly, non-speaking job: Sometimes on a film set the director suddenly discovers that a speech (even just one single word) is needed from a member of a crowd and it has to be someone other than one of the principal cast members. An extra player is usually chosen to say the speech, and for saying just that one speech---even *just that one word*---is "being bumped" into a speaking bit role; is not only eligible (because of that one speech) to immediately become a Screen Actors Guild member; but also will be added to the cast payroll for the picture and be paid the minimum Screen Actors Guild day player salary (as this book is written, at least $448!) for that one single day's work.

Even if you aren't "bumped" into a speaking role on the set, look at what you're learning: You're rubbing shoulders with some well known Hollywood actors, many of whom are really cordial, friendly people. One or more of them may find you interesting for some reason and, being seen befriending you, may increase your chances of being chosen to say that one speech if the opportunity comes up. You're watching how films are made. You're learning film set language. You're observing who does what on a film set, and how they do it, for that later time when it's *you* in front of the camera and, after enough *extra*-ing experience, knowing what you're doing.

For *extra*-ing jobs, you might want to take along a book you're reading, just in case. There'll be lots of waiting around time. You may be needed on camera for only one or a few short scenes, depending on what kind of scene or scenes you're to work in. But those few short scenes can take hours! And there'll be *many different "takes"* of whatever sequence it may be. A party scene, for instance, will take most of a day or perhaps two days, since the principal actors' dialogue scenes, with all the extras in the background, will be shot from a number of angles, and there'll be many *"atmosphere"* shots, involving only the extras. If it's a classroom scene, the same applies . . . there'll be all kinds of shots, some of only the extras with no principal actors involved. A courtroom scene, a busy office, a sightseeing tour group and other sequences involving many people will keep an extra on salary for at least one day and in some cases for a week or two.

If you do decide to start seeking "extra" work in location film and television projects, and manage to be hired for even one day, at that approximately $50 pay, you'll find that the extras are treated as more part of the background---which they truly are---and you'll find that when lunch is served by a catering organization for the principal cast, the production people and the crew members, you as an extra will not usually be able to join the others at the catered buffet lunch. In most location filming the extras are provided with cold sandwiches and beverages. Don't make the mistake of pouting or complaining. Accept the discrimination gracefully....which leads to another important thing that should be mentioned:

On a location film set, everyone---from production executive and director down to the lowliest grip (one of those people who move things when needed)---is under pressure. There's a lot of time and budget stress for everyone, and everyone is trying to work as comfortably and happily as possible in spite of that pressure. All professionals on a film set try to keep everything happy and pleasant. Even as an *extra*, you should do the same. Smile. Be pleasant and cheerful. It will be appreciated, and someone may notice....and if one of those magic opportunities arises where a single speech is to be given to an extra it could fall to you if everybody likes you.

Those are the available manners of starting....often available right in your own backyard. The only materials you'll need to begin seeking thost beginning opportunities are the addresses and telephone numbers you'll find in the Addenda Section of this book---and the two basic items that every actor is expected to have....a good professional photo and a correctly prepared résumé.

Before you start contacting either talent agencies or casting people in your area make sure that you have a supply of professional photos and résumés ready so you can

7

leave at least one of each with each person you hope will keep you in mind for calls. _Don't waste your and their time with appointments until you have your photo and résumé ready to leave with them!_

3

The Professional
Photo and Résumé

Even though you're not in Hollywood, when you're hoping for film and television work of any kind you're being considered by _Hollywood people_. The top brass of the production and several of the creative staff are the ones you'll be auditioning for. And even before you have opportunities to audition for them, to acquire a talent agent franchised by the Screen Actors Guild in your own home state, or to persuade a location casting person in your area to call you in to interview for a role, you need to present yourself in a totally professional manner...and that means having a supply of _glossy, 8x10 copies of a good professional photo_ (many people call them "headshots") to leave with agents, casting people and commercial and other producers, always with a _correctly prepared résumé_ pasted on the back. (See the examples of the right kinds of photos later in this Chapter.)

Get help with choosing which photo to use (from the many shots on a sheet of contact proofs), and get help with preparing your résumé in the form that is preferred industy-wide by film and television people. Any knowledgeable acting teacher can help you with these. And if there's no "knowledgeable acting teacher" available in your area whom you feel you can contact, then at a meeting with an agent or casting person show them your pages of proofs and ask their advice as to which shot(s) should be printed in glossy, 8x10 size for use as your main professional photo(s). (If an agent or casting person finds you interesting enough in person---even without a photo printed up to leave with them---they may be willing to give you this help in selecting a productive photo from among your proofs. Don't go into their office without at least _proofs_.

As for help with your résumé, there are some tips and clear examples later in this chapter that can help you put a good beginning résumé together for yourself---one that will suffice until you have some "credits" (jobs) to enter on it.

Your Professional Photo is Serious Business!

Don't get a friend to take photos intended for professional use. You can waste a lot of money and time trying with friends. And some photographers available in outlying cities are more accustomed to taking family photos or modeling photos, etc., and they may as a result specialize in certain types of shots that aren't right for actors. Ask to see samples of the photographer's main body of work. Those who do many head shots---rather than models' bodies and family and baby portraits---are best.

In choosing a photographer, probably the first consideration is their charge. It varies widely from photographer to photographer. Don't expect to pay less than $50 for a sitting fee for "theatrical" portraits (just head shots) and perhaps (but not always) a few 8x10 prints of your choice included. Some photographers require deposits ahead of time. Appointments for shooting should be made at least a week ahead of time, and in some cases there may be a wait.

Inquire about the fee; any deposit required; the amount of time afforded at that price for a sitting; whether they shoot indoors or outdoors or both and in what kinds of locations (because while outdoor shots are usually okay for men, women should be shot in studio lighting); ask what amount is payable at the sitting or when the money is to be paid; the number of proof pages (there are about 36 or 72 to a page usually) or the number of total shots that are included; how many original 8x10 prints come in the package at that price; the cost of any 8x10 original prints over and above the number included in the price; and whether they release the negatives to you (most don't); how soon proofs may be expected; how long any ordered prints should probably take; what kind of wardrobe the photographer recommends; any other questions you can think of.

The best kind of photo for use by actors is one which shows the whole head, with the face either directly toward camera or faced a little (not too much) past the camera. No wild expressions! Both eyes should be visible to some extent, whether in three-quarters angle (turned just a little sideways) or fairly straight front. Simply your face, either calmly serious or smiling. And when the photographer "crops" the photo, make sure that there's not much empty space at the sides and top of the shot and that the bottom cropping is approximately at the bodice collar for women and at the open shirtcollar first button for men.

Backgrounds of medium greytones, whether leaves of trees or buildings or simple studio backing sheet, are best. No dramatic black and white contrasts to distract from your face. There should be a little brightness (sunlight or artificial studio lighting) in the pupils of the eyes. And don't have the photo "raked" or "airbrushed" to take out a mole or lines or wrinkles or dimples.

Don't wear a hat in the photo. Don't have a hand anywhere in the frame. Don't wear dramatic black and white contrasts to distract from your face. Don't let the photographer shoot you in a black turtleneck, as some unaware photographers like to do. And don't wear the kind of jewelry that can distract.

For *Young Men*, open shirt collar is usually good, perhaps with a not too neat denim or outdoorsy jacket. If your hair looks best neatly combed, have it that way. If mussed hair is good for your look, have it that way. Dress for this important photo the way you see yourself most useable in roles. There are different potential casting categories.....straight leads, heavies, characters, street people, executive suite people, etc. Your appearance and personality automatically place you in one or two of these catgegories whether you like it or not. Each category certainly requires the basic likeness and exploitation of your own unique personality, but there are other considerations as well: If you're a healthy, outdoorsy-looking, sports-bodied type, for instance, say so subtly with your photo.

Ingenues (pretty young women) shouldn't use "cleavage" (low or nonexistent bodice) shots unless that's what they want in terms of roles. Such photos won't generally produce any other kind of job consideration and sometimes bring unwanted kinds of telephone calls. Don't let your wardrobe or the pose attract too much attention from your face, and be careful to not have on too much makeup.

Leading Women tend to be immediately categorized photographically by their choice of wardrobe, even more than men. Express your own taste and personality, with some indication of social level in your choice of what to wear.

Character People usually need at least three or four different shots suggesting their various casting categories. Agents like to have several different photos of "character" people, in order to submit the most appropriate shot of you for specific roles. And character people should exploit anything that makes them different and special. If they have any facial, body or other features which are unusual or even abnormal in their own estimation, those things they may hate about their own appearance are probably what they should exploit most prominently in their photos. Character roles, by their very label, demand characters!

Order three or four 8x10 originals from the photographer, whether that many are included in the photographer's basic fee or not, so that you can see more vividly which is the best for you. Then, if you're not in Hollywood or within traveling distance, mail your chosen original to a _Quantity Photo Reproduction Lab_, have the lab make a "_dupe neg_" (duplicate negative) and have the lab print at least 100, perhaps more copies, in your first print run.

You may want to have your name typeset and printed at the bottom of your photos. The lab can do this.

If you prefer to have your quantity printing done in Hollywood, _Duplicate Photo Labs_, located one block north of Sunset Boulevard on Highland Avenue, is fine for quantity reproduction. So is _Quantity Photo_, at 5432 Hollywood Boulevard, and there are others. Those are the two that seem to this writer to be the most often used, and they're both excellent for 8x10 glossy black and white photos...your standard "headshots". Get their current telephone numbers from Hollywood Information (Area Code 213) and call them for current prices. These two companies usually have a quick, three-day turnaround on orders from the time they receive the print desired to be duplicated.

For people located in the Midwest there's another quantity print shop that does good work....._ABC Pictures_, at 1867 East Florida, Springfield, Missouri 65803.

Here are some examples of the most productive "cropping" for actors' professional photos. Industry people want to see them like this:

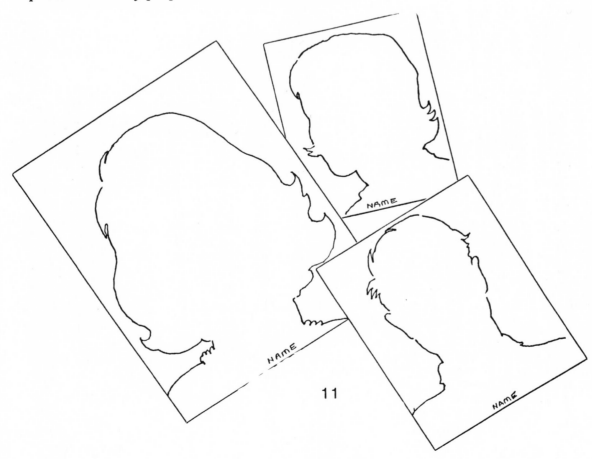

11

Examples of Photo Arrangements for Reverse Side of Commercial Composites

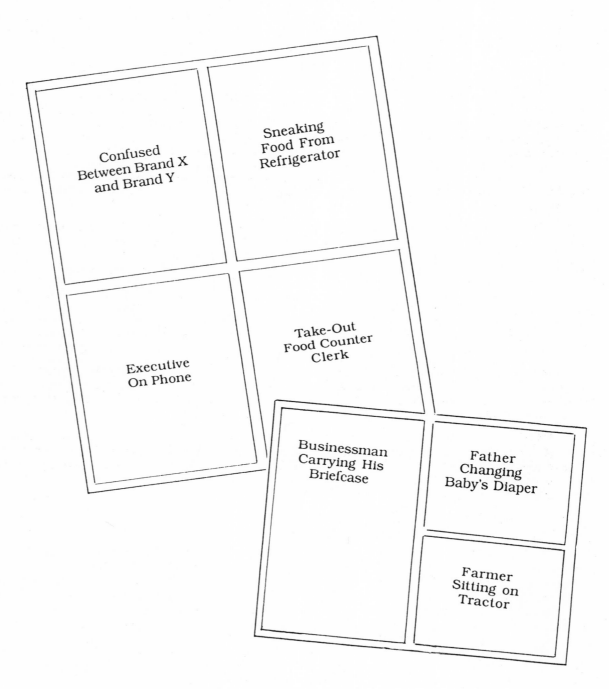

You Need A Résumé Also....It's Your "Ad Copy"!

On the back of each of your photos to be handed out at offices should be a copy of your résumé. It should be rubber-cemented or otherwise pasted securely onto the back of the photos so it won't tear off when stuffed into casting or agency files. Have it typewritten or word-processed neatly, along the lines suggested below, then cut to 8x10 size so it won't stick out past the photo when pasted onto the back of it.

There is a standard form recommended by the Casting Society of America which has been adopted industry-wide and is now the form in which producers, directors, casting and agency people expect to see it. (See the samples of correctly formed résumés at the end of this Chapter.)

Your name should run across the top center in large, heavy type---perhaps a pasteup strip from your personal stationery, or a specially typeset version in heavy bold type, so the name stands out, or you can simply type your name there in capital letters and perhaps underline it to make it stand out as prominently as possible. One of the first pinciples in advertising---which is what a résumé is---is that the name of the product should appear in larger size type than anything else around it, and this is equally true in any "advertising" the actor does. So start observing that principle with your résumé.

About one or two type lines lower, at the top of the left side of the sheet, list, one after another down the margin, *Height:, Weight:, Hair:* and *Eyes:*, with the correct information shown for each item.

Some actors, following the author's suggestion, made their "Hair" item more interesting by calling it, perhaps, "Prairie Dog Brown" rather than just brown; by calling grey eyes perhaps "Hungry Coyote Grey" or "Hit Man Grey". These kinds of far more descriptive comments also arouse interest. They show that the actor has a vivid imagination.

In the upper right corner, directly across from the Height, Weight, etc. entries, enter information as to how to contact you if you don't yet have an agent representing you. You can of course enter your home phone number there, but it's best to use a telephone message service number to avoid getting bothersome phone calls from people you don't know. After leaving your photo and résumé in an office you never know whose hands it may fall into.

Once you have an agency representing you that section of the résumé should be left for your agent's or the agency's name and telephone number, because once you have an agent all calls for you should be (and usually are) routed through the agency by casting and production people.

In the center, at the top, just under your name, when you become a member of one or more of the performing unions---SAG (Screen Actors Guild), AFTRA (American Federation of Television and Radio Artists) and Equity (Actors Equity Association)---you should enter that information. Just "SAG" or "SAG / AFTRA / Equty"...or whichever item or combination applies.

Then drop down about five or six lines below your *Height, Weight, Hair, Eyes* data to start your listing of your "credits" across the page..

If you have no motion picture or television credits yet, then list any theatre background under the centered, all capital letyters, bold type heading THEATRE. Perhaps underline that title so it stands out. Then drop down two more lines and at the left margin show the first play title; in a centered column across from the title name the role and (some do) in parenthesis add (Lead) or (Starring) or (Featured). Across from these entries, at the right, list the theatre and perhaps the city and year if you like.

But if you do have some (any kind of) film or television background---even extraing, the first centered title (instead of THEATRE) should be the one of those two in which you have the most credits---either MOTION PICTURES or TELEVISION. List all your credits, down the page one after another, in the category to which they apply, using the same basic layout as described for Theatre, except that in the case of motion pictures the right hand column should show the studio or production company and, if you like, the year in which produced. Some like to also list the name of the director, but if there isn't room across the page to do this neatly, don't.

For television, if the appearances are in episodes of series, the left hand column should name the series first, in bold caps, and the episode title (also bold) in parentheses; the middle column should name the role you played and if you like, in parenthesies, the billing---(Starring), (Costarring), (Featured)....or you could, as some do, after the episode and role names put in a one, two or three word description of your character...like (The nasty nurse), (The kidnap victim), (Slinky's Boyfriend). The latter entries make even a bit role appear to have been more important, and also give opportunities for you to subtly advertise the kinds of roles you'd like to play more often.

The foregoing titles sequence...first MOTION PICTURES or TELEVISION, then the other of those two, then THEATRE (last, because you're pushing for film and television) and following those, two more centered titles...COMMERCIALS and OTHER.

Under the COMMERCIALS heading the usual entry is simply "List Available Upon Request" (whether there's been even one commercial to list thus far or not). The reason for this very common phrase is that if people have actually done several commercials it signals potential hirers that they should check with the actor's agent to make sure there hasn't been a "conflict"---a commercial job for a conflicting product---i.e., a previous commercial for a soft drink of any kind when someone's being considered for a Coca Cola or 7-Up commercial.

Under the OTHER title should go entries of Variety experience, Dance, Musical Groups, Industrials, Training Films, Modeling, Singing, etc.

At the bottom left corner, list SPECIAL SKILLS or title it MISCELLANEOUS, and under that title list things like Swimming, Skiing, Skydiving, Gymnastics, All Field and Track Sports, Snakedancing, etc. The importance of listing *every ability you have* can't be too strongly stressed. When the author was casting the *"Sea Hunt"* series, for instance, many actors got their first film roles because they listed *Scuba, Snorkeling, Spelunking,* etc., among their special skills and that series needed those skills. When casting the *"Bat Masterson"* series, many new actors got first roles simply because they claimed they were *Expert Riders*.

Across from that, at the right bottom, under the title TRAINING, list the names of the best known coaches or training establishments, what was studied with each, and where the study occurred. (If you were in Hollywood you'd of course list any Hollywood, New York, London or important other coaching or study first.

If you have any ability with dialects or speak an additional language or two, list those in the bottom center, under the title LANGUAGES AND DIALECTS. But be absolutely objective by not listing any language or dialects with which you're not *expert*. You might add in parentheses after a listed language or dialect a word like "fliently" or "fair". Do not, repeat *not*, list a dialect ability that isn't totally convincing!

On the following pages are some examples of correctly prepared résumés.

Examples of Actors' Résumés
in the Industry-Recommended Form

This résumé layout is recommended for the actor or actress who *has* a number of film and television credits as well as theatre background.

JAMES HARPER

SAG / AFTRA / Equity

Height: 6' 1"   Warner / Phillips Agency
Weight: 160 lbs.   Helen Phillips (212) 650-2111
Hair: Dk. Brown
Eyes: Spooky Grey

MOTION PICTURES

DEER VALLEY	Jake, The Hunter (Co-Starring)	Columbia (90)
WALLABEES	The Out Back Hermit (Featured)	Univ. (89)
THE LONG WALK	Juniper, the AWOL (Top Featured)	Lorimar (88)

TELEVISION

BITTER SEED	Paul, The Cellmate (Co-Starring)	NBC MOW (90)
FANTASY CHILD	William, The Threatener (Cameo)	CBS MOW (90)

THEATRE

Leading roles in **JUNO & THE PAYCOCK, WELL BORN, PSYCHICALLY SPEAKING, BOYLAN & SON**, Circle Players, Off Broadway NY; Summer Theatre, 4 seasons at Ogunquit Playhouse, Maine (1985-1988)

COMMERCIALS

List Upon Request

MISCELLANEOUS SKILLS   **TRAINING**
Most Field Sports, Team Roping,   Neighborhood Plhs. (NY)
Heavy Equip. of All Kinds   Uta Hagen (2 Yrs)

This form of résumé might ideally serve a newcomer who has no film or television credits yet but who has much theatre background:

Deborah Cramden

Equity

Height: 5' 6"
Weight: 110 lbs.
Hair: Flax Blonde
Eyes: Soft Lavender

Tel. Messages: (310) 275-8298

THEATRE

A DOLL'S HOUSE	Nora (Title Role)	Greenwich Playhouse NY, '87
DESPERATE JOURNEY	Maybelle (Lead)	ANTA Theatre NY, '86-87
HELLO OUT THERE	The Girl (Lead)	National Tour for CFI, '88

and **many seasons of Summer Theatre** in top roles, at Keene Summer Theate, Long Island Players (Bridgehampton), Ephrata Star Playhouse, Boothbay Theatre, etc.

MOTION PICTURES

None Yet....Just Starting in Hollywood in 1991

TELEVISION

Same...None Yet

COMMERCIALS

Many Non-Union Commercials in New York for
Local and Regional Market Products and Services

MISCELLANEOUS SKILLS

Wordprocessing & Computer Skills,
Mountainclimbing, Snake Dancing,
Gemologist, Horticulturist, Ecol. Nut

TRAINING

Sanford Meisner (4 Years), NY
Lawrence Parfke (Hwd), Now
Jeanne Hartman (Reading)

4

Making Your First
Industry Contacts

In the Addenda Pages at the back of this book are lists of State and City Film Commissions, Talent Agencies, Modeling Agencies and Location Casting Directors located throughout the United States. You can start your "Contact" List with those in your state and in neighbor states. Those lists have been updated to early 1993 and will probably still apply for the most part for a number of years to come.

We believe you'll be *amazed* at the completeness of these lists. There is nowhere else we know of where so total lists exist. They've been painstakingly gathered from all the Film Commissions and other sources, to help readers find these organizations easily.

Once you have a good professional photo and résumé ready, those are the offices, people and organizations you should begin contacting. You can opt to first get additional acting training---preferably with a coach or teacher with some personal background in film and television action, or you can simply start contacting the agents and casting people and asking them to help you start.

Don't be shy about promoting yourself with these folks. They actually need you, the actor, almost as much as you need them. Location Casting Directors---those who offer themselves to "location cast", providing actors for auditions for visiting film and television projects---need to know of all the talent available to be called for either "bit roles" or extra work. And talent agents in most cities and areas of the country as well as in the production centers such as Hollywood and New York need to have all kinds of actors---cross-sections of all ages and types, all racial and ethnic categoies---ready to suggest to casting people for roles, to advertising agencies for commercials and advertising print work and to industrial and training film producers for their non-theatrical projects.

In most areas of the country outside those principal production centers mentioned above you'll find both agency and casting people at least moderately receptive to meeting new talent. If you come to them with at least a professional photo and résumé in hand they'll treat you with professional courtesy and consider you.

17

If you're a newcomer with absolutely no background, in all probability they'll consider you first as a potential "extra", but they'll usually give you a chance to read (act) something for them in their office to find out whether you have at least enough natural talent to be considered for some of those "bit role" auditions. Some will offer you a chance to prepare a short monologue to do for them, or an invitation to prepare a scene with a partner that can be performed in their office. You'll normally be given some kind of opportunity to earn their serious consideration.

Some agents (especially) will simply like your *look* and consider you on that basis, in case your "type" is likely to be called for for something that doesn't require experienced, professional level *talent.* Those early opportunities do exist---for extra-ing (playing background) in films, television projects, commercials, etc. It's seldom that a talent agency in an outlying area of the country will have too many of any type. Their doors are remarkably open for most who contact them for representation.

The Right Manner of Contacting Casting and Agency People

You'll have your best chance of getting some positive response from either an agent or a casting person---and you should immediately begin contacting both---if you mail a short note to them and enclose your photo and résumé with it. If you attempt to contact either of them by telephone first it's probable that they'll instruct you to do just that anyway. People in the industry want to know *what kind* of actor is asking to be interviewed. This rule of thumb applies in outlying talent offices just as it does in Hollywood and New York. They want to know what you look like, what your photo suggests in casting terms, what you've done or not done---from your résumé, and any talents (other than acting), miscellaneous skills, etc., that may appear on your résumé.

Write that very short note and send it, enclosing your material. It's expected. And keep your note to a single paragraph. To an agent, simply say, for example, "I'd appreciate your meeting me and considering representing me" or "I'm seeking agency representation and would appreciate an appointment with you at your earliest convenience." Honestly, any longer letter filled with persuasive details would mark you as less professional! In Hollywood and other top production centers anything longer than such a brief, one paragraph note is a *definite no-no!*

To a location casting director, keep your cover note equally short. The same reasons apply. Perhaps "I'd appreciate the opportunity to meet you and be considered for upcoming film and television casting" or perhaps "Not yet having agency representation, I'm writing to ask for a brief personal interview at your convenience." Short notes such as these will normally receive the optimum consideration and response.

In the case of both talent agents and casting directors, *following up* is respected. Often both offices have quite a number of such requests with photos included that are left sitting on their desks to be responded to "later"....but "later" may never come. Usually a phone call, simply asking (1) whether they received your note and material and (2) whether you may have an interview, will give you your best chance for one, while all those other submissions on their desks may lie unanswered forever. After all, even the *beginning* of an acting career is a business. Following up is considered businesslike and is respected. Swallow your shyness and make that follow-up call.

And if you have a car and gas money, and would be able to take off from whatever you're doing---job, school or whatever, mail your notes and materials to agencies and casting people in cities farther from where you live. Send them to agencies and casting people in *neighboring* states as well as your own. Often there is much more film and television location activity just over the state line in another state. The more of such activity there is, the more responsive both agencies and casting people will be. Many enterprising new actors obtain agency representation in their own locales and also in nearby states.

18

5

What Talent Agents Do...
And How They Do It

A talent agent---whether in Hollywood or New York or in your own or a neighboring city--- interviews and agrees to represent actors, models, voice-over people, sometimes writers, producers and directors, sometimes standup comics, sometimes musicians, composers and musical groups.

Some agencies are franchised by (1) the Screen Actors Guild to represent actors for film and *filmed* television, commercials, modeling and print work, etc., (2) AFTRA---the American Federation of Television and Radio Artists---to represent actors, announcers, soap opera and other players for *taped* performances and *radio* performances, (3) Actors Equity Association, to represent actors, singers and dancers for theatre performance of all nature, (4) AGVA---American Guild of Variety Artists, to represent variety performers and specialty acts for clubs, etc., (5) AGMA, to represent musicians and singers for all kinds of engagements, (6) The Writers Guild of America (WGA) and The Writers Guild of America West (WGAW), to represent screenwriters for television and feature film assignments.

Some other agencies are _not franchised_ by any of the above unions or guilds. Some of those agencies aren't even licensed by their State Labor Commissions and some aren't registered with DBA's ("doing business as" business titles) in the City Clerks' Offices of their cities to legally do business in the cities.

In the "Talent Agencies" listings in the Addenda Section of this book, where possible there's indication as to which agencies are franchised by the Screen Actors Guild and which aren't. The important difference is that in many states (as in Hollywood) Screen Actors Guild Members---which all professional film actors must be---may not be represented by agencies that aren't franchised by SAG.

When it's possible for the new actor to become represented by one of the _union-franchised_ agencies, it's much to be preferred. The franchised agencies usually get first notifications of upcoming location projects and other opportunities, simply because they usually represent more professional talents than do the unfranchised agencies, therefore their clients are usually among the first thoughts of the casting person and calls for them to come for audition go out to those SAG agencies first. As stated above, a Screen Actors Guild member actor is not permitted by the union---at least in most regions of the country---to be represented by an unfranchised talent agency. Although most outlying casting directors will call the unfranchised agenies as well as the SAG-franchised ones for their talents to audition, the SAG-franchised agencies' talents are auditioned first. And often a film or television producer will specifically limit the casting process to SAG members or at least to SAG-franchised agencies' talents. They simply trust the "professionals" more, and don't want to take time to meet the lesser agencies' people if there are enough candidates among the franchised agencies' people.

To obtain union and guild franchises, those agencies who hold them have (in most states) first had to obtain Artists Manager Licenses from their State Labor Commissions, have then had to apply to the National Offices of the Screen Actors Guild and AFTRA in Hollywood, furnishing much documentation and verification of their stability, professional experience whether as agent or otherwise, etc. They usually have to have a business office other than a corner of their home living room. In some states, just as in the large production centers, they have to deposit large bonds with the unions and guilds to insure their operating of their business according to rules and regulations of the unions and guilds.

You may be certain that most _union-franchised_ talent agencies are on the up and up and that their business practices are sound. If there are any complaints by their clients to SAG or AFTRA about mismanagement of their clients or failure to conduct their business with legitimacy, they must answer to the union in hearings and risk losing their franchises.

An _unfranchised_ agency may be just as honorable, but it isn't subject to certain of the same professional constraints concerning its manner of operating. It in fact usually doesn't have to answer to _anyone_ as to how it handles its talents, their salary checks and commissions due the agency, the promotion of its clients' careers, etc.

A _franchised_ agency cannot require that a prospective actor client have professional photos taken by a specific photographer of the agency's choice, or require that the actor attend specific workshop classes to quality for representation, or require that the actor also sign with a personal management firm or person to be represented. Each of these "qualifying requirements" may be open to what's called "kickback" arrangements whereby the fees paid to those outside the agency may be shared with the agency. This can and sometimes does happen with an unfranchised agency. The problem for the new, not yet union member actor, is that if one of these "scams" is discovered or even suspected because one of these requirements is placed upon the applicant for representation, the new actor has no recourse to any supervisory organization or bureau. The Screen Actors Guild or AFTRA cannot be responsive to the new, non-union actor's complaint. But it can deal quickly and objectively with any such complaint that comes from one of its own members. A SAG or AFTRA-franchised agency, therefore---if it's currently in business at all---is much less likely to be involved with any of these actor-exploiting schemes.

Another word of advice: If the agency is operated in conjunction with a school of any kind and paying for training by that school is a condition for representing you, pass. Where a school is operated by or in association with the agency, it---the school---is usually the main operation of the organization, with its "talent agency" title simply tacked on as a "come-on" to increase its school attendance. Also, if the agent asks for any money at all out front to accept you for representation, again pass. There are other agencies in your area.

As to _what a talent agency does, and how it does it_ : It agrees to represent a fairly large list of actors---called "clients" by the agency---for all nature of professional work. It finds its "clients", as mentioned earlier, from photos and résumés being submitted and their senders being subsequently interviewed and accepted, or sometimes from seeing the actors work in a local theatre and liking their work. At other times a client of another agency, with quite an extensive background, whether locally or from Hollywood or New York, may be unhappy with the other agency and want to be represented by an agent about

20

whom they're heard enthusiastic reports. Sometimes a casting person, producer or director or someone else in an important industry position will call an agent they respect and suggest the agent interview and consider representing the actor they're recommending.

The agency, upon taking a new client, will normally request quite a supply of photos and résumés from the actor; will discuss the manner in which they feel the actor should best be handled; will get several telephone numbers for contacting the actor; and some agencies will have the actor sign the standard union contracts to make the representation official. Some agents operately solely on a "handshake" basis, however.

If the agency is in a small city, chances are that agency will want to handle the actor *exclusively* for "theatrical" (motion pictures and television roles), commercials, modeling, voice-over (off-camera voice work), etc. But in the much larger cities it's not uncommon for agencies to allow the actor to be represented by their agency for just one or two areas---often just motion pictures and television, or just commercials and modeling and voice-over, understanding that the two areas of representation involve totally different legwork and promotion and knowing that the actor will be best served if allowed to be with one agency that specializes in one or the other area and be with another agency that specializes in another. (This is especially true in Hollywood, where many actors have one agent for "theatrical", one for commercials, one for voice-over work and another for fashion, runway or print work.)

In Hollywood and the other main production centers, talent agents know that they must *continually promote* their clients; must try to have casting people meet and consider them; must subscribe to what's called the "Breakdown Service" to be quickly aware of what's being cast and just as quickly suggest their clients to the casting people. This is usually not as true in outlying cities. Some agents in those smaller, outlying cities consider it "spinning their wheels" to keep going around trying to promote their clients when there are only sporadic demands for actors and any casting opportunities will automatically come to them by phone as soon as they come up.

When there's something being cast---for motion picture or television, for a commercial of any kind, for a modeling job whether fashion runway or print, the agency is first called and told of it by the casting person. What's needed is described, whether it's a single actor or model or a large list of characters for which many actors will have to audition in readings. In some outlying areas the agent is permitted by the casting person to send the agent's own selection of people to try for the roles. That manner of casting is usually called "Cattle calls". In other cases where the casting director is more conscientious and is continually meeting and becoming better acquainted with all the talents he or she can find, the casting director will ask the agent to set appointments for specific people selected by the casting person.

In either kind of casting, the agent sets the appointment times and tells its clients where to report, what time they're to arrive and also perhaps the best ways to dress because of the kinds of characters involved. The agent's job for each client is done then until the call may come from the casting person either asking that the actor return for a "callback" audition---probably to read for the producer or director or both. Again the client is called with the encouraging news and the agent must simply wait and hope.

When a casting person makes the call to actually cast the actor who has won a role, usually in "location casting" it's most often simply to inform the agent that the production wants the actor for the role, approximately when the role will be filmed or begin filming, and the salary that will be paid.

Usually in location casting there's no discussion or negotiation of the salary unless the agent asks for at least "scale plus ten"....the union minimum usually paid by location film companies for minimally experienced (and even some more experienced) actors, plus an additional ten percent to cover the agent's ten percent commission without reducing the actor's "minimum" salary. In some cases penny-pinching productions won't pay the "plus ten" and in some states the agent therefore isn't entitled to receive the ten percent commission. In other states the actor is allowed to pay the commission out of his or her salary. (Each state's SAG Council may vote to allow this or may prohibit it on the basis that the "minimum" of the union is exactly that and if the agent isn't able to negotiate the "plus ten" that agent isn't entitled to receive any commission on the job.)

When you're with an agent, there are things you can do to help your agent and help yourself:

When you're appearing in a play---no matter where or how unimportantly---ask the agent to come, and arrange for two complimentary seats for him or her. The theatre may require you to pay for them, or it may not. Inform the agent of the "ticket pickup" deadline required, so that if they don't attend the tickets can be returned to the rack for sale and that way you certainly shouldn't be charged for the seats.

And send postcard notifications to any casting directors in your area, asking them to come see your work. Be sure to offer those two complimentary seats. Again, if someone says they intend to come be sure to inform them of the "ticket pickup" deadline required by the theatre, for the same reason as in the last previous paragraph.

If you're in an acting class, ask the agent to come observe your work if the teacher will permit it. (Most will and are happy for the industry attention.)

When you finish a role, volunteer to go into the agency office and personally write in the new "credit" on the agent's supply of your résumés. (Of course immediately do the same on your own supply at home.)

When you come out of a casting interview or reading for a role, call the agent and report what happened, whether good or bad, encouraging or discouraging. They're part of your team and want to know.

If the agent doesn't have you sign what are called "Check Authorization Forms" when the agent agrees to represent you, then you will receive your salary checks direct from production companies, in which case you should immediately upon receipt of your check take the agent's 10% commission in to him or her. (If you've signed Check Authorization Forms" at the agency, then the agent submits one of those forms to the Payroll Dept. of the production company and the check goes to the agency. At that point, the agent deposits your salary check in the agency's Clients' Account and issues the agent's own check to you, always enclosing a photocopy of the original salary check for your information and records.)

In the Addenda Section of this book are listed all of the talent agencies located in most of the cities throughout the country. The list includes both union-franchised and non-union agencies, since from time to time a non-union agency decides to become franchised. These lists have been furnished for this book as recently as November 1992 by the National Office of the Screen Actors Guild and by the State and Film Commissions located throughout the country. It will save you time and effort to use these lists, rather than local telephone directories, in putting together your mailing and telephone contact list.

Start contacting agency after agency as soon as you have your professional photo and résumé ready. Hopefully, one will acept you for representation.

6

What Casting Directors Do...
And How They Do It

When actors are just starting out, they often think casting directors are some kind of gods or something. Not so. They're hired by production companies or studios to bring in for auditions and readings the actors whom they feel to be the most right for the roles being cast. That's the extent of their influence in the casting process. Then, after all roles are decided the remaining step is to handle the last negotiations with actors or their agents as to salary, billing, etc. The most the casting director can do for you is (1) appreciate your talents, (2) call for you to come in to read for roles, (3) help you gradually obtain better salary and billing and of course (4) have you come in many interviews and readings at their suggestion. That's how it works in Hollywood and how it usually works with location casting directors in outlying areas.

There's one difference, though: In other areas of the country some of the casting people cast only the _speaking roles_ that remain to be cast locally at the location, while others, working with the Location Casting Director, cast only the _non-speaking "extras"_. For the purposes of this book there's no indication in the big list in the Addenda Section (except in a few specific cases) as to which casting people handle which. New talents should make themselves known to _all_ of them.

In Hollywood, casting people have no obligation to treat all agencies fairly with respect to informing them of roles being cast. It's up to the agencies to subscribe to "The Breakdown Serivvce" which publishes all casting information on sheets delivered to subscribing agency offices early every morning. The agents then submit their suggestions of their clients for the roles announced. Sometimes the agencies are ignored because the casting person has his or her own suggestions ready and doesn't need any more ideas.

Generally, in outlying cities and areas the _location_ casting person is required by the Screen Actors Guild Regional Office to inform _all_ talent agencies that are franchised by SAG when there's casting to be done, with description of the roles available. Usually the casting person contacts not only the franchised agencies but also the non-union ones. If s/he has vast and qualitative knowledge of most actors in the area, s/he will probably put together a list of between five and ten possibilities for each role and set appointments for them. Some other location casting people, perhaps because they know the actors of the area less well, prefer to afford time periods for the individual agents to bring or send in their clients whom _they_ think are possibly right for what's wanted after having the available roles described to them by the casting person. Since from time to time the manner of cast-

23

ing may vary, even with individual casting people, you can see how important it is that you make sure that the casting people, as well as your agent, all know you and your talents.

At the auditions, with many actors called to read for the available roles, the casting person usually has an assistant present to check the actors in as they arrive for their appointments. When it's an actor's turn to go inside to read s/he is brought inside by the casting person. Sometimes the casting person is the only one there for first auditions and is holding this original "elimination" audition to eliminate the less desirable actors. Then, for later auditions for the producer and director, called "callbacks", the best people from the original interviews are brought back. They're that much closer to the possibility of getting the role.

At some auditions---even the early "elimination" auditions and often the later ones for producers and directors---your readings will be <u>videotaped</u>. If they are, you'll often be asked to first state on tape your name, the agency that represents you, then commence reading your lines with another person reading other characters lines opposite you.

And you'll <u>certainly</u> always be videotaped when you're auditioning for a <u>commercial</u>, since your audition must be shipped to the distant advertising agency producing the commercial for a national sponsor, for the ad agency back east of elsewhere and the sponsor whose product the commercial will represent are the ones selecting the actors.

Reporting in for a <u>commercial</u> audition, sign in on the SAG-required *Sign-In Sheet* which bears the product name at the top. Entries are name, agency, time of arrival, time of appointment, etc. Leave the "sign out" item blank until you're leaving and fill it in then. (SAG regulations limit the length of time actors may be held at commercial auditions.)

There'll be copies of the "*Copy Sheet*" next to the Sign-In Sheet. Take a copy and begin preparing the lines.

When called inside to be taped, take your photo and résumé inside with you and lay it on the table where other photos lie. There'll be marks on the floor for you to step into. When asked to, announce your name and your agency, then deliver the lines. When finished, thank them and leave.

When the producer and director have made the final choices among the actors they've auditioned for the roles in a film, television or commercial project, the casting person has the task of calling those actors' agents and making the final deals with any negotiation necesssary. Usually there's *no* negotiation about salary or billing for roles cast with local actors. The exceptions are those cases where an actor with a vast background of film and television roles happens to currently live in the location area. Those actors often request and receive larger salaries and, if the roles warrant, better billing. If the actor's background and (in some cases) recognized name value warrants, his or her "salary quote"---the salary usually received in the past and easily verified with other production companies---will probably be paid by the location company without any negotiation if the actor's agent is adamant from the start.

It's vitally important for actors to make sure *every casting director in or near their area* knows about them and likes their work. The actor needs to have impressed the casting person with a ready talent or an outstanding personality or both because, even with a talent agent representing the actor, it's often, though not always, the *casting director* who decides who's to be called for interviews.

In the Addenda Section of this book most individuals and organizations that do <u>location casting throughout all parts of the country</u> are listed with their addresses and telephone numbers. These have been supplied for this book as recently as early 1993 by State and City Film Commissions. Most should therefore be current, and it can help you locate the ones nearest where you are.

7

Many Actors Get Their Starts
As Models...

It's interesting how many young actors overlook or even sneer at the thought of doing modeling, whether parttime or full time, as a manner of starting and as a supportive income for the early years. Yet many of today's top stars started out as models, and many others did and still do modeling for a second income source. Certainly the very attractive women and men have good chances of working as models, but so do the very _un_-pretty people who are often much in demand as "commercial" models and who are sought out by advertisers for commercial print work.

Whichever group you may be in strictly on the basis of appearance, modeling offers excellent pay for a few hours of work . . . and it's _acting for the camera_, after all.

Any medium to large city in the country also has a number of _advertising agencies_ located in its downtown area. Those advertising agencies prepare the local (and sometimes even national Class A) commercials for their clients' products or services. They use both actors and models of all kinds in those commercials. They prepare display advertising for other clients' products, and they hire "commercial print" models---both attractive and unattractive folks---for those newspaper, magazine, flier and billboard ads and signs. Those faces are actors who are also models just as often as they are models for whom modeling is their only career.

In most cities there are several agencies that would be happy to represent new people for modeling jobs whether the same agencies want to handle them for acting or not. And each modeling job of only a few hours work at least earns as much as or substantially more than the actor could make in a week at a nine to five job somewhere.

For actors who want to add modeling of whatever kind to their beginning career, the steps---in the most productive order---are: (1) Find a good agent who will represent you enthusiastically. (2) Gather a portfolio of good photos. To do that, set appointments with a number of photographers to look at their books. After a photo shoot get your _agent_ to pick the shots you should use. (3) With your agent's help, prepare a "comp card", probably 5x8, with several shots on it along with your measurement statistics. The "comp card" is for leaving at offices when you go on appointments. The comp card should show you in several different manners. (4) Let the photographers with whom you've worked or whom you've

25

met know that you'd be happy to do some "test" shoots for them. . . which are "free photos" opportunities for the model in return for letting the photographers use you for testing some technical aspect of their own photography. Doing these "test" shoots for photographers helps build your portfolio with the prints you're given by the grateful photographers.

If you get into modeling more seriously as you find yourself called for time after time by the same ad agencies and others, you'd be wise to also put together and have handy at all times a "Tote Bag" that contains all the items a model needs to be fully prepared for any booking that may come up suddenly.

For women, such items as makeup hood, deodorant, facial tissue, underarm shields, anti-static spray, mirror, sewing kit, assorted neutral lingerie, assorted shoes (seasonal), assorted pantyhose, accessories, clothing brush, breath spray, a roll of masking tape (wide), etc.

For men, jockey shorts (not boxers), athletic supporter, shaving equipment, comb and hair brush, hair spray (if used), shirt collar tabs, assorted ties, deodorant, anti-static spray, lint brush, safety pins, suspenders, posing strap, dress shoes (brown and black), socks (over-the-calf length, in dark colors), socks (athletic), cuff links, belts (mixed), facial tissue, hand mirror, etc.

The points to be considered by beginning actors who *can* add modeling as a second career are that (1) the pay is very good for even short shoots of just a few hours, (2) the same advertising agencies that hire models for all kinds of shoots hire *actors* for the commercials they prepare for other sponsors, and (3) modeling is, after all, _acting for the camera_!

A final point in favor of considering modeling as perhaps an early door that will open before an acting role comes along is that it may help you persuade a talent agency to represent you, since they can put you up for both acting and modeling opportunities!

8

Start Networking!...

No matter where you're located, there are bound to be many other actors---some just beginning; some vastly experienced in film, television and theatre and frequently hired for film and television projects locationing somewhere nearby. Some of the more experienced professionals may be teaching university, college or private classes or heading area theatre companies. Some of the less experienced---perhaps just beginning---actors may be attending professional acting workshops. Some have talent agencies representing them for acting or modeling; some are members of local technical unions who are hired by film and television location companies for sound crew, transportation, lighting crew, production assistant and other categories of location filming employments.

You don't need to wait until you're a working actor to begin making friends with and exchanging tips with other actors. You can begin any time. . . and the sooner the better.

Simply *go where other actors are*! A good film-oriented acting class is one of the best places to start. There are surely one or two acting classes where, in addition to developing your talents, you're able to hear of films planning to come to your area or commercials being cast. If a talent agency is representing you there are often agency parties where their top clients can meet and enjoy getting to know you, perhaps help at some point by recommending you to someone. Agency clients, like fellow acting class members, like to talk. And when the agency sends you for an interview introduce yourself to other actors there to audition. There are theatre groups where extra unpaid help is always welcome, and where actors exchange news with each other. There are usually "hangout" places . . . small restaurants and diners where actors socialize after acting classes or theatre rehearsals. There are always organizations of arts orientation, and at meetings the members often exchange information with their friends.

Make contact with the people at the State Film Commission Office. In exchange for some kind of help you can offer that office from time to time perhaps they'll let you know ahead of time when a production company is setting up its location production office. If you have some particular technical ability that films require, try to contact the *Location Manager* at that office as soon as it's set up.

Even if you can't be hired for a role or for some crew job on a film, you can still find out where the film is shooting on a given day and go there, observe the filming, and perhaps make a new friend or two who'll remember you later. On any film set there are some of each technical crew's union who've been brought from Hollywood or New York, while there

27

are others who've been hired locally. Whether from Hollywood or local, most film crew technicians are friendly and may allow you friendly favors if they discover that you're interested in what they do and how they do it. In the bargain, you'll be observing how films are filmed; how shots are set up; how professional actors work in front of cameras; who does what on film sets and the language that would be gibberish to you if you haven't learned what the different words and phrases mean.

Develop the art of _collecting telephone numbers_ of all kinds! And begin conscientiously _collecting mailing addresses_ for your own promotion when you have something to promote.

Wherever the Screen Actors Guild Office is for your area---in some larger cities it may be in your telephone book, in other locations there should be one in a large city nearby, contact that office---even as a non-member---and ask whether there is any membership "open window" planned . . . a period within which the local union has been permitted (by the National Office of the Guild in Hollywood) to accept membership applications and confer SAG membership without the requirement of a SAG signatory employment.

Some actors personally make the rounds to their areas' advertising agencies and television production companies also. The advertising agencies often film or tape commercials for local businesses, using actors and models. The production companies film or tape those commercials not shot by the ad agencies, also often film training films, etc. Some of those offices keep their own talent files, and you should make sure that your photo and résumé are in any such files in those companies' offices. And every so often drop in and say hello to whoever's handling their casting and ask whether anything's coming up you might be right for. In many locations the main body of their commercials and print work employs non-union actors. In others, commercials' casts employ mostly union actors as "principals" (speaking or visually featured roles) and a number of non-union actors as "extras".

The important thing to remember is that in the beginning period of an acting career it's strictly a "single proprietor business". Nobody else is going to do all the promotion for you. Visibility counts from the very start, and even throughout later years of advanced careers it's what keeps you in industry people's minds when opportunities come up. It's why, as acting careers move forward into much higher levels, actors hire press agents. That being impractical for newcomers, it's important to "network" in any manner possible to start people thinking of you.

Organizational Work, Joining and Volunteering...

No, we're not wandering from our subject. We're still talking "networking". And there's one kind of networking open to all actors, regardless of the current levels of their careers. It's _Organizational Work, Joining and Volunteering!_ Some excellent industry contacts and ongoing friendships that can speed your career progress can come from volunteering to work with and for some of the organizations that are even peripherally involved with the entertainment industry---including, of course, Screen Actors Guild branch offices', AFTRA offices' and Actors Equity offices' activities and committees, once you're a member of one or more of those performing unions.

The entertainment community is less centralized than it once was. No longer do all of the top stars live in Hollywood or New York. Many now commute regularly between Hollywood and their homes in several Florida cities, the Sundance community in Utah, New Mexico's Santa Fe / Taos artist colonies, Aspen and Vail chalets in Colorado, Maine and Martha's Vineyard beach homes, Scottsdale mansions in Arizona and Wyoming cattle ranches and two or three Nebraska and Iowa farms. One actress purchased a small city in Alabama and plans to live there. Jane Fonda works with a high school project in Atlanta where she lives. Burt Reynolds founded and still works occasionally with a small theatre in Florida. Marlon Brando spends time helping the Indian reservation causes in his native

Nebraska and neighbor states. Greer Garson contributed a complete film sound stage complex in Santa Fe where she lived until recently. Several stars helped found and still sit on the Board of a Chicago theatre group. Some top stars operate race horse farms in Southern Florida and Kentucky.

It's not unusual for the arts organizations of any city in the country to have one or two entertainment industry luminaries on their Boards. And most of those organizations are heavy with clout but usually short on "gofers" who are willing to "go fer" whatever's needed for their activities. You can usually find one or two or many of them ready and happy to have your help in some "gofer" capacity.

The point---from the standpoint of your self promotion through 'networking'---is that in an organization that has even one or two industry people in its comittees or special activity groups you'll be able to rub elbows with and become acquainted with people who are in a position to help you if they happen to take a personal interest in you.

Even before you're a card-carrying member of one of the performing unions like SAG, AFTRA and Equity, you can find out where *their* office is and offer yourself as a volunteer to help the union in any capacity where you can be of value. If you have some special ability or professional expertise in a peripheral field that committees and projects often need---typing, wordprocessing, printing, graphic design or whatever---all the better. You can rapidly gain a far broader knowledge of the industry and industry practices and probably have occasion to meet some industry bigwigs for the first time in a peer relationship, either on union business or socially, through this contributing of your valued help.

Even as a "gofer", you'd probably be in some of the photographs taken at special events, standing beside someone important and as a result looking more important yourself than you yet are. You might be called to attend emergency meetings at stars' homes if they're chairpersons of committees having trouble getting things together. You'd be meeting people by the dozens that you wouldn't otherwise stand a chance of meeting for many years.

Even in running errands as a "gofer" you'd be given those luminaries' home phone numbers, probably meet their families, learn what projects they're working on at the time which might offer opportunities for you, etc.

Since it may be hard for some to envision how productive this volunteering and "gofering" can be as a manner of early (and even much later) self-promoting through "networking", I'm going to give you some examples out of my own biography to illustrate how the many things you involve with in this manner can mushroom into huge and unexpected results later.

In my own personal case I rather got drawn into most of these things one after another more than calculatedly getting into them with thoughts of what they could do for me, though I won't deny the ego-gratification that came with each request for my help. In hindsight I have certainly recognized the great richnesses my years of "pitching in and helping things" . . . volunteering myself . . . have brought me.

In New York in 1946, my first professional "volunteering" was for the Equity Library Theatre's Executive Board. Equity Library Theatre was and still is today a special "showcasing production" organization subsidized by Actors Equity Association. The Executive Board Members receive no pay. Their administering of the organization is strictly volunteer work on their part. I've never known why a close friend nominated me---an Equity member for only a year---for election as a Board Member in a Board that included theatre stars Peggy Wood, Sam Jaffe, Aline MacMahon, Florida Friebus, Osceola Archer and others. Perhaps it was the words "Good Gofer Material" which were probably written all over this energetic newcomer's face. In any event, my friend nominated me, I accepted nomination and was elected.

Soon there was the post of an Assistant Executive Director to be appointed for the exciting new Equity Community Theatre project which would be taking specially produced ELT productions to outlying theatres after their closings in Manhattan. Who better than the new "gofer" in the ranks to do all the hard work that the Executive Director, busy character actor Leon Askin, wouldn't have time to do?

Working my tail off on promotion for that project put me into unexpectedly close and continuous contact with the New York Times' dean of New York critics, the late Brooks Atkinson, and the New York Post's theatre editor Vernon Rice. Both of these gentlemen becoming friends, together they soon observed my hard work and results and delegated me, as their representative, to go around and meet with many of the separatist, unconnected Off Broadway producers---then still operating in isolated aloneness without any central organization, to urge and foster---as official delegate of those two leading critics---the forming of an Off Broadway League with those two critics' daily support in their columns. The Off Broadway League became a reality shortly thereafter and still exists today as the League of Off Broadway Theatres.

Again working my tail off on that wortwhile project, I learned so much that was to benefit me tremendously many years later toward helping form both the Equity Library Theatre West and the ANTA Repertory Theatre West in Hollywood in 1958 and be appointed Co-Chairman for those organizations' inaugural seasons. But what I learned was to be even more important when in 1972 it provided the base knowledge and perspective for me to personally bring together fifty Hollywood and Los Angeles theatres to form the League of Los Angeles Theatres and be elected president of that organization to serve it---most say very effectively---for its first three terms.

It didn't hurt that among the first theatres to join the new Los Angeles League were two of the most respected that were headed by producers who had been part of the original cadre of the Off Broadway League in New York, whom I'd come to know personally through helping form that earlier organization.

There were other benefits from that very first (Equity Library Theatre) volunteering, too. Peggy Wood, its president at that time, became a friend, invited me to join her and others in the Episcopal Actors Guild, where I met and worked closely with still more leading players that I wouldn't have met so soon otherwise. And almost eight years later, I'm sure it was Peggy again who had me brought in as Papa's Office Manager, Mr. Jenkins, for the last season of her "Mama" television series.

And there's still more! From working closely with top critics Vernon Rice and Brooks Atkinson on the two projects mentioned came the surprises that Mr. Rice, in 1947---after confiding that he wouldn't have found time to come see *"A Doll's House"* in its Off Broadway run if I hadn't been in it---honored me with his Off Broadway Award that year for my performance as Torvald in that play. And, two years after that, while we were still involved with forming up the Off Broadway League, when he made a special trip to Keene, New Hampshire to meet with me on details of the then rapidly progressing League, and saw my summer theatre production of *"An Inspector Calls"*, he voted me his Summer Theatre Direction Award that year!

And Mr. Atkinson too, by then a supportive friend, after a meeting about the League back in New York, stayed to sit in on my acting class and, later commenting briefly about my teaching in one of his columns, afforded me one of the critical comments of which I shall always be most proud.

And I firmly believe that I must attribute many of my early "Golden Age of Television" roles as an actor to contacts made and visibility promoted during the helping of those organizations I've mentioned thus far. At least many more people had become quickly acquainted with me than would have if I'd been simply "making the rounds" of offices daily begging for handout roles. I'm sure it all helped.

By then I was "an experienced gofer" and one was needed at that time by the brand new United Cerebral Palsy Foundation headed by Leonard Goldenson---a Hollywood film producer himself, and someone suggested "gofer" Parke to do the promotion and phoning to form up the National Sports and Entertainment Committee for the UCPF.

In setting that up and arranging its kickoff luncheon at "21 Club", I became fairly well acquainted with world champion fighter Sugar Ray Robinson and noted playwright Ben Hecht. Some results? In 1950 Sugar Ray and his then wife Edna Mae helped finance and continued supporting my first summer theatre venture as a producer-director, at Pompton Lakes, near his training camp, and in 1960 (ten years later in Hollywood) Ben Hecht asked me to work with him on the adapting of his play *"Winkelberg"* into its musical version *"Bodenheim"*.

My friend Peggy Wood, always a bigger star in London than in New York, volunteered me as official New York boat meeter and liaison for Colonel Alexander's International Artists and Artistes, a leading London talent agency for stars. Meeting Sir Laurence Olivier's ship when he arrived to play the "Cleopatras" at the Ziegfeld Theatre in the 50's produced an acquaintance with Sir Laurence which was to later make possible his coming to see and his fervent endorsement of one of my plays, *"The Cage"*, during its commercial run in Hollywood in 1964-65, which helped obtain several productions of it in world theatre capitals later.

In 1956, it was handling English television star Terry-Thomas's arrival and early managerial details in New York---again for Colonel Alexander's London agency---that put me in first contact with Ziv Television Programs, which eventually---I hardly remember how now---led to my role as "Luke" in Ziv's *"Harbourmaster"* television series, filmed at Rockport, Mass., and during that filming it was my unpaid volunteer help with some of the administrative details on location that led, when the series finished shooting, to my being brought to Hollywood by the studio's president in 1957 and being afforded a hands-on education in all departments of film and television production . . . at a very nice salary.

Forming the League of Los Angeles Theatres in 1972 and serving as its president for three years---again at no salary and again doing all the "gofer" work---brought appearances before City Council, Chamber of Commerce gatherings, etc. And my meeting and becoming acquainted with two top City Councilmen during this period on League business resulted in both of those gentlemen helping me obtain the financing for the European Festivals appearances and the subsequent European theatre capitals tours of my environmental theatre piece *"Minus One"* which had been selected by the French World Theatre Festival as that year's American entry.

Now? I've long since stopped "gofering" to devote myself to my own activities. But the foregoing are put down here as examples of the advantages which can accidentally and unexpectedly accrue from volunteering your help---especially in your early years---wherever you observe an organization that can use it. "Networking" in this manner, starting early and continuing it for as long as you want to, can bring amazing results!

But don't limit your networking to those people whom you know to already be important. In acting classes you'll meet others who, like yourself, are just starting out. They certainly don't appear to be important at that early time . . . but you never know. Through some stroke of luck they might get exciting opportunities and begin moving upward quickly. They may before long be in a position to remember you and your fine talents and recommend you for something that you wouldn't have a chance at otherwise.

In other words, "networking" doesn't just mean grabbing onto the coattails of those who are already in high positions in the industry. It means making friends, exchanging information and favors with *literally everybody.* News of projects currently being cast or scheduled to begin casting can come from just about anyone around you. And helping those others around you can produce many tips and favors in return.

31

Don't be afraid to *"pick others' brains"* for advice, information about anything you need advice about, addresses and telephone numbers, scuttlebutt about who's doing what, candid appraisals of theatres' quality or special seminars' worth, or anything at all. In a so professionally selfconscious world as acting, it's easy to be shy about risking appearing self-pushing, and many young actors hesitate to be outgoing and friendship-building with those around them. But in the end networking is *Public Relations,* often producing many unexpected and career-advancing opportunities that will never come if you don't get out among others in the industry and get involved with anything and everything around you in whatever manner you can. And it's much cheaper than paying for expensive advertising and publicity.

9

Start Tailoring Your
Professional Image...

It's never too soon to start thinking about *your professional image!* To be remembered by the people who might consider you for roles you must be *something*. . . it doesn't matter what . . . just *something.*

It's not uncommon for new actors and actresses---long before even their talents are developed---to go out and get expensive photos made, start grabbing any and all kinds of showcasing opportunities, start agent-hunting and casting director mailouts---without any thought of *what they are or have* that may interest the industry people they're trying to impress.

Your general appearance, your outstanding qualities and everything about you needs to be consciously considered and perhaps consciously adapted toward presenting yourself---in person and in your professional photos---in your most employable manner.

If you put this off, you'll waste a lot of money on early photos that you'll have to throw out later, clothes that you'll later realize are killing your acting role prospects, etc., because they confuse people, distract from your unique personality and often leave no definite impression at all.

Start thinking like a casting director, a producer and a director. Look in the mirror. Really examine yourself. Is there *anything* about your appearance that can whet industry people's interest to meet you and that will help them actually remember you afterward? If what you see in the mirror doesn't suggest some general casting category and some types of acting roles, then it's time to start doing something about it.

Don't delude yourself that your acting talent alone will get you into agency offices or casting interviews. Anyone who claims to be an actor, even a beginning one, is assumed to have talent.

Like a product on a supermarket shelf, there has to be some kind of special "packaging" that will make it stand out from all those other brands. In manufacturing it's called "product engineering", "point of sale appeal" and other very clearly sales-oriented things. Every possible device is used to attract buyers. That's what film and television industry people are . . . buyers! And you the actor are the product. An actor can't act without a job, and to get a job you must somehow manage to be "purchased" and "hired" by someone in the industry who needs what you have and are.

Manufacturers are wise enough, calculating enough, to not have their products displayed on shelves before all those _buyer-oriented devices_ are designed and in place. Actors should do the same . . . _sooner_, not later.

Following are some items that even beginning actors should consider, should do, should obtain and should painstakingly prepare before even thinking of having expensive professional photos taken, before any kind of showcasing, before asking agents to consider representing them, and before sending out mailings asking for any kind of film and television industry employers' attention:

Interview Yourself In The Mirror

This is step one. In your mirror appears a would-be actor whom you as a casting director must find interesting. As a "casting director", you have all kinds of roles to cast day after day and there are always a few of them small enough that you can dare to cast a newcomer in almost exclusively physical appearance terms, with little consideration for talent. Like most other casting directors, imagine that you maintain reminder files of different "types" for such "bit role" casting oppotunities. As you look at the actor staring at you from your mirror try to decide where in your casting reminder files that actor's photo and résumé should be filed.

Is the actor there in the mirror athletic, outdoorsy? Extremely handsome? Very unattractive? Scroungy? Hard, mean and streety looking? Executive suite? Skid Row? If his appearance doesn't suggest being dropped into one of your specific reminder file categories the photo may well go into the wastebasket with all those others that don't suggest something.

Is she glamorous and high fashion? Tomboy? Flashy and cheap-looking? Executive suite? Frumpy? Natural beauty? Frazzled housewife? Librarian / Spinster? Prison matron? You should hope that one of these is staring back at you.

Men's Image Concerns

If you're obviously _athletic and outdoorsy_, keep your body in shape with some muscles or get it that way. Muss your hair slightly for a careless look. Keep about half a tan. Stock up on plaid and plain blue denim shirts, jeans and work pants. Go to the corner barber, not a "Rodeo Drive" hair stylist. Throw away most of your ties, especially the school stripe kind. Keep a few shirts and jackets unpressed, and don't hesitate to wear them to interviews. If you've studied speech---perhaps to get rid of a regional accent, then get rid of those perfectly aspirated and dotted t's and d's, popped p's and b's, and any other speech sophistications that don't fit that wide range of _middle class, Middle American, blue collar_ types that appear in every script.

Unless a beard or mustache sets off your features and adds to a slightly rough-around-the-edges masculinity, don't grow either. They limit the spectrum of acting roles for which you can be considered. But if you have one or both of them already and are positive it's a plus, keep it, even though either or both can keep you out of the runing for some roles. And either beard or moustache will certainly limit your chances for commercials. If on the other hand you're a really scruffy-appearing fellow, either or both could help.

If you're basically _unattractive_, don't let it bother you in acting terms. Notice how many of today's top stars are fairly unattractive. Simply make sure that you can peg some casting areas where your lack of attractiveness can be a plus. Many producers and directors nowadays look for and value the "offbeat" look. If you have it, flaunt it. Make sure your shirt colors don't go with your pants colors, that your hair is just as unattractive as you feel your facial features are. Never go to either interviews or photo sessions dressed up.

If you're one of the _biker, pusher and street gang_ types, play it to the nines. Remember, we're talking appearance and manner of presenting yourself. You may be a well bred intellectual inside, but the outside is what counts in visual entertainment mediums and you should keep your Socrates and R. D. Laing hidden in a pocket when you're around industry people. Certainly keep your hair long and unkempt or in some un-dressy hair style.

If you're more the *Executive Suite or Yuppie* type, subtly say so with what you wear. Just don't go overboard and appear too selfconsciously dressy. Keep your hair well groomed and avoid the faddish long hair at the back of the neck. Again, beards and mustaches would limit you. In the 80's and 90's especially, the writer has counselled many young actors who should aim for this category to get rid of those popular long hair styles. After first resisting the advice, when they finally got business world haircuts they started working almost immediately in commercials and in those good starting-out "bit" roles for which their long-hair friends couldn't be considered.

Women's Image Concerns

Regrettable as it is, there still is and apparently always will be the inclination on the part of industry hirers to give preferential consideration to women who have natural beauty when they're casting leading roles. This is more prevalent in Hollywood casting, however, where the top leading roles are cast. Fortunately for those less attractive young women starting film and television acting careers in areas across the country, most location film and television projects' female leads have already been cast in Hollywood and the remaining small "bit" roles needn't be concerned with anything but "type" . . . and "types" come in all shapes and sizes and appearances . . . from pretty to quite unattractive.

For most new young actresses, if you're *attractive* it needn't be stressed. What needs to be there in your photos is whatever else you want to say about yourself. . . slightly tomboyish, direct and challenging, cheerleaderish, etc. For most young women, regardless of type, simple, conservative dresses are best at all times. Learn what colors compliment your hair and eyes. Don't wear more than a bit of jewelry if any . . . jewelry tends to categorize you into very limited areas. Don't have low neckline photos. Don't let too much hair dominate your photos or your office meeting impressions.

Most young women should consult hair stylists and try different hairstyles and different lengths of hair until they have what they know sets off their features. If you're not expert at putting long hair up attractively, be careful of keeping too much or too long hair. Hairstyles that are close to the outlines of your head can compliment your features without distracting by too much mass. Bangs should be kept to a minimum and the forehead should have some open space to lengthen the face. You don't see too many actresses in film with their foreheads covered.

If you happen to be *unattractive* of face, don't try to downplay this uniqueness. There are so often roles for your type in the supporting cast roles. Dress in whatever manner emphasizes the basic type into which your appearance falls. If, no matter what your inner personality, you appear *facially hard* or *streety* or *severe*, consider what your external appearance suggests and subtly tailor your wardrobe and hairstyle and manner to fit the rest.

If you're glamorous and a *high fashion* type---which of course includes the height consideration that you're probably minimum 5'9" or 5'10", quite thin and graceful of manner---you're somewhat limited in casting terms of any category but what your appearance and manner so obviously suggest. If you want to be considered for good dramatic roles those "runway model" items need to be downplayed. Your height alone limits you for any and all roles that appear in scenes with top male stars. It's unusual for a leading male star to appear shorter than the women appearing in scenes with them.

All the regimes taught at modeling schools apply for you, and you should certainly learn them and in every way aim to include top modeling among your career goals. Many top models have later become top film and television actresses . . . after they've been scouted as top models. There isn't much hope for you to make much of a mark in acting roles until you're discovered by a producer, director or casting director accidentlly watching you as a game show hostess, a Clairol spokesperson or a Paul Mitchell hair tosser in a commercial. And unfortunately you won't be expected to be a good actress at first. The fact that you may be that as well as a top model will help when the chance comes to work in a scene of whatever size with a tall leading man.

If, try as you always have tried to hide it, your mirror tells you that there's a _cheap, flashy or streety_ look about you, no matter how much or how little makeup you wear or avoid, go for it. Don't try to be like all the others. Fill your closet with fairly low-cut necklines, bright colors that may even clash, jewelry that has to be Home Shopping Club CZ because it's too flashy to be real, and higher than comfortable heels.

Actually, if you fall into the latter category, you're probably one of the ones who'll be given top consideration for the "interesting" bit roles in visiting films and television projects. It's not easy for the pretty people to change their images in any substantial degrees for different types of roles. For you in this less pretty type range it's so easy to subtly adapt to whatever one of those early bit roles calls for.

First Impressions Are Lasting Ones . . . Or They're No Impression At All!

Tailor your image early . . . _before_ you get photos, start showcasing your talents to get attention, start seeking an agent or start contacting casting directors for appointments. You'll spin your wheels for a long time if you don't do this!

10

First Interviews With
Location Casting Directors...

It may be difficult to persuade one or more of the people who handle "location casting" for films and television projects in your general area to grant the time to meet you for the purpose of acquainting themselves with your personality and your casting category, perhaps even your talents. Unlike their counterparts in Hollywood and New York, they usually have another business activity or two on which they depend for income during the long timespans between assignments to cast visiting projects. A number of these folks would probably prefer--- for that reason primarily---to simply receive your photo and résumé and keep you in mind to be called in---perhaps first for only "extra" jobs if for anything at all.

But there are some more conscientious location casting people who do really want to know not only what you look like but also _what you are_ in casting category terms and also _whether you can act_. This kind of casting person might well be responsve if s/he receives in the mail from you a decent-looking photo and even a bare-bones, almost empty résumé enclosed with a single paragraph note requesting an appointment. If you're somebody just starting out, with no "credits" (jobs to list) yet, consider it encouraging . . . and at least partially a favor . . . if one of them will actually afford you an appointment.

If you do get an appointment, understand that it's simply what's called a "General Interview" . . . a meeting to get acquainted. That's better than nothing.

Certainly consider the casting category impression you want to leave with the person. Wear the right kind of clothes to help leave that impression. And at least subtly behave in the interview itself in a manner that will help do the same. All the advice in the "Image" chapter applies at such a meeting. Don't appear "dressed up".

Be sure to bring a photo and résumé with you to leave with the person, even though you've already sent them with your request for the meeting.

Don't try to impress them with how _versatile_ you are. To be remembered, you must be remembered as _something definite_. And don't be a "Big Smiler" and wipe out any possible serious consideration. Maintain a serious, direct manner that allows your particular personality and casting category to be easily apparent. A "Please like me", perpetual smile will tell them nothing. And if you've been doing theatre, don't "project" and sound like a stage actor. Talk on a strictly "living presence" level, just as you would on a film set.

If you're really at heart a moody, serious person, make sure that's easily detectable. There are many more roles of all kinds for disturbed, troubled young people than for nextdoor nice guys and girls.

It's unusual for a new actor to be asked to "audition" at such a meeting, but it could happen, and be happy if it does. You might be handed a short piece of script or a bit of commercial copy to read after you've taken some moments to look it over. If it's even slightly dramatic, don't try to make it *more* dramatic to exhibit your talent. Keep it simple. And if it's some commercial copy simply keep it bright. Location casting people know that the habit of <u>overacting</u> will kill any chances for you in auditions for film and television people.

If asked to prepare and present a scene or monologue for a film-oriented casting director, the worst thing you can do is choose a loud, wildly dramatic piece! It's the most common mistake actors can make when asked to bring in something to help agency or casting people judge your talents. When yelling and in violent action and histrionics---thinking that kind of work will show how *dramatic* you can be, you're not only showing your ignorance of the kind of dramatics appropriate for most film work but you're also making it impossible for the person viewing the piece to observe your personality, your subtleties and even your normal speaking voice! Working at such a peak level completely wipes out those qualities that set you apart from other actors!

Ideal is a scene or monologue involving deep feelings, of course, but one that allows you more "between the lines" (non-dialogue) moments spinkled throughout. Film is a visual medium, remember.

And don't go in to present a scene or monologue half-prepared. Either be ideally ready or don't go in with it. And never, after finishing, say something like "It didn't work right that time. Can I do it again?" It's the mark of an amateur, and you'll be witten off.

Expect to be in the office or the casting person's living room for no more than about fifteen minutes or a little longer. The longer the meeting, the better the impression you're making. If you're just starting out, the most important thing to leave them with is the fact that you'd be happy to be called for <u>anything</u>, whether a tiny bit role or even an "extra" job. And you'll know when the meeting is over. Simply thank them for meeting you and leave.

11

Role Interviews, Readings
and "Extra" Auditions...

In Hollywood, if you're trying for a *speaking* role---even a tiny one, you'd be meeting and reading for either the producer or the director or both. If it's for an *extra* job you'd simply be called for, perhaps even sight unseen, by the First Assistant Director. But location casting is most often handled differently.

For location casting of even tiny bit roles, the casting person, thinking you *may* be right for something, may call you in to read for him or her privately first. You'll be told where to come to pick up your "sides"---the script pages from which you'll be reading. You'll be able to take your "sides" home to study them.

Dress for a casting interview with some thought about the character. Producers, directors and casting people as well often form their impressions visually the minute you walk into the room. If what you're wearing is at least somewhat right for *who and what the character is and the situation it's in,* you won't be ruled out in those first moments.

There may be some suggestions made in that first audition, to help prepare you to do your best when you meet the location production people. Following that private "coaching" session, you may or may not get a "callback" to audition for someone else. If the Hollywood casting director comes to the location, as they sometimes do to oversee even the local casting, the next step---if you're called back---will be to read for the Hollywood casting person. Chances are that you won't yet be reading for the director or producer (unless they're terribly pressed for time). Again, if you're considered a possible, there may be a bit of "coaching" by the Hollywood person. If after reading for the Hollywood casting person you're still in the running---or if the Hollywood person isn't coming to location and your only preliminary reading will have been with the location (local) casting person, your "callback" will be to read for the director or producer or both immediately upon their arrival at location from Hollywood.

Arrive at least a half hour before your call time for all these appointments. To appear professional, immediately report in at the receptionist's desk. Give him or her your

39

name and be checked off. You'll be called in the order of scheduled times. Hold onto your "sides", even if you think you're secure with you line(s). The people interviewing don't expect you to know your lines at those readings. And, nervous in the interview, you'll likely forget and fumble even if you felt secure before coming to the interview.

When shown inside to read for the production head(s), you'll be briefly introduced and probably invited to sit for the reading (unless it's mostly physical appearance and manner they're looking for). You'll be invited to read immediately.

If you need to refer to the "sides" to keep up with your dialogue, hold the page(s) as low as possible and refer to them if you need to when *not talking*. Keep your face up, at an acceptable film level, when talking, just as you'd have to do in the actual scene.

If it's a *tiny bit* role with only one or a few speeches, talk directly into the eyes of the casting person reading opposite you. You're expected to keep it simple. Such roles should not be too interesting or they might distract from the leading or supporting actor who's going to be playing opposite you. You're visually right, and have the right manner for that tiny role or you wouldn't be on callback. Simple, good line readings, coupled with how you look and sound, are what are expected and hoped for . . . completely natural, but not interesting enough to be distracing!

But if you have a larger role, with quite a few speeches and perhaps some action involved, they'd like you to be more interesting, and they'll be hoping that there's more of the character's experience---its mood, feeling and human colors---than they'd want in a tiny bit role. For this size of role, appear to have to think of what to say, not be so glib with your lines that they appear to be known ahead of time. For this kind of somewhat larger role you're allowed the luxury of having an attitude and being a total human being.

In both of these types of role interviews it's common for new, very nervous actors to forget to *listen to the other character and react while they're speaking!* The new actor is often so nervous about his or her own lines that this is overlooked. Remember that in either type of role *listening and reacting* may be your main contribution to the scene.

You won't be told after your reading whether you have the role or not. There are others competing for the same role and the director and producer need to confer with each other after all have been auditioned. You'll either be called later (in perhaps a day or two or perhaps the same afternoon)---by your agent if you have one, or direct if you don't---and told they want you, or there'll be no call and you'll know somebody else has been cast.

And don't despair if you *don't* get the role. Don't think it was some failure on your part. There are so many other considerations in casting . . . too tall, not the ideal look, a bit of local accent or the absence of one, etc., etc.

When the author was a talent agent in Hollywood he had a very heavy woman client with a broad Texas accent named Pollyanna Houston. She was sent out for many interviews and wasn't cast. In my office one day I told her how sorry I was that she wasn't getting roles. She smiled and said "Don't worry, honey. Every time I miss out gets me that much closer to the one I'll get." Within weeks, she was cast as "Mrs. O'Grady", his acid-tongued landlady, in Robert Blake's *"Baretta"* television series at Universal! In the series she seldom had more than one or two speeches, but she was happy and worked nearly every week over a period of time.

The latter example brings to mind another point for actors seeking casting on location: If you're cast in a small role in a single episode of a television series, don't be dismayed. It's quite possible that if you do an excellent job and depending on the milieu of the series you may wind up with what's called a *recurring role*---one that will be brought back for several more episodes of the series.

12

Your First Film
Acting Role!...

It will come if you keep trying. Some location production will eventually want you for the role. You need to know what that first speaking role involves.

If it's a union signatory production, as most Hollywood producions shooting on location are, then you have the opportunity to join the Screen Actors Guild . . . and if you're serious about your career you certainly should. There's a big advantage to joining the Guild in your own area. In many states outside the Hollywood and New York production center territories it costs much, much less to join. In one state, New Mexico, it costs just $150 for the membership initiation fee, plus the first six months' dues of $42.50 . . . a total of only $192.50! If you don't join before moving to Hollywood someday it will cost over $800 for the membership initiation fee, plus, again, the six months' dues of $42.50! And after that first role, if you then have your SAG membership card, you'll be considered "a professional" by other location productions coming to your area.

It should be added that, when and if you do move to Hollywood or New York later, you will have to pay the difference---in the foregoing example, between $192.50 and close to $900---but while you're still building your professional credits in your own area you'll have that card that says you're a professional actor, and when you do move to Hollywood to advance your career you'll already be a SAG member. The SAG membership card is even more important in Hollywood.

To join the SAG, simply locate the Local or Regional Office of SAG that has jurisdiction in your area and ask for the application forms. That office will have already been made aware of your being cast and is simply waiting to find out whether you want to join the Guild or do your first role under the *Taft-Hartley Law*, which is your option.

If you decide to do the first speaking role under that Law you're permitted to. However, after that first role you're allowed to do another role under that Law *only within a thirty day period.* The next role, whenever it comes, will require SAG membership.

41

The only exception to this is in a "Right to Work" state, where by Law you cannot be refused any kind of employment because you're not a member of whatever union generally applies to such employment. That includes SAG in these states.

Anyone will tell you: Join SAG at your first opportunity! It's not only required of all professional film and television actors; it's also another valuable venue for *networking*, increasing your visibility in professional circles. Start attending all Membership Meetings, meeting experienced professionals and listening to their points of view in the open discussions at meetings. There are always SAG programs that can be of benefit to you. And there are committees formed in SAG local chapters where an amount of participation and work on committee activities is repaid in new friendships formed, information exchanged among fellow committee members, increased knowledge of the entertainment industry and its language and terms, opportunities to display and perhaps develop abilities that others in the committees don't have, and sound professional advice and support for each other in problem times.

New SAG members that volunteer themselves for such committees and really dig in and help in whatever manner they can will always find their industry knowledge growing and their industry contacts expanding swiftly.

But, most important of all . . . belonging to SAG means you're *a professional film and television actor!*

13

The Film Job,
Step By Step

In so many of the seminars conducted by the author for film actors in Hollywood, some who've been working in film and television for years have come up to me afterward to say "I never knew that!" and other similar comments about some of the items which are included in this chapter. Often they've even been actors whose work I've seen in a number of films.

Of course in an actor's first film job a director is prepared to have to teach the basics of acting for the camera at many steps along the way. But if armed with enough foreknowledge about _what to do each step along the way_---from getting the role through to getting more roles because of the manner in which each is carried out---an actor can appear to be a seasoned professional on a film set the very first time he works. If _ignorant_, on the other hand, of the many, many things that should be known, checklisted to be done and systematically and professionally taken care of---before, during and after the job---the actor can suffer many indignities on the set, may never work for the director again, may have his role reduced to shreds on the cutting room floor because of problems, and may be too embarrassed to try again.

So, here we go . . . into the many things that _can_ be done, _should_ be done, and in some cases _must_ be done to make each film role---whether the first or the hundred and first---a stepping stone to more and better roles and to optimum upward mobility in a film acting career.

It all starts with being hired.

When You're Told You Have The Role...

If it's your first job you won't care about the salary or billing. Even if it's another in a building list of credits, as long as you're a locally cast actor in a location film or television project, you can't expect much if any more in salary than "scale" (SAG minimum) or perhaps "scale plus ten", with the extra ten percent allowed to cover your agent's commission. As to billing, you'll be happy enough to see your name at the end of all the other names, but if your role has any size you may find yourself automatically listed in the end credits ahead of some of your friends in lesser roles. Even if you're not in a position yet to demand specific billing, if the role and your performance warrants it you'll be given it.

You'll be called to pick up your script and, while in the casting office, probably be asked to _talk to Wardrobe_ by phone. (On location, sometimes you're told that Wardrobe will call you later.) If it's a role that requires only your own available street clothing that's how it will be handled. If on the other hand you have to go to a special location and meet with the Wardrobe person for a _fitting_, because special wardrobe is required, a _fitting fee_ will be added to your pay check automatically.

If you're a _day player_---working for only one day or perhaps two or so, but hired at a "daily" salary rate---you won't sign your contract in the casting office. That will be done, along with other employment papers of the production company, when you report for your first day's work. The Second Assistant who checks you in when you first report for work will hand you your contract, a W-4 (tax withholding) form and any other employment papers the company requires. Fill in the blanks and sign all these papers quickly and get them back to the Second Assistant so they can be on their way to the Payroll Department.

Sometimes the script is delivered at your door by courier---yes, even if you have just one or two speeches! The script you receive first---either in the casting office or at your home---will be _"the whites"_---that's what the final shooting script is called. Sometimes there are _"revision pages"_ delivered along with the white pages, in which case you're expected to insert the revision pages, substituting them for their similarly numbered white pages. Revision pages are most often (but not always) blue for first revisions, yellow or pink for second, green for third, etc.

Women will be told to _talk to the Hairdresser_ and will be instructed as to what to do. Usually they're told to set their own hair in their accustomed manner the night before but _not comb out_. The Hairdresser must do the comb-out the next morning just before filming.

If you're brave enough to start self-promoting at this point, call the local newspaper's City or Entertainment Editor and tell them you've been cast. Sometimes your nearby papers are happy to write a special article about local actors cast in film roles.

You'll probably receive with your "white pages" script a _Shooting Schedule_, indicating which scenes are expected to be shot on which days, and where.

Learn your lines cold! No actor should ever arrive on a film set in less than totally secure condition with lines. Too many things happen on film sets that disrupt the actor's concentration, so if you're less than secure on lines it will be found out quickly, and you'll be in very hot water and cause shooting delays and retakes.

When you receive "revision pages" to put into your script, check and make sure that your original script lines haven't been changed. If they have, learn the new lines quickly.

The Night Before You Work...

Don't party the night before you're scheduled to shoot! Be by your phone until you get your _Work Call_, telling you where and what time to report, and to whom, the next morning. Be sure to get all the details clearly. In the call, if they use the phrase "Ready by---", which they may not with newcomers, "Ready" means in makeup and wardrobe, at the place indicated, at the exact time set . . . ready for filming.

If you've been hired to work more than one day your call will also include the _scene numbers_ you'll be in the next day, so you can concentrate more specifically on the next day's filming, perfecting the lines involved and reminding yourself of ideas you have for different moments in the scenes involved. If you've received a _Shooting Schedule_ with your script you'll find each day's planned scene numbers in it. (In film scripts, the Scene Numbers are the numbers running down the side of the pages, while the _page_ numbers appear at the top right corner, with a period after the number. Some new actors don't know.)

Be sure to _set your alarm clock_ before you accidentally nod off and sleep through after studying your lines into the night. If you're late for your morning call arrival and reporting in all hell breaks loose and it can start your day off miserably. Film Set union crews cost big money. And lay the script out for taking with you in the morning.

Speaking of the script . . . from the first telephone call or meeting with the casting person, then the producer and director, then Wardrobe, Makeup and Hairdresser people, _start jotting down those people's names_ somewhere . . . just inside the front of the script is a good place. And when you get to the set, continue this name-jotting, filling in names you haven't already gotten . . . the Second Assistant Director who checks you in, the Wardrobe supervisor (if you haven't already talked with him or her), Makeup, Props, etc. It makes you more a professional if you call them by name. It's a "grace note" that can bring extra considersation. They're artists, just as you are. If your job is for several days you'll feel more like, and be accepted more as, a member of "the family".

For your work day, you'll either be picked up at your home or hotel and driven to the location, or you may be expected to drive yourself to some designated place.

Any _clothing from your own personal wardobe_ that you've been asked to bring for the role must not be what you wear to and from the set. Sometimes they'll ask you to bring several articles for last-minute choosing from among several articles. And what you're to wear in the role, if you're working more than one day, is expected to be _left in your dressing room_ at the end of the shooting day so it can be cleaned or laundered during the night hours, if necessary, for the next day's shooting.

Women _shouldn't wear any street makeup to the set_! Any makeup you might have on---out of ignorance of this standard procedure---would have to be taken off before Makeup can "give you your face" before shooting. You're expected to know this. Street makeup is not film makeup. It must be done---from start to finish---by the expert who's paid good money to make you look good or look whatever way you're supposed to look for your role.

People On The Set---Working With Them...

The minute you arrive at location, _report in at once to the Second Assistant_. Until you've done that you haven't reported in. Since you won't have met him or her, and won't know what he or she looks like, ask the first person you can "Who's the Second, and where is he?" Someone will point out the man or woman.

This "Second Assistant" is in charge of the actors . . . getting them to Wardrobe or Makeup, getting them transported to the set if it's not nearby, knowing exactly where they all are every minute. And you'll be getting your next day's call from him or her at the end of the day if you're working more than the one day.

After noting your arrival time on a Timesheet and having you sign it, the Second will show you where your _dressing room_ is. You'll find your _wardrobe_, if you haven't brought it from home, with your character's name pinned to it, neatly hung in the dressing room closet. If you've brought your own wardrobe for Wardrobe's selection, show them the articles for their choice. If the cast for the day's filming is small you'll have your own private dressing room. If there are many actors working that day you'll share with another actor.

Actors who work often know this: The dressing rooms are usually located at one end of the "_honey wagon_". The honey wagon has men's and women's bathrooms in it. Not having to ask where yours is will again make you look professionally experienced. Small point.

The "Second" will have you sign your contract and the other employment forms. As mentioned earlier, get them back quickly so they'll be on their way to Payroll. Even before you have time to fill them out the Second will get you to Wardrobe or Makeup---whichever you're needed to go to first.

45

Even _in the Makeup chair_ you can appear professional or amateur by what you do or don't know. The Makeup person will smooth the base on your face. Next comes the blush and other colorings for women and sometimes a bit for men too. The next step is the tell-tale one for fellows . . . the eyelining pencil (the "ouch stick" that men aren't used to if they haven't done a lot of film). It helps the Makeup person if you close your eyes and actually look down with them closed while the top lid is being lined first, then have them wide open and looking far upward while the bottom lining is being applied. Actors who work often in film do these two steps this way by second nature.

Powdering down presents no problem. But then comes another telltale operation when the Makeup person says he or she wants to "give you your hands." Don't ask what is meant. Just make sure your sleeves are rolled up past the wrist and hold out your hands palms down. Makeup will dawb some base onto the backs of your hands. It's then your job to spread the makeup evenly over your hands and up onto the wrists or even onto the arms as far as needed to meet your wardrobe. Then wipe off the palms of your hands on tissue from the box in front of you on the Makeup Stand so you won't get makeup all over your wardrobe. Powdering down of the hands and wrists after makeup is usually done for you, after you've spread the base evenly. This hands makeup is necessary so that in shots your face won't be one color and your hands stark white as they'd appear by contrast if not also made up.

The facial tissue that's put inside your callar or dress bodice by Makeup should be left there until just before an actual filming, to protect your wardrobe. When a shot is finished, if there's to be some time between it and the next shot you're in, get another tissue from Makeup to put in its place.

Once you're in makeup and wardrobe, it could be a good idea to _wander near to where the Director is and simply say "Good morning" or something_, so he can take a hurried look at you and either approve of your wardrobe and how you look or call for something to be changed. Don't hang next to him. He's very busy. You've simply given him a chance to check how you look and save time at the last minute later.

Be prepared to stand around or sit somewhere waiting, sometimes for hours, before they're ready for your first scene. Finally . . . about the time your nerves are shattered from the long wait . . . you'll be called to rehearse one of your scenes, first for _blocking_ and getting your _marks_, then on camera. It may be the first time you'll meet several people close up that you've only watched from a distance throughout the waiting for your turn.

Others On The Set...

The _First Assistant Diretor_ (called simply _"The First")_ is the person who bellows out "Quiet! . . . Give us a bell! . . . Kill the blowers! . . . Roll 'em! (or Roll Sound)," etc., when everything's ready for a take. This person is the "Sergeant Major" on the set . . . the "Straw Boss". While the Director is responsible for the creative element in filming, _The First_ is responsible for all the technical aspects, through "pre-production" (rounding up technical crews, supervising things with Carpentry, Set Decoration and other crews). S/he prepared the Breakdown (what to shoot when and where, with what physical production elements and what casts). S/he arranged for use permits to shoot on private property locations. At the end of the shooting day, when everybody else goes home for the night, s/he's starting another long night preparing the next day's shooting. Then s/he's up ramrodding everything by daybreak! Don't bother this busy person. No contact is expected with the actors.

The _Script Supervisor_ is the person with the script on a clipboard or stand, with a ruler and stopwatch hanging from around his or her neck, who's usually busy marking down each take on pages of the script as to "story minutes" and "minutes on film", etc. The Script Supervisor's copy of the script is the one used later by the Editor as reference as to what takes there are of every scene, what different versions of the same brief scenes there are, etc. The Script Supervisor also constantly monitors "matching" details as to wardrobe, hair, etc., in case something doesn't match the way it was, or was done, in another angle of the scene.

The *Cinematographer* (whose other titles are *Director of Photography* and simply *Cameraman)* rides the camera setting up best angles and frames with the Director. After making sure that lighting is perfect, the right filters are being used, that actors are going to remain in focus easily, etc., he sometimes climbs off the camera and---union featherbedding being what it is, at least in Hollywood more than on location shoots---turns the camera over to his second, the *Operator* (or *Assistant Cameraman)*, who will actually shoot the scene most of the time unless the Cameraman opts to do the shots himself.

During rehearsals prior to the actual shots, experienced actors ask the Cameraman "When am I in?"---which an actor needs to know when walking into a shot; "When am I out?"---when exiting a continuing scene and having no other way of knowing when he's out of the camera's frame; or "Where are you cutting me?"---to find out where to hold a prop to have it appear in the frame, etc.

One with whom you'll have little or no contact is *Slates*, who holds the clapboard with scene number, location, director's name, participants in the shot and the take number chalked on it, and claps it loudly, barely missing your nose---because it has to be in focus as well as your face is. Slates usually rides the side seat on the camera dolly and continually adjusts focus to preset marks during camera or action moves.

The *Grips* are the men who move things and carry things and hold things. They're headed by the *Key Grip*.

The Lighting Crew, who set and adjust the lighting, is headed by the *Gaffer* (the head honcho), assisted by the *Best Boy* (his No. 1 assistant) and several others you'll seldom notice. Some of them are on the catwalk over the soundstage floor or standing behind the individual lights brought in to supplement the natural lighting.

The Sound Crew includes the *Recorder* (whom you probably won't ever see, because he stays hidden away in the soundproof sound truck at the edge of the set), the *Mixer* (who adjusts the dials on his console next to the set for best recording of dialogue and sound) and the *Boom Man* who on location stands next to scenes in progress most of the time and extends the microphone boom out over the actors' heads, flipping the mike back and forth toward whichever person has the next line).

Others you might never actually meet personally are the *Stand-ins*, including your own. But there's something you need to know: When you hear the call *"First Team!"* that means you, the actors. You're being called back for shooting with that yell. Before that, the Director has rehearsed you and blocked you into positions, establishing your "Marks". Then you'll hear *"Second Team!"*. That means you should leave the set as the Stand-ins (the "Second Team") come to the set and literally "stand in" your positions while lighting is being adjusted on your marked positions.

Film Acting Requires Working With The Camera

Although if you're a beginning actor cast in your first role in a location production you're not expected to know many if any of the basics, you can understand how relieved and pleased the Director will be if you know some or all of the following things, so he won't have to take time during filming to teach you.

First off . . . *Left Frame* is to your right when you face the camera. *Right Frame* is to your left in the same position. Rarely will the Director use these phrases to a newcomer, but if he does you'll know.

Before your scene is shot there'll be at least one *Dry Run* or rehearsal of it---sometimes no more than just that one or perhaps two at the most---for setting your positions and giving you your *"Marks"* on the floor or sidewalk, to set camera angles and movements, and to make sure everything that happens in the shot is right.

When everything's right from the camera's standpoint a fellow with a piece of chalk or some white tape will *"give you your marks"*---outline where your feet must wind up when you stop someplace or stand someplace. You'll be expected to be able to walk onto those marks skillfully (and stop directly on them) without looking down at them. Actors who can always "hit their marks" time after time work more often than the less accomplished in this always required, very technical feat. Actors who can't "hit their marks" cause many interruptions of takes and cost precious minutes of time.

There are various approaches for "hitting your marks", but there are only two that are that dependable. What might be called *peripheral vision* or *relative position* means estimating how far you're to wind up from one or two objects . . . perhaps a chair on one side and a table on another; a tree trunk on one side and a rock pile on the other. You need to estimate how far you are to wind up from these objects both to the side and to the front.

There's really *only one very exact method* for hitting your marks when there aren't enough pieces of furniture or other objects to relate to in knowing exactly where to stop. The best of all manners involves what surveyors and photographers use: *Lining Up* or *Crosshairs* or whatever you want to call it.

This method, when you're given your marks as to where you're to wind up after a move, and the direction you're to be looking is established in the blocking, means that you should *line up*---both vertically and horizontally, one nearer and one more distant object, or a point on each, making sure neither object or point is going to be moved. Stationary objects only! . . . building roofs, trees, desks, lamps, windows, streetlights, pictures on walls . . . . whatever. Notice exactly where two imaginary points intersect. Then, if in moving back to that spot later you wind up even inches to the right or left or in front of or behind your marks the intersecting point won't be quite the same and you can easily correct your position as you "settle in" on your marks without anyone being aware of the small adjustment.

When you hear *"First Position!"* called out, you should get onto your marks. At that point, just before starting the take, you may hear *"Powder down!"* called out by the Cameraman if he detects some perspiration shine on the actor's face. Makeup will scurry to the actor and "powder down" the offending perspiration spots.

The actual filming will probably be *Master Shots* first . . . shots which involve any large or moving action, or perhaps some complicated camera dollying or panning, etc. A newcomer, already very nervous to do everything right and remember lines, often forgets that s/he must also bear in mind *exactly how* s/he stood, how a prop was held, the angle of the head, what was being done with hands, etc. There are normally more and different camera angles (called *"coverage"*) taken of the actor in each of those positions later. Those "coverage" shots will include your *Closeups*---usually your head only, *Medium Shots*---usually the top half of the body, often including two actors, *Reverses*---probably shooting from behind one actor's head toward another actor who's in closeup, *Over-The-Shoulder Shots*---the same as "reverses" but usually framing the shot with the side of one actor's head and shoulder. There are all kinds of shots---different *"angles"* that may be taken of the same short scene. And you must "match" your body use in all of them!

For film acting it's ideal to make *extremely conscious, definite and precise movements* at all times . . . not only for the "matching" reason, but also so the camera can comfortably keep you "in frame" in a particular way and anticipate every move. The camera doesn't like surprises.

Top film actors also know that it helps keep film frames interesting visually---while it also duplicates our unconscious real-life body involvement more truly as well---if a hand is used in some manner around or on the head some of the time. Lean on a hand, perhaps, to think . . . remembering exactly how you do it, of course. Play with a collar or

48

something . . . again remembering exactly what you do. Hold your disturbed forehead . . . and remember how you do it. A face and nothing else in a closeup can become a little dull after a few moments. Use your taste and judgment, of course, but it's worth keeping in mind and trying.

Hold the head fairly up almost all the time. The face and eyes need to be visible to the lens. This is fairly standard as a requirement . . . and experienced actors know it.

On film sets you sometimes see the Director stand near the camera during actors' closeups or some two-shots (with two people in frame) and hold his or her hand at *lens level, about three feet from the camera, to its right or left,* telling the actor to "Look at your thoughts and what you're talking about over here most of the time." There are several reasons . . . some being simply technical for the camera; some being more aesthetic . . . for this being the spot where you may be asked to look and think most of the time:

(1) The lens is the viewer's horizon level as the scene is viewed later in a film or television piece. The viewer, with the actor's horizon being the same as his own, can forget that it's film being observed and feel like an unobserved bystander to the action;

(2) When looking or talking at that angle the actor's two eyes and the thoughts and processes behind them are clearly visible to the lens;

(3) That point where the Director is indicating is where the other character's face supposedly is in many cases, since most camera recording of interaction is done at an angle which places the viewer almost (but seldom exactly) in the direction being talked toward. Almost never will you be asked to talk directly to the camera lens, except as a spokesperson in a commercial or as a threatener in a horror picture;

(4) The "horizon" level is really more truthful for the actor as well, since people being talked about, things being reenvisioned, etc., literally lie out there on the true horizon over which they disappeared. Similarly, tomorrow's hopes and dreams lie somewhere out there on the same true horizon.

Cultivate this manner of working . . . before a Director has to stop to teach you one of the things every film actor must learn.

Some Definite No-No's for Film Actors!...

Word-Jiggling and *Syllable-Shaking* is something some actors and other people aren't aware they're doing. This teenage habit---usually developed in the years when there's insecurity as to one's ability to communicate effectively---looks terrible on film! It works well for a bubbly, bouncy Drive-in car hop, or in a teens scene in a high school corridor, or in a teenage boys' or girls' gym descriptions of their previous nights' conquests. In adult film roles it might be allowed for a glib, talkative character of little or no depth and probably little honesty, but for few other types of characters. It's one of the most distracting habits an actor can bring to a film set, and the camera hates it!

Watch leading actors and actresses and top players in film and television more closely. There's none of that jiggling and shaking to simply talk. Observe how much more clearly you can see their inner thoughts, attitudes, fragmented inner processes . . . because they're not shaking their heads and jerking around when they're talking. The habit doesn't work for film acting and it's seldom allowed to even get onto a film set.

Quick, unpredictable or jerky movement of any kind is sometimes impossible for the Cameraman to hold ideally in frame. Experienced actors know that the camera makes most movements appear a little more rapid than they actually are.

Weavers and *Drifters* are guilty of wasting a lot of film. The "Weaver" is the actor who keeps shifting his or her weight unconsciously from one foot to the other for whatever reason, usually nervousness. The "Drifter" is the "I'm very involved" actor who drifts

49

across the shot in order to achieve the ultimate in his or her version of deep feeling experience. Both the Weaver and the Drifter cause many interruptions of shots by the Cameraman.

The *Bouncer*, too, causes problems. He is one of two things . . . either an actor talking wth hands too much (therefore causing his head to jiggle up and down in the shot) or an actor who's so nervous that he simply bounces up and down like a selfconscious Freshman, pressuring himself to remember his lines successfully . . . meanwhile, making the wallpaper or trees in the background bounce with him if the camera is to hold his face in center frame as planned. For some characters bouncing is appropriate, but when it is the camera simply doesn't bounce up and down with the character, thereby emphasizing it as a character trait.

There are what are called *Haystack Actors*, too. When their heads and face are constantly down and you can't see anything but their blonde or brunette "haystacks" of hair, somebody's going to yell "Cut!" quickly to teach the actor the correct head and face angle for film.

Some actors are incurable *Overlappers* of others' dialogue or action. In your closeups or other shots involving <u>only you</u> in the shot, you should wait a beat before responding with your lines, no matter how false it may seem the first few times. This isn't true in "group shots" or shots involving two people, but it's desired in your own closeups.

This is a film acting requisite because sound recording of the "dialogue track" is on tape. Scissors have to get in between the last sound before your words and the start of your voice, so that your closeups can be cut into the picture . . . otherwise you're "overlapping". If you're a hopeless ovrlapper who can't be persuaded out of the habit on the set you'll spend a lot of time at the ends of shooting days in the *Looping Stage*'s soundproof booth re-recording your own dialogue. But the bigger problem with "overlappers" is that other players whose dialogue you've overlapped will have to be sent to the Looping Stage too. It becomes costly for the production in terms of additional time and payroll money.

And there's *Visual Overlapping* as well. Body movements which are to accompany your dialogue shouldn't begin too suddenly after the other person's speeches when your closeups are being filmed. Otherwise, the Editor will have to cut into the end of your body's adjustments in the Editing Room, losing some of your action in moving, so that the previous speaker's speech can be totally cut into the film. The Editor cutting the picture detects such problems quickly and the number of your own closeups eventually cut into the picture may be approximately zero as a result. And even the leaping into physical movement the split second the Director yells "Action!" will be overlapping, because his voice is still ending on the tape and, again, there's no space for the scissors to cut between the two.

Hands-Talking is a big problem actors may have and may not know they have. "Matching" becomes involved, even if constant "frame-jiggling" doesn't. The "hands-talker" (who can't talk without using his hands to help say words and accompany every speech in some manner) can't possibly match in a later shot what he did in an earlier version of the same sequence.

An example out of the past: There used to be what were called *"Zasu Pitts Cutaways"*. Miss Pitts, in those old films, constantly fluttered her hands along with her quavering speeches and still fluttered them in her silent moments. It was one of the things audiences found "charming" and certainly unique. But it was impossible for her hands to be in the same fluttering positions in all the angles of shots in continuing sequences. Her closeups couldn't possibly be cut directly into any other kinds of shots of the same scenes. So the solution became one of shooting "cutaway" shots---of maybe ducks on a pond (for no reason) or of an old hound dog scratching fleas outside a screen door (again, for no reason). This allowed for cutting away from one of Zasu's closeups to the scratching dog or the ducks, then back to Zasu, and it didn't matter what position her hands had been in in the previous moment. In today's more rapid-paced industry, few people are afforded the luxury of Zasu Pitts cutaways.

Some Basic Film Techniques and On Set Behavior...

Learn to Cheat! When playing the foreground (closest to camera) position in a "two shot" that involves two actors---one in closeup and the other farther from the camera, with both players facing generally forward in the direction of the camera---which saves time and money by obviating the reversing of lighting and camera positions continually, you need the "soap opera actor's" ability to be talking to another character who's standing behind you on the other side of the frame of the shot. Some actors have difficulty making this convincing because they've been in classes where they've worked straight into others' eyes all the time.

Foreground acting requires expert, convincing "cheating" . . . when talking to people behind you; when listening to them; when sharing and relating with them equally as much as if you were also looking at them. Actors who can't do this in a convincing and comfortable manner usually wind up in the background---and as a result smaller in the frame, but even there they need to be able to talk to where they know the foreground player's eyes are without having to lean out on their side of the shot to look into those other characters' eyes.

You should learn to do this "cheating" convincingly and become totally comfortable with it. As mentioned above, the soap opera actor has to do it in almost every single shot where there are two actors. Learn it! Get used to doing it!

For actors who are trained to focus on *their characters' own experiences* (rather than on the other character) it's "duck soup" and totally fulfilling, but for those who are taught to "get everything from the other character" or continually "do something to the other character"---which is lousy training for a film actor to begin with, it can be an uncomfortable manner of working. Face it. Get used to it. Come to enjoy it. It's an often encountered manner of working before the camera.

Also, get used to *stopping dead and standing still* just out of the shot when you have to exit a continuing shot. Don't continue walking. Experienced actors simply step out of the camera's frame, then stop dead in their tracks till the shot in progress is completed. The reason? Their footsteps which would be disappearing in the distance will be dubbed in on the Dubbing Stage later. They'll be the right kind of footstep sounds, whereas yours, perhaps stepping from a carpeted set onto a wooden floor, wouldn't match, sound-wise. It's simply the way this is done. You're expected to know.

When you're in a group scene of any kind but have observed that for a time you're not on camera, *stay in character anyway!* Don't goof around, even in a camera rehearsal or run-through of any kind. And don't just "go dead" just because you know the camera's not on you during a part of the shot. If you believe that what you're doing won't be in the shot you might even be mistaken and cause a stoppage and be bawled out.

If you remain in character and keep doing what your character should be doing, it's even possible that the Director or Cameraman might notice and, even though they haven't planned to "cut away" to your piece of activity, they might suddenly decide that they should do an extra shot of you and what you're doing . . . affording you some more footage in the scene. Act and react, in other words, even when the camera's off of you, until the scene ends. It has often paid off for the actors who do it. Anything else on your part can be distracting and annoying to the Director.

Bring more than your lines to the set! Generally, these days, you won't have even gotten past the reading for the role if the lines are all you know to bring. If there are more than one or two lines for your role, you'll probably have gotten the role in the first place because you've brought to the reading more of the character and its personal experience than others did in their readings.

51

Once you've gotten one of those roles with two, three or more speeches, the process mustn't stop. You've been hired because the Director realized that he wouldn't have to spoon-feed to you those interesting "character's experience" moments or inventive ideas. He'll expect that, in homework preparation, you'll come up with still more little touches for those generally "between the lines" moments as well as for those moments involving dialogue.

Between shots, it can be a good idea to jot down on you copy of the script, in the appropriate spots in dialogue and action, any _changes_ that may have occurred to your hair, wardrobe, props or body during the scene just finished, to assist in the "matching" process in subsequent scenes or coverage (different angle) shots. The production's _Continuity_ person (or the Script Supervisor) will probably have caught the change and noted it too, but you can help. And they'll appreciate it if they see that you remembered. If the wind blew your hair awry during the scene, notice it, so that in the next shot it will be the way it wound up in the other shot. If a cigarette was half smoked, notice it for matching in the next shot. If you buttoned or unbuttoned something, notice it and mark it in the script.

The foregoing is especially vital when, out on a location somewhere, you walk up to a building door to enter---at which point the action will be "Cut!"---and perhaps days or weeks later must enter through what looks like that same location-filmed doorway, with everything about you in the same exact shape . . . in a building or set miles away!

A small point . . . sort of a "grace note", but not just that: If you don't have to go off alone and woodshed your lines for upcoming scenes, stand or sit and _watch some of the other scenes being filmed_. Often the people involved are favorites and often-used friends of the Director. They're often part of his "stock company", and seeing you interested enough to watch their work might . . . just might . . . seem an indication that you like his choices among actors and that you're interested in and enthusiastic enough about his work to watch it. He may not even look in your direction in any obvious way. After all, he's busy and rushed. But he's probably at least conscious of who is interested in what he's doing and who's bored by it. It could even illuminate for you the Director's points of view and biases, as well as his personal style, for your own work in your later scenes with him.

Another small point, but one which experienced professionals know . . . .Often a Director will ask you to make some adjustment in your position, the manner in which you move from one point to another, or the manner of handling a prop. Don't try to read his mind and jump to make the adjustment you _think_ he's going to ask for. _Listen carefully until he's finished_ telling you what to do. Otherwise, you may guess wrongly and he'll be annoyed to have to start all over again telling you exactly what he does want. Simply wait till he's finished, then do what he's asked of you. He'll appreciate it and time won't be lost because of your well-intentioned but over-eager leaping to the wrong guess.

At The End Of The day....

If you're still on the set at the end of the shooting day you'll hear _"It's a wrap!"_ called out. It means that everything's finished for the day. But it doesn't mean _you're_ officially released to go home until you've been released by the Second Assistant. Either earlier in the day or at the "Wrap" time, you'll probably be given your _Next Day's Call_ if you're working another day . . . again by the Second. If there's some problem, though, and he doesn't yet have the "calls"---which happens often on a location, you'll be getting your call by telephone later that night when the next day's schedule is finished in the Production Office. Be home to get the call's details accurately, to avoid somebody else getting a detail or two incompletely or wrong.

When releasing you, the Second will have you sign the _Time Sheet_ with the correct releasing time shown on it before he lets you go.

If the Second tells you _"You're slopping!"_ , it doesn't mean you're doing a sloppy job, as a nervous newcomer might fear at hearing those words. It means, in film lingo, that they haven't finished with you as expected and that you're to work the next day again, or at some later time, and are still on salary unexpectedly. Actors love to "slop" after they've learned what the word means.

If you're working again, either the next day or later, *don't wear even one item of your character's wardrobe home!* Hang every bit of it in your dressing room closet where you found it (unless you brought your own from home). In either case, leave *every item* of it hanging in your dressing room. The Cleaning and Laundry people must have it available so they can have it freshly readied and back in the closet for you before your next filming, even if it's the next day. This applies whether it's production-supplied or your own brought from home. Somebody may have a heart attack if you've taken something home and forgotten to bring it to the set the next time you work.

At the end of the day, or when you're being released earlier, it's not a bad idea to be cordial to the people of all kinds that you've worked with. If it's the end of your job, it's good to thank everybody personally. . . even the Director who may have yelled at you during shooting and left you thinking he didn't like you or was impatient with you. Thank him especially. He was probably only yelling at you so he could be heard over the noises on a busy set.

If you have an agent, as soon as possible be sure to call the agent and let them know you've finished. That way, they'll know you're free to go on more interviews immediately.

And before you go to bed that night after you've finished filming, why not enter the new credit in the appropriate place on your own copies of your résumé? You'll want that new credit to be on your résumé when you hand it out at somebody's office perhaps the next day. You might write the credit in ink, to more vividly point out the fact that you've worked too recently for printing of a new résumé.

Also, ask your agent, if you have one, if he'd like you to come around and make the same entries on the copies of your résumé that are being held at the agency for its use. The agency might forget to enter the new credit, and it's important to get the word out quickly that you've worked.

After The Job . . . Some Things You Can Do

You might send *Thank You Notes* . . . to the Casting Director---saying how much you enjoyed doing the role and appreciating their thinking of you; to the Director (in care of the studio or production company if you can't get their mailing address elsewhere)---saying something nice, of course; and maybe to the Producer also.

For a television program, sometimes producers will send cards later notifying actors of scheduled air dates. But often those notifications, if sent at all, are received by the actor too late to be used effectively in the actor's promotion.

The best way to be informed ahead of time about a scheduled airing of a television program is to find out what network it's going to run on and then call the network from time to time until they can tell you the air date. The *Network Scheduling Department* will usually be cooperative in response to such inquiry. If you forget to do this, at least keep checking the *TV Guide* so you'll know maybe a week or so ahead of time.

As with everything else you do with regard to displaying your talents, be sure that *everybody* is informed whenever you're appearing---on television, in a film playing in theatres, in a theatre production. This applies as much in your home state and neighboring states' casting offices and production companies, etc., as it always will when and if you later relocate in Hollywood. An actor's self-promotion never stops.

And as mentioned earlier, the minute you receive your salary check take or send to the agent his or her 10% commission! Agents quickly sour on clients who don't get those commissions to their agents quickly. After all, that 10% commission is what helps the agent pay office rent, phone bills, lunches paid for to promote you and others, etc. _You_ are the _employer_, remember. The agent _works for you_ . . . is a member of your staff (even if the only one), and like any employee deserves to paid and paid promptly. Keep on the good side of your agent and keep him or her working hard for you by getting their 10% commissions to them promptly!

If you've had a fairly good role in a television episode, movie of the week or a feature motion picture it's not beyond possibility that you may receive an invitation---or may somehow be able to wangle entré---to attend a _screening_ of the finished film. These screenings are usually attended by the producer, director and members of the production staff, plus friends of those folks and any network people involved if it's for television. You can sometimes find out from the producer's secretary in Hollywood when and where such screenings are to be held. Even though your role may not seem all that important to you, it could be a good idea to call the producer's office in Hollywood and ask to be allowed to attend---if you're willing to spend the air or car fare to get there. Seeing the finished film will let you know how your work came off or whether you're even still in the finished film, since in Editing sometimes entire sequences are cut out.

If you do attend a screening and like what was done in editing your performance, _then_ is the time for a nice letter to the Producer thanking him or her for the opportunity to appear in the film and appreciating how your performance was handled. Remember, this is something you can do if your role is a fairly good one. Otherwise, simply wait and see it when it's aired or is being shown in movie theatres.

At least, if you get to see it ahead of time, you'll know whether to ask a lot of people to be sure to see it.

14

Hollywood Later? . . .
The Decision Is Yours

If you really use the advice in the foregoing chapters and the contact address listings in the Addenda pages that have thus far applied for you, it's quite possible that you could earn a decent living and be happy remaining where you are. You'd sooner or later be working in most of the film and television projects shooting on location in your state and in several of the other states in your area.

But most actors want to move into the mainstream after earning a sufficient number of film and television credits in location projects and locally produced television and theatre. There's a limit to how far an actor can go without going where most of the action is and where upward mobility is unlimited. That usually means Hollywood, where there's more continuous employment and where actors, if they're talented, lucky and prepared, can advance their careers swiftly.

Bear in mind, if that's what you want, that you're _either "in Hollywood" or you're not_. There's no half-way for actors. Until you're broadly known in Hollywood production circles it's just not possible to remain living in your home town somewhere else in America and hope for any employment opportunities or career advances in Hollywood. That can only work for Hollywood leading actors broadly known in the industry who don't need to be auditioned for roles, who are known to most Hollywood producers, directors and casting people and who can simply be sent scripts through their agents for their consideration and, if they decide to do a role, are set for it and are put up in a hotel in Hollywood for the duration of their employment.

Beware any Hollywood agent who might offer to represent you in Hollywood while you're still living elsewhere and are still an unknown talent. Nine times out of ten it's an agent who has schemes for separating you from your money . . . there are a few such agents in Hollywood. They come to outlying cities, hold "seminars" of one kind or another, meet many eager young people and "sign" them for representation in Hollywood . . . and within a short time if not immediately begin bilking those unsuspecting "easy marks".

Also, don't fall for the diabolical scam of that national magazine that every so often runs ads in your neighboring cities' Sunday papers headed "Hollywood Comes To (City)!", holds very impressive "free one-day seminars" that are actually advertising pitches to get would-be actors and models to run their photos in their huge, full-color magazine that's loaded with such photos ranging from small ones costing around $300 up to full page photos costing several thousand dollars. This scurrilous publication claims that "Hollywood uses this publication to find new talents!" Not so. In Hollywood this organization is recognized for what it is---a money-scrounging scam---and its very attractive publication, distributed free to casting and production offices, is usually thrown away immediately. Hollywood doesn't like scams any more than the rest of us do.

And don't think you can obtain decent Hollywood agenting until you're actually there. Hollywood agents aren't anxious to represent unknown actors when they know that those folks can't be available for short notice interviews. Interviews are scheduled that way in Hollywood, and any respectable Hollywood agent representing you would have to decline most if not all such opportunities. You need to be _living in Hollywood_ before you seek a Hollywood agent. Nothing else works. And you really should have your SAG Membership Card, a decent (even if small) list of film and television speaking roles on your résumé, and a list of contacts and friends already in Hollywood and involved in the industry there who can help make your transition easier.

Before you move, it's a good idea to subscribe to _Drama-Logue_, the weekly actors' newspaper that is issued every Thursday in Hollywood. It's full of film, television and theatre news, items and columns that offer many suggestions, ads for services like acting workshops, photographers, answering services, showcase organizations, etc., and all kinds of orientation about the Hollywood acting milieu. You could continue receiving your subscription to this publication after your move to Hollywood. You can subscribe from Drama-Logue Inc., P. O. Box 38771, Los Angeles, California 90038-0771. The cost is $55 for 52 weeks or $33 for 26 weeks. It's sent by 2nd Class mail. The telephone number is (213) 464-5079. Its newsstand price is $1.85 per issue.

Also, _before_ you move, so you can start studying its total career advice and avoid making early mistakes in Hollywood, you should order from Acting World Books a copy of _The Film Actor's Complete Career Guide_. This 304-page paperback book by the author of the book you're reading is a bestseller at Samuel French and other actors' bookstores in Hollywood and New York and is loaded with clear, step by step advice on what to do, how to do it for best results, and page after page of insider, behind-closed-doors information that many actors take years to learn. It costs $24.95 and can be ordered by mail ahead of time from Acting World Books, P. O. Box 3044, Hollywood, California 90078.

Once you're _actually in_ Hollywood, at Samuel French Theatre Bookshops, 7623 Sunset Boulevard in West Hollywood, pick up the current copies of _The Agencies---What The Actor Needs To Know_ ($10) and _The Hollywood Acting Coaches And Teachers Directory_ ($12.50). The former lists all SAG-franchised agencies with their staffs' names, the kinds of talents they represent, the areas they represent for, and in most cases brief comments about their reputations and how they prefer that actors submit themselves for consideration. It's published with the cooperation of the Agency Department of the National Office of the Screen Actors Guild in Hollywood, a consulting panel of casting directors who work with the agents every day, and the agents themselves in keeping their listings up to date. The latter lists most acting coaches and teachers, describes what and how they teach, and in most cases gives their backgrounds.

Also once you're there, always available at Samuel French and many newsstand locations throughout Greater Los Angeles are the two daily "trade papers" of Hollywood--- _Daily Variety_ and _The Hollywood Reporter_. Both carry news items and columns about the studios, production companies, new developments, ratings, etc. But _The Reporter_ also carries, each week, a complete list of filming projects that are in the early stages of preparation, scheduled to begin filming and where and with complete staffs listed, and others currently filming, filming in the future, etc. Each listing includes the production company name, executive producer and other producers, directors, writer and sometimes even the casting director's name if one is set by then. The listings include international listings as well as those in Hollywood and in locations in the U.S., with the same total details.

Just before making your move to Hollywood, be sure to write or phone any friends or acquaintances there to let them know you're moving there. Some may volunteer temporary apartment-sharing or other accommodations, and most will offer to help in any way they can. Don't wait till you get there to notify them.

Especially important is any production company person with whom you've become friends while working with them in location films back home. Most, even though probably busy, will or at least can and might help with a suggestion or two, perhaps even a valuable referral to an agent or casting person. Depending on how well you got to know them earlier, some minor miracles could occur in those phone calls. One actor, having become good friends with a Second Asst. Director on location, called her ahead of time and was told she was immediately leaving for a film in Africa and the actor could house-sit her house, rent free, until she returned in several months. Another actor called the casting director who had helped cast him in a decent-sized role on location and was told to come sooner than planned to try out for a small role in a motion picture the casting person was starting to work on. The actor accelerated his move, was there at the right time, and got the role!

You see, many of those now producing, directing or otherwise involved in those films shot on location in your home state either still are or have been actors, have had top agencies representing them for years and are probably still represented by those top agencies. If they've appreciated your talent enough in the location filming with you they can give you what are called "industry referrals" (to friend agents and casting people) that carry enormous clout and influence, toward getting you started in Hollywood.

∞∞∞∞∞∞∞∞∞∞

These chapters are about the sum total of what advice you can be given for the early period of *starting* your film and television acting career *before* moving to Hollywood if you do decide to make the move later to continue expanding your career.

And, as a puchaser of this book, once you're actually in Hollywood and may have a question from time to time, this book's publishing company, Acting World Books, has an *Actor Information Service* which receives actors' questions (in letter form only) and replies with information and sometimes with advice as well. If you mention in such a written inquiry that you purchased this book earlier your question will receive whatever extra details as may be available to the Service.

Good luck!

Addenda

FILM COMMISSIONS OF ALL U. S. STATES AND TERRITORIES

ALABAMA

Alabama Film Office
340 North Hull St.
Montgomery, AL 36130
205-242-0486

ALASKA

Alaska Film Office
3601 C Street, Ste. 700
Anchorage, AK 98503
907-562-3575

ARKANSAS

Arkansas Motion Picture Office
1 State Capitol Mall
Little Rock, AR 72201
501-682-7676

Eureka Springs City Offices
44 South Main
Eureka Springs, AR 72632
501-253-9703

ARIZONA

Arizona Film Commission
3800 N. Central Av., Bldg. D
Phoenix, AZ 85012
602-280-1380

Flagstaff Film Commission
211 W. Aspen
Flagstaff, AZ 86001
602-779-7658

Lake Havasu Area Film Commission
1930 Mesquite Ave., Ste. 3
Lake Havasu City, AZ 85403
601-453-3456

Page / Lake Powell Film Comm.
PO Box 727
Page, AZ 86040
602-645-2741

Phoenix Motion Picture Coord. Ofc.
251 W. Washington
Phoenix, AZ 85003
602-262-4850

Scottsdale Film Office
3939 Civic Center Plaza
Scottsdale, AZ 85251
602-994-2636

Sedona Film Commission
PO Box 2489
Sedona, AZ 86336
602-282-7722

Tucson Film Office
110 E. Pennington, City Hall Annex
Tucson, AZ 85726
602-791-4000

Wickenburg Film Commission
216 N. Frontier St., PO Drawer CC
Wickenburg, AZ 85358
601-684-5479

CALIFORNIA

California Film Commission
6922 Hollywood Blvd., Suite 600
Hollywood, CA 90028
213-736-2465

Big Bear Lake Film Commission
PO Box 2860
Big Bear Lake, CA 92315
714-866-6190

Crescent City-Del Norte Film Comm.
1001 Front St.
Crescent City, CA 95531
707-464-3174

Eureka Cty. Conv. / Visitors Bureau
1034 2nd St.
Eureka, CA 95501
707-443-5097

Los Angeles County Film Office
6922 Hollywood Blvd., Ste. 612
Los Angeles, CA 90028
213-957-1000

Los Angeles Motion Picture Div.
6922 Hollywood Blvd., Ste. 612
Los Angeles, CA 90028
213-461-8624

Oakland Film Commission
505 14th St. #601, 1 City Hall Plaza
Oakland, CA 94612
415-273-3109

Oxnard Film Office
300 W. 3rd St.
Oxnard, CA 93030
805-984-5611

Palm Springs Film Office
69-930 Highway 111, Ste. 201
Rancho Mirage, CA 92270
619-327-8411

San Diego Motion Picture Bureau
402 W. Broadway
San Diego, CA 92101
6I9-234-3456

San Francisco Film Commission
Mayor's Office / City Hall
San Francisco, CA 94102
415-554-6144

San Jose Film & Video Commission
333 W. San Carlos, Ste. 1000
San Jose, CA 95110
408-295-9600

Stockton Film Office
445 W. Weber Ave., Ste. 220
Stockton, CA 95203
209-466-7066

COLORADO

Colorado Film Commission
1625 Broadway, Suite 1975
Denver, CO 80202
303-572-5444

Breckenridge Film Commission
PO Box 7579
Breckenridge, CO 80424
303-452-0568

Canon City Chamber of Commerce
1032 Royal Gorge
Canon City, CO 81215
719-275-5149

Colorado Springs Film Commission
104 S. Cascade Ave., Ste. 104
Colorado Springs, CO 80903
800-FILM-695

Denver Film & Television Office
216 16th St. Mall, Ste. 1000
Denver, CO 80202
303-572-4600

Grand Junction Film Commission
PO Box 117
Fruita, CO 81521
303-858-9335

Greeley/ Weld Cty Film Commission
1407 8th Avenue
Greeley, CO 80631
303-351-3566

Trinidad Film Commission
309 Nevada Avenue
Trinidad, CO 81082
719-846-9412

CONNECTICUT

Connecticut Film Commission
865 Brook St.
Rocky Hill, CT 06067
203-258-4301

DELAWARE

Delaware Development Office
99 Kings Highway, PO Box 1401
Dover, DE 19903
302-739-4271

FLORIDA

Florida Film Bureau
107 W.Gaines St., Rm 430
Tallahassee, FL 32399
904-487-1100

Clearwater Film Commission
112 S. Osceola, 3rd Floor
Clearwater, FL 34616
813-462-6206

Gainesville Chamber of Commerce
300 E. University
Gainesville, FL 32601
904-336-7100

Jacksonville Film & Television Ofc.
220 E. Bay St., 4th Floor
Jacksonville, FL 32202
904-630-1073

Miami Dept. of Development
300 Biscayne Blvd. Way, Ste. 400
Miami, FL 33131
305-579-3366

Orlando Film Commission
200 E. Ropbinson, Ste. 600
Orlando, FL 32801
407-422-7159

Tampa Motion Picture / TV Devel.
306 E. Jackson
Tampa, FL ·33602
813-223-8419

GEORGIA

Georgia Film & Videotape Office
PO Box 1776
Atlanta, GA 30303
404-656-3591

HAWAII

Hawaii Film Industry Branch
PO Box 2359
Honolulu, HI 96804
808-548-4535

Maui Motion Picture Coord. Comm.
380 Dairy Rd., PO Box 1738
Kahului, Maui, HI 96732
808-871-8691

DAHO

Idaho Film Bureau
700 W. State St., 2nd Floor
Boise, ID 83720
208-334-2470

IOWA

Iowa Film Office
200 East Grand Ave.
Des Moines, IA 50309
800-779-3456

Des Moines Conv. / Visitors Bureau
309 Court Ave., Ste. 240
Des Moines, IA 50309
515-286-4971

Dubuque Film Bureau
770 Town Clock Plaza
Dubuque, IA 52001
319-557-9200

Fort Dodge Mayor's Office
819 1st Avenue South
Fort Dodge, IA 50501
515-472-7144

ILLINOIS

Illinois Film Office
100 W. Randolph
Chicago, IL 60601
312-814-3600

Chicago Film Office
174 W. Randolph, 3rd Floor
Chicago, IL 60601
312-744-6415

INDIANA

Indiana Tourism & Film Devel.
1 Noth Capitol
Indianapolis, IN 46204
317-232-8829

KANSAS

Kansas Film Commission
400 W. 8th
Topeka, KS 66603
913-296-4927

Lawrence Film Office
734 Vermont, Box 586
Lawrence, KS 66044
913-865-4411

Oveland Park Film Commission
10974 Benson, Ste. 290
Overland Park, KS 66210
913-491-0123

Topeka Film Office
3 Townsite Place
Topeka, KS 66603
913-234-1030

Wichita Film Office
100 S. Main, Ste. 100
Wichita, KS 67202
316-265-2800

KENTUCKY

Kentucky Film Office
Berry Hill Mansion, Louisville Road
Frankfort, KY 40601
502-564-7588

LOUISIANA

Louisiana Film Commission
PO Box 44320
Baton Rouge, LA 70804
504-342-8150

New Orleans Film Commission
1300 Perdido St. City Hall #2W17
New Orleans, LA 70112
504-565-6580

MAINE

Maine Film Office
State House Station, Ste. 59
Augusta, ME 04333
207-289-5705

MARYLAND

Maryland Film Commission
217 E. Redwood
Baltimore, MD 21202
301-333-6633

Baltimore Film Commission
303 E. Fayette #300
Baltimore, MD 21202
301-396-4550

MASSACHUSETTS

Massachusetts Film Office
10 Park Plaza, Ste. 2310
Boston, MA 02116
617-973-8800

MICHIGAN

Michigan Film Office
525 W. Ottawa, PO Box 30225
Lansing, MI 48909
517-373-FILM

Detroit Film & Television Office
1126 City/County Bldg.
Detroit, MI 48226
313-224-4733

MINNESOTA

MinnesotaFilm Board
401 N. 3rd St., Ste. 460
Minneapolis, MN 55401
612-332-6493

MISSOURI

Missouri Film Commission
PO Bx 118
Jefferson City, MO 65102
314-751-9050

Kansas City Film Office
920 Main, 6th Floor
Kansas City, MO 64105
816-221-2424

St. Louis Film Partnership
100 S. 4th St., Ste. 500
St. Louis, MO 63102
314-231-5555

MISSISSIPPI

Mississippi Film Office
1200 Walter Sillers Bldg.
Jackson, MS 39205
601-359-3297

Columbus Film Commission
PO Box 789
Columbus, MS 39703
601-329-1191

Natchez Film Commission
311 Liberty Rd.
Natchez, MS 39120
601-446-6345

Oxford Film Commission
PO Box 965
Oxford, MS 38655
601-234-4651

Tupelo Film Commission
PO Box 1485
Tupelo, MS 38802
601-841-6521

Vicksburg Film Commission
PO Box 110
Vicksburg, MS 39180
601-636-9421

MONTANA

Montana Film Commission
1424 Ninth Ave.
Helena, MT 59620
800-548-3390

NEBRASKA

Nebraska Film Office
PO Box 95143
Lincoln, NE 68509
401-471-2593

Lincoln Film & Television Office
129 North 10th St. #111
Lincoln, NE 68508
402-471-7432

NEW HAMPSHIRE

New Hampshire Film & TV Bureau
172 Pembroke Rd., PO Box 856
Concord, NH 03302
603-271-2598

NEW JERSEY

New Jersey Motion Picture & TV
PO Box 47023
Newark, NJ 07101
201-648-6278

NEW MEXICO

New Mexico Film Commission
1050 Old Pecos Trail
Santa Fe, NM 87504
505-827-7365

Albuquerque Film & Television
PO Box 1293
Albuquerque, NM 87103
505-768-4512

Las Cruces Conv. / Visitors Bureau
311 North Downtown Mall
Las Cruces, NM 88001
505-524-8521

NEVADA

Nevada Motion Picture Division
3770 Howard Hughes Pkwy, #295
Las Vegas, NV 89158
702-486-7150

NEW YORK

New York Govt. Office for MP/TV
1515 Broadway
New York, NY 10036
212-929-0240

New York Ofc. Film/Theatre/Bcstg.
254 W. 54th St., 13th Floor
New York, NY 10019
212-788-2990

NORTH CAROLINA

North Carolina Film Office
430 N. Salisbury
Raleigh, NC 27611
919-733-9900

Wilmington Film Commission
PO Box 1810
Wilmington, NC 28402
919-341-7810

NORTH DAKOTA

North Dakota Film Commission
604 E. BoulevArd Ave.
Bismarck, ND 58505
701-224-2525

OHIO

Ohio Film Bureau
77 S. High St.
Columbus, OH 43266
614-466-2284

Cincinnati Film Commission
264 McCormick Place
Cincinnati, OH 45219
513-784-1744

OKLAHOMA

Oklahoma Film Office
440 S. Houston, Room 505
Tulsa, OK 74126
918-581-2844

Lawton Film Commission
607 C Ave., PO Box 1376
Lawton, OK 73502
405-355-3541

Tulsa Convention/Visitors Bureau
616 S. Boston
Tulsa, OK 74119
918-585-8386

OREGON

Oregon Film Office
775 Summer St. NE
Salem, OR 97310
503-373-1232

PENNSYLVANIA

Pennsylvania Film Bureau
Forum Bldg., Room 455
Harrisburg, PA 17120
717-783-3456

PUERTO RICO

Puerto Rico Film Commission
PO Box 362350
San Juan, PR 00936
809-758-4747

RHODE ISLAND

Rhode Island Film Commission
150 Benefit St.
Providence, RI 02903
401-277-2102

SOUTH CAROLINA

South Carolina Film Office
PO Box 927
Columbia, SC 29202
803-737-0400

SOUTH DAKOTA

South Dakota Film Commission
711 Wells Ave.
Pierre, SD 57501
605-773-3301

TENNESSEE

Tennessee Film Commission
320 6th Ave. North
Nashville, TN 37219
615-741-3456

Memphis/Shelby Film-Tape-Music
245 Wagner Pl., Beale St. Landing
Memphis, TN 38103
901-527-8300

TEXAS

Texas Film Commission
816 Congress Ave., 12th Floor
Austin, TX 78701
512-469-9111

Amarillo Film Office
1000 S. Polk St.
Amarillo, TX 79105
806-374-1497

Austin Film Commission
PO Box 1088
Austin, TX 78767
512-322-3661

El Paso Film Commission
1 Civic Center Plaza
El Paso, TX 79901
915-534-0698

Houston Film Commission
3300 Main St.
Houston, TX 77002
713-620-6614

Irving Texas Film Commission
6301 N. O'Connor Road, LB119
Irving, TX 75039
214-252-7476

San Antonio Conv / Visitors Bur.
PO Box 2277
San Antonio, TX 75298
512-270-8700

UTAH

Utah Film Commission
324 South State, Ste. 230
Salt Lake City, UT 84111
801-538-8740

VERMONT

Vermont Film Bureau
134 State St.
Montpelier, VT 05602
801-828-3236

VIRGIN ISLANDS

Virgin Islands Film Promotion Office
PO Box 6400
St. Thomas, USVI 00804
809-775-1444

VIRGINIA

Virginia Film Office
PO Box 798
Richmond, VA 23206
804-371-8204

Metro Richmond Film Bureau
300 E. Main St., Suite 100
Richmond, VA 23219
804-782-2777

WASHINGTON

Washington State Film & Video
2001 6th Ave., Ste. 2700
Seattle, WA 98121
206-464-7148

Tacoma Film Production
747 Market St., Ste. 1036
Tacoma, WA 98402
206-591-5209

WEST VIRGINIA

West Virginia Film Industry Devel.
2101 Washington St. East
Charleston, WV 25305
304-558-2286

WISCONSIN

Wisconsin Film Office
123 W. Washington
Madison, WI 53707
608-267-3456

Milwaukee Film Commission
PO Box 324
Milwaukee, WI 53201
414-223-5790

WYOMING

Wyoming Film Office
1-25 & College Drive
Cheyenne, WY 82002
307-777-7777

Cody County Film Commission
109 W. Yellowstone
Cody, WY 82414
307-527-6256

Sheridan Film Promotion
150 S. Main
Sheridan, WY 82801
307-672-2481

TALENT AGENCIES (BOTH FRANCHISED AND NON-UNION) IN ALL U.S. STATES

Every effort was made to obtain all states' Talent Agencies, however two states were not responsive, *even after a number of attempts to obtain their information. For the lists of the two states for which lists are not printed herein---Connecticut and Rhode Island, actors should contact those states' Film Commissions and ask for them. The Connecticut Film Commission tel. no. is 203-258-4301 and the Rhode Island Film Commission's tel. no. is 401-277-3456. That failing, talent agencies are usually listed in area telephone directories under the heading "Theatrical Agencies" for easiest locating.*

ALABAMA

Beau Monde Prods. Unlimited Inc.
1827 Coral Lane
Montgomery, AL 36116
(205) 386-3696

Cynthia's Modeling & Talent
3814 Harrison Road
Montgomery, AL 36115
(205) 272-5555

E'lan Agency
3000 Riverchase Galleria, Ste. 705
Birmingham, AL 35244
(205) 985-3001

Executive Management & Talent
110 C South Florida St.
Mobile, AL 36606
479-9629

Fast Traxx
4653 Benson Road
Mobile, AL 36619
(205) 661-1000

Gulf Coast Talent
PO Box 908
33915 Highway 98
Lillian, AL 36549
(205) 962-2000

Images Unlimited
1212 Wilmer Ave.
Anniston, AL 36201
(205) 236-0952

Kiddin' Around / Real People
700 28th St. South, Ste. 210
Birmingham, AL 35233
(205) 323-KIDS (5437)

Cathi Larsen Models
1628 6th St. NW
Birmingham, AL 36215
(205) 871-2718

Macy's Modeling Agency
20-1/2 East 12th St.
Anniston, AL 36201
(3205) 236-3597

Mannequins, Inc.
2026 14th Ave. South
Birmingham, AL 35206
(205) 933-2996

Marie Prater Agency
2642 O'Neal Circle
Birmingham, AL 35206
(205) 822-8135

Model Concepts
PO Box 241361
Montgomery, AL 36124
(205) 277-5378

Rare Quality Model & Talent
224 N. Foster
Dothan, AL 671-2200
(205) 671-2200

Star Quality
2210 Mountbrook Drive SE
Decatur, AL 35601
(205) 350-6005

Vandaza Model & Talent Agency
Madison Square Mall
5901 University Drive #28
Huntsville, AL 35806
(205) 430-0904

Wil-Bea Productions
1802 Logan Street
Tuskegee Inst., AL 36088
(205) 727-4674

ALASKA

Carlson't Co. of Models & Talent
4011 Arctic Blvd., Ste. 206
Anchorage, AK 99503
(907) 561-2454

Thompson Media Talent
11522 24th Ave. NE
Seattle, WA 98125
(206) 363-5555

ARKANSAS

A. R. Productions
25 East South
Fayetteville, AR 72701
(501) 443-7897

Entertainment, Etc.
P. O. Box 9261
North Little Rock, AR 72119
(501) 372-2772

Ferguson Modeling & Talent
1100 West 34th St.
Little Rock, AR 72206
(501) 375-3519

P-B-C Entertainment
13715 West Markham
Little Rock, AR 72211
(501) 221-1070

Professional Models Assn.
6616 Hawthorne
Little Rock, AR 72207
(501) 666-2178

The Agency
916 West 6th St.
Little Rock, AR 72201
(501) 374-6447

The Four Seasons Models
P. O. Box 683
Mayflower, AR 72706
(501) 450-9205

ARIZONA

ACT & Grissom (SAG)
6264 E. Grant Road
Tucson, AZ 85712
(602) 885-3246

Robert Black Agency (SAG)
725 S. Rural Road #C201A
Tempe, AZ 85281
(602) 966-2537

Blue Ox Talent Agency
4130 N. Goldwater Blvd., #121
Scottsdale, AZ 85251
(602) 312-8669

Dani's Agency (SAG)
1 East Camelback Road #550
Phoeniz, AZ 85012
(602) 263-1918

Emerging Talent Network
18658 N. 4th St.
Phoenix, AZ 85024
(602) 230-5349

En Avant Agency
4500 S. Lakeshore Dr., Ste. 400
Tempe, AZ 85282
(602) 839-1969

Flair Parisienne Agcy. (SAG)
6700 N. Oracle Road #501
Tucson, AZ 85704
(602) 742-1090

Fosi's Model & Talent Agency (SAG)
2777 N. Campbell Ave. #209
Tucson, AZ 85719
(602) 795-3534

Pam Grissom Talent Agency
6264 E. Grant Rd., #261
Tucson, AZ 85712
(602) 327-5692

Leavey & Associates
9029 N. 43rd Ave., Ste. 229
Phoenix, AZ 85051
(602) 864-6766

L'Image / Casablancas
4533 N. Scottsdale Rd.
Scottsdale, AZ 85251
(602) 941-4838

International Model & Talent Agcy.
6209 N. 21st Drive
Phoenix, AZ 85015
(602) 242-0306

Leighton Agency, Inc. (SAG)
3333 N. 44th St.
Phoenix, AZ 85018
(602) 224-9255

New Visions Model /Talent Ctr.
P O Box 372
Prescott, AZ 86302
(602) 445-3382

Pet Counselor Talent Agcy.
3651 E. Baseline Rd., Ste. 234B
Gilbert, AZ 85234
(602) 279-6229

Sedona Model & Talent Agcy.
PO Box 10141
Sedona, AZ 86336
(602) 284-0914

Signature Talent Agency (SAG)
725 S. Rural Road #201
Tempe, AZ 85281
(602) 966-1102

Studio 2000 Modeling & Talent
1661 N. Swan Rd., Ste. 244
Tucson, AZ 85712
(602) 323-1106

Talent Marketing Specialists
1116 W. Freemont
Tempe, AZ 85282
(602) 831-8084

CALIFORNIA

Hollywood & Greater Los Angeles

New actors must realize that the talent agencies in this film industry center are extremely selective as regards the clients they represent. Some will consider new talents, but many represent top players with established backgrounds in film and seldom will consider a new talent not yet a member of the Screen Actors Guild. Some have offices in New York as well, and some have offices in Europe and other global entertainment centers. Since there is rapid turnover of agencies here, we do not represent that the following list will be either complete or current when the reader is reading or using this book. All agencies shown are franchised by SAG. If we have omitted any agencies we're sorry. For actors in the Los Angeles Area, the currently updated listings are always available in The Agencies---What The Actor Needs To Know, sold at Samuel French and other stores.

A.S.A.
4430 Fountain Ave #A
Los Angeles, CA 90029
(213) 552-9787

Larry Abbott & Associates
10153 Riverside Drive
Toluca Lake, CA 91602
(818) 761-4777

Abrams Artists & Assoc.
9200 Sunset Blvd. #625
Los Angeles, CA 90069
(310) 859-0625

Abrams-Rubaloff & Lawrence
8075 W. 3rd St. #303
Los Angeles, CA 90048
(213) 935-1700

AFH Management
7250 Beverly Blvd. #102
Los Angeles, CA 90036
(213) 965-8780

The Agency
10351 Santa Monica Blvd. #211
Los Angeles, CA 90025
(310) 551-3000

Agency For The Performing Arts
9000 Sunset Blvd. #1200
Los Angeles, CA 90069
(310) 273-0744

Aimee Entertainment
13742 Victory Blvd.
Van Nuys, CA 91401
(818) 994-9354

Allen Talent Agency
10850 Wilshire Blvd. #770
Los Angeles, CA 90024
(310) 474-7524

Bonni Allen Talent, Inc.
260 S. Beverly Drive, 2nd Flr.
Beverly Hills, CA 90212
(310) 247-1865

Carlos Alvarado Agency
8150 Beverly Blvd. #308
Los Angeles, CA 90048
(213) 655-7978

Ambrosio / Mortimer
9150 Wilshire Blvd. #175
Beverly Hills, CA 90212
(310) 274-4274

Amsel, Eisenstadt & Frazier
6310 San Vicente Blvd. #407
Los Angeles, CA 90048
(213) 939-1188

Angel City Talent
8228 Sunset Blvd. #311
Los Angeles, CA 90046
(213) 650-1930

Chris Apodaca Agency
2049 Century Park East #1200
Los Angeles, CA 90067
(310) 284-3484

Irvin Arthur Assoc.
9363 Wilshire Blvd. #212
Beverly Hills, CA 90210
(310) 278-5934

Artist Network
12001 Ventura Place #331
Studio City, CA 91604
(818) 508-6397

The Artists Agency
10000 Santa monica Blvd. #305
Los Angeles, CA 90067
(310) 277-7779

Artists First, Inc.
450 S. Wetherly Drive
Beverly Hills, CA 90211
(310) 550-8606

Artists Group, Ltd.
1930 Century Park West #403
Los Angeles, CA 90067
(310) 552-1100

Artists Management Agency
835 5th Avenue, Ste. 411
San Diego, CA 92101
(619) 233-6655

Atkins & Assoc.
303 S. Crescent heights Blvd.
Los Angeles, CA 90048
(213) 658-1025

Avenue "C" Talent
12405 Woodruff Ave.
Downey, CA 90241
(310) 803-5775

B.O.P. - L.A. Talent Agency
1467 Tamarind Ave.
Los Angeles, CA 90028
(213) 466-8667

Badgley • Connor
9229 Sunset Blvd. #607
Los Angeles, CA 90069
(310) 278-9313

Baldwin Talent, Inc.
1801 Avenue of The Stars #640
Los Angeles, CA 90067
(310) 551-3033

Bobby Ball Agency
8075 W. 3rd St. #550
Los Angeles, CA 90048
(213) 964-7300

Rickey Barr Talent Agency
1010 Hammond #202
Los Angeles, CA 90069
(310) 276-0887

Bauman, Hiller & Assoc.
5750 Wilshire Blvd. #512
Los Angeles, CA 90036
(213) 857-6666

BDP & Associates
10637 Burbank Blvd.
North Hollywood, CA 91601
(818) 506-7615

Belson & Klass
144 S. Beverly Drive #405
Beverly Hills, CA 90212
(310) 274-9169

Lois J. Benson
8360 Melose Ave. #203
Los Angeles, CA 90069
(213) 653-0500

Marian Berzon
336 E. 17th
Costa Mesa, CA 92627
(714) 631-5936

Beverly Hills Sports Council
9595 Wilshire Blvd. #711
Beverly Hills, CA 90212
(310) 858-1872

Bigley Agency
19725 Sherman Way #200
Canoga Park, CA 91306
(818) 368-7280

Yvette Bikoff Agency
8721 Santa Monica Blvd. #21
Los Angeles, CA 90069
(213) 655-6123

Nina Blanchard Agency
957 North Cole Ave.
Los Angeles, CA 90038
(213) 462-7274

J. Michael Bloom
9200 Sunset Blvd. #710
Los Angeles, CA 90069
(310) 275-6800

B.O.P.-L.A. Talent Agency
1467 Tamarind Ave.
Hollywood, CA 90028
(213) 466-8667

Borinstein-Oreck-Bogart Agency
8271 Melrose Ave., Ste. 110
Los Angeles, CA 90046
(213) 658-7500

Brand Model & Talent Agency
17941 Skypark Circle #F
Irvine, CA 92714
(714) 261-0555

Paul Brandon & Associates
1033 N. Carol Drive #T-6
Los Angeles, CA 90069
(310) 273-6173

Brandon's Commercials Unlimited
7361 Beverly Blvd.
Los Angeles, CA 90036
(213) 937-2220

Bresler, Kelly & Kipperman
15760 Ventura Blvd. #1730
Encino, CA 91436
(818) 905-1155

Alex Brewis Agency
12429 Laurel Terrace Dr.
Studio City, CA 91604
(818) 509-0831

Jim Bridges Enterprises
5000 Lankershim Blvd. #7
North Hollywood, CA 91601
(818) 762-9892

The Brustein Company
10850 Wilshire Blvd. #560
Los Angeles, CA 90024
(310) 470-8342

Don Buchwald & Assoc. / Pacific
9229 Sunset Blvd.
Los Angeles, CA 90069
(310) 278-3600

Burkett Talent Agency
1700 E. Garry #113
Santa Ana, CA 92705
(714) 724-0465

Iris Burton
1450 Belfast Drive
Los Angeles, CA 90069
(310) 652-0954

Bush & Ross Talents
4942 Vineland Ave.
North Hollywood, CA 91601
(818) 762-0096

C. L. Inc.
843 N. Sycamore Ave.
Los Angeles, CA 90038
(213) 461-3971

C.P.C. (Susan Nathan & Assoc.)
8281 Melrose Ave. #200
Los Angeles, CA 90046
(213) 653-7573

Cactus Talent Agency
13601 Ventura Blvd. #112
Sherman Oaks, CA 91423
(818) 986-7432

Calder Agency
17420 Ventura Blvd. #4
Encino, CA 91316
(818) 906-2825

Camden • ITG
822 S. Robertsonf #200
Los Angeles, CA 90035
(310) 289-2700

Barara Cameron & Associates
23548 Calabasas Rd. #204
Calabasas, CA 91302
(818) 591-1495

Capital Artists
6255 Sunset Blvd. #1926
(Los Angeles, CA 90028
(213) 463-1424

William Carroll
120 S. Victory Blvd. #204
Burbank, CA 91502
(818) 848-9948

Cavaleri & Assoc.
6605 Hollywood Blvd. #220
Los Angeles, CA 90028
(213) 461-2940

Century Artists Ltd.
9744 Wilshire Blvd. #308
Beverly Hills, CA 90212
(310) 273-4366

Chasin Agency
190 N. Canon Drive #201
Beverly Hills, CA 90210
(310) 278-7505

Jack Chutuk & Assoc.
2121 Ave. of the Stars #700
Los Angeles, CA 90067
(310) 552-1773

Circle Talent Associates
433 N. Camden Drive #400
Beverly Hills, CA 90210
(310) 285-1585

C'La Vie Inc.
7507 Sunset Blvd. #201
Los Angeles, CA 90046
(213) 969-0541

W. Randolph Clark Co.
2431 Hyperion Ave.
Los Angeles, CA 90027
(213) 953-4960

Colleen Cler Modeling
120 S. Victory #206
Burbank, CA 91502
(818) 841-7943

CNA
1801 Ave. of The Stars #1250
Los Angeles, CA 90067
(310) 556-4343

Coast To Coast Talent Agency
4942 Vineland Ave. #200
North Hollywood, CA 91601
(818) 762-6278

Colours Model & Talent Mgmt.
7551 Melrose Ave. #6
Los Angeles, CA 90046
(213) 658-7072

Kingsley Colton
16661 Ventura Blvd. #400
Encino, CA 91436
(818) 788-6043

Contemporary Artists
1427 Third St. Promenade #205
Santa Monica, CA 90401
(310) 395-1800

Coppage Company
11501 Chandler Blvd.
North Hollywood, CA 91601
(818) 980-1106

Coralie Jr. Agency
4789 Vineland Ave. #100
North Hollywood, CA 91602
(818) 766-9501

Robert Cosden Enterprises
7135 Hollywood Blvd., Phse. #2
Los Angeles, CA 90046
(213) 856-9000

Cox Talent Agency
4310 Cahuenga Blvd. #103
Toluca Lake, CA 91602
(818) 752-4000

Craig Agency
8485 Melrose Place #E
Los Angeled, CA 90069
(213) 655-0236

Creative Artists Agency
9830 Wilshire Blvd.
Beverly Hills, CA 90212
(310) 288-4545

Susan Crow & Associates
1010 Hammond #102
West Hollywood, CA 90069
(310) 859-9784

Lil Cumber Attractions
6363 Sunset Blvd. #701
Los Angeles, CA 90028
(213) 469-1919

Cunningham, Escott & Dipene
261 S. Robertson Blvd.
Beverly Hills, CA 90211
(310) 855-1700

Dade / Schultz Associates
11846 Ventura Blvd. #100
Studio City, CA 91604
(818) 760-3100

Richard DeGrandcourt Talent Agcy.
5927 Franklin Ave., Pthse.
Los Angeles, CA 90028
(213) 460-2529

Devroe Agency
3365 Cahuenga Blvd.
Hollywood, Ca 90068
(213) 666-2666

Diamond Artists Ltd.
215 N. Barrington Ave.
Los Angeles, CA 90049
(310) 472-4911

Efendi Talent Agency
6525 Sunset Blvd. #207
Los Angeles, CA 90028
(213) 957-0006

Elite Models / John Casablancas
345 N. Maple Drive
Beverly Hills, CA 90210
(310) 274-9395

Ellis Talent Group
6025 Sepulveda Blvd. #201
Van Nuys, CA 91411
(818) 997-7447

Emerald Artists
6565 Sunset Blvd. #210
Los Angeles, CA 90028
(213) 465-2974

Epstein / Wyckoff & Associates
280 S. Beverly Drive #400
Beverly Hills, CA 90212
(310) 278-7222

Estephan Talent Agency
6018 Greenmeadow Rd.
Lakewood, CA 90713
(213) 421-8048

F.P.A.
4051 Radford Ave. #A
Studio City, CA 91604
(818) 508-6691

Eileen Farrell Talent Agency
18261 San Fernando Mission Rd.
Northridge, CA 91326
(818) 831-7003

Favored Artists
8150 Beverly Blvd. #201
Los Angeles, CA 90048
(213) 653-3191

William Felber
2126 Cahuenga BVlvd.
Hollywood, CA 90068
(213) 466-7629

Feldman-Gold Agency
19301 Ventura Blvd. #202
Tarzana, CA 91356
(818) 776-1900

Liana Fields
3325 Wilshire Blvd. #749
Los Angeles, CA 90010
(213) 487-3656

Film Artists Associates
7080 Hollywood Blvd. #704
Hollywood, CA 90028
(213) 463-1010

First Artists Agency
10000 Riverside Drive #6
Toluca Lake, CA 91602
(818) 509-9292

Flick East-West Talents, Inc.
9057 Nemo St., Ste. A
West Hollywood, CA 90069
(310) 247-1777

Judith Fontaine Agency
1720 N. LaBrea Avenue, 2nd Flr
Los Angeles, CA 90046
(213) 969-8398

The Barry Freed Company
2029 Century Park East #600
Los Angeles, CA 90067
(310) 277-1260

Fresh Model Management
8490 Santa Monica Blvd. #4
West Hollywood, CA 90069
(310) 659-5001

The Gage Group
9255 Sunset Blvd. #515
Los Angeles, CA 90069
(310) 859-8777

The Gaines Agency
9220 Sunset Blvd. #220
Los Angeles, CA 90069
(310) 274-4209

Helen Garrett Agency
6525 Sunset Blvd., 5th Flr.
Hollywood, CA 90028
(213) 871-8707

Dale Garrick International
8831 Sunset Blvd.
Los Angeles, CA 90069
(310) 657-2661

Russ Garrison & Associates
260 S. Bevrly Dive, 2nd Flr.
Beverly Hills, CA 90212
(310) 275-8184

The Geddes Agency
8457 Melrose Place #200
Los Angeles, CA 90069
(213) 651-2401

Laya Gelff Associates
16133 Ventura Blvd. #700
Encino, CA 91436
(818) 713-2610

Paul Gerard
2918 Alta Vista Drive
Newport Beach, CA 92660
(714) 644-7950

Gerler / Stevens & Associates
3349 Cahuenga Blvd. West
Hollywood, CA 90068
(213) 850-7386

The Gersh Agency
232 N. Canon Drive
Beverly Hills, CA 90210
(310) 274-6611

Georgia Gilly Talent Agency
8721 Sunset Blvd. #103
Los Angeles, Ca 90069
(310) 657-5660

Harry Gold Talent Agency
3500 West Olive Ave. #1400
Burbank, CA 91505
(818) 972-4300

Gordon / Rosson Talent Agency
12700 Ventura Blvd. #350
Studio City, CA 91604
(818) 509-1900

Gores / Fields & Associates
10100 Santa Monica Blvd. #700
Los Angeles, CA 90067
(310) 277-4400

Gray / Goodman Talent Agency
211 S. Beverly Drive #100
Beverly Hills, CA 90212
(310) 276-7070

Vaughn D. Hart
200 N. Robertson Blvd. #219
Beverly Hills, CA 90211
(310) 274-7887

Harter / Manning / Woo
201 N. Robertson Blvd. #D
Beverly Hills, CA 90211
(310) 278-7278

Heacock Literary Agency
1523 6th St. #14
Santa Monica, CA 91401
(310) 393-6227

Beverly Hecht Agency
8949 Sunset Blvd.
Los Angeles, CA 90069
(310) 274-7815

Henderson / Hogan Agency
247 S. Beverly Drive
Beverly Hills, CA 90212
(310) 274-7815

Hervey / Gimes Talent Agency
14200 Ventura Blvd. #108
Sherman Oaks, CA 91413
(818) 981-0891

Howard Talent West Agency
12229 Ventura Blvd. #201
Studio City, CA 91604
(818) 766-5300

Martin Hurwitz Assoc.
427 N. Canon Drive #215
Beverly Hills, CA 90210
(310) 274-0240

Image Talent Agency
259 S. Robertson Blvd.
Beverly Hills 90210
(310) 277-9134

Innovative Artists & Literary Agency
1999 Ave. of The Stars #2850
Los Angeles, CA 90067
(310) 553-5200

International Creative Management
8899 Beverly Blvd.
Los Angeles, CA 90048
(310) 550-4000

Intertalent
131 S. Rodeo Drive #300
Beverly Hills, CA 90212
(310) 858-6200

It Model Management
941 N. Mansfield Ave., Unit C
Los Angeles, CA 90038
(213) 962-9564

Jackman & Taussig
1539 Sawtelle Blvd.
Los Angeles, CA 90025
(310) 478-6641

George Jay Agency
6269 Selma Ave. #15
Los Angeles, CA 90028
(213) 465-0232

Tom Jennings & Assoc.
28035 Dorothy Drive #210A
Agoura, CA 91301
(818) 879-1260

Joseph, Heldfond & Rix
1717 N. Highland Ave. #414
Los Angeles, Ca 90028
(213) 466-9111

Joseph / Knight
1680 N. Vine St. #726
Los Angeles, Ca 90028
(213) 465-5474

Len Kaplan Associates
1800 N. Highland, Ste. 405
Los Angeles, CA 90028
(213) 871-2555

Kaplan-Stahler Agency
8385 Wilshire Blvd. #923
Beverly Hills, CA 90211
(213) 653-4483

Karg / Weissenbach & Associates
329 N. Wetherly Drive #101
Beverly Hills, CA 90211
(310) 205-0435

Kelly Blue Talent Agency
12301 Wilshire Blvd. #205
Los Angeles, CA 90025
(310) 207-4542

Tyler Kjar Talent Agency
10653 Riverside Drive
Toluca Lake, CA 91602
(818) 760-0321

A. Koch Talent Agency
1783 Westwood Blvd.
Los Angeles, CA 90024
(213) 962-7308

Paul Kohner, Inc.
9169 Sunset Blvd.
Los Angeles, CA 90069
(310) 550-1060

Victor Kruglov & Associates
7060 Hollywood Blvd. #1220
Los Angeles, CA 90028
(213) 957-9000

L. A. Artists
2566 Overland Ave. #600
Los Angeles, CA 90064
(310) 202-0254

L. A. Models
8335 Sunset Blvd.
Los Angeles, CA 90069
(213) 656-9572

L. A. Talent
8335 Sunset Blvd.
Los Angeles, CA 90069
(213) 656-3722

Stacey Lane
13455 Ventura Blvd. #214
Sherman Oaks, CA 91423
(818) 501-2668

The Lawrence Agency
3575 Cahuenga Blvd. West #125-3
Hollywood, Ca 90068
(213) 851-7711

Guy Lee & Associates
8235 Santa Monica Blvd. #202
Los Angeles, Ca 90046
(213) 650-1300

Levin & Lorant Talent Agency
16530 Ventura Blvd. #211
Encino, CA 91436
(818) 990-1171

The Levin Agency
9255 Sunset Blvd. #401
West Hollywood, CA 90069
(310) 278-0353

Terry Lichtman
12456 Ventura Blvd. #1
Studio City, CA 91604
(818) 761-4804

Robert Light Agency
6404 Wilshire Blvd. #800
Los Angeles, CA 90048
(213) 651-1777

The Light Company
1148 4th St.
Santa Monica, CA 90403
(310) 451-3660

Ken Lindner & Associates
2049 Century Park East #2717
Los Angeles, CA 90067
(310) 277-9223

Johnny Lloyd Talent Agency
6404 Hollywood Blvd. #219
Los Angeles, CA 90028
(213) 464-2738

The Loft Agency
9713 Santa Monica Blvd. #201
Beverly Hills, CA 90210
(310) 576-9012

Los Angeles Sports Talent Agency
2121 Ave. of The Stars, 6th Flr.
Los Angeles, CA 90067
(310) 551-6500

Lovell & Associates
1350 N. Highland Ave.
Los Angeles, CA 90028
(213) 462-1672

LW1, Inc
8383 Wilshire Blvd.
Beverly Hills, CA 90211
(213) 653-5700

Lynne & Reilly
6735 Forest Lawn Drive #313
Hollywood, CA 90068
(213) 850-1984

Alese Marshall Model / Comm Agcy.
23900 Hawthorne Blvd. #100
Torrance, CA 90505
(310) 378-1223

Martel Agency
1680 N. Vine St. #203
Hollywood, CA 90028
(213) 461-5943

Maxine's Talent Agency
4830 Encino Ave.
Encino, CA 91316
(818) 986-2946

James McHugh Agency
8150 BVeverly Blvd. #303
Los Angeles, CA 90048
(213) 651-2770

Media Artists Group
6255 Sunset Blvd. #1926
Los Angeles, CA 90028
(213) 463-5610

Metropolitan Talent Agency
9320 Wilshire Blvd., 3rd Flr.
Beverly Hills, CA 90212
(310) 247-5500

MGA / Mary Grady Agency
150 E. Olive Ave. #304
Burbank, CA 91502
(818) 843-1511

Gilbert Miller Agency
21243 Ventura Blvd. #243
Woodland Hills, CA 91364
(818) 888-6363

Miramar Talent
9157 Sunset Blvd., Ste. 300
Los Angeles, CA 90069
(310) 858-1990

Mishkin Agency
2355 Benedict Canyon
Beverly Hills, CA 90210
(310) 274-5261

Patty Mitchell Agency
11425 Moorpark St.
Studio City, CA 91602
(818) 508-6180

Mod Model / Talent Mgmt.
6310 San Vicente Blvd. #500
Los Angeles, CA 90048
(213) 936-5808

Tracey Moechel Agency
200 N. Robertson #224
Beverly Hills, CA 90211
(310) 276-9321

Monteiro Rose Agency, Inc.
17514 Ventura Blvd., Ste. 205
Encino, CA 91316
(818) 501-1177

Willam Morris Agency
151 El Camino Dive
Beverly Hills, CA 90212
(310) 274-7451

H. David Moss & Associates
8019-1/2 Melrose Ave. #3
Los Angeles, CA 90046
(213) 653-2900

Mary Murphy Agency
6014 Greenbush Ave.
Van Nuys, CA 91401
(818) 989-6076

Omni Artists International
9107 Wilshire Blvd. #602
Beverly Hills, CA 90210
(310) 858-0085

Omnipop, Inc.
10700 Ventura Blvd., Ste. C
Studio City, CA 91604
(818) 980-9267

Pacific Artists
515 N. LaCienega Blvd.
Los Angeles, CA 90048
(310) 657-5990

The Parness Agency
1901 Ave. of the Stars, Ste. 385
Los Angeles, CA 90067
(310) 551-0071

The Partos Company
3630 Barham Blvd. #Z108
Hollywood, CA 90068
(213) 876-5500

Perseus Modeling & Talent Agency
3807 Wilshire Blvd. #1102
Los Angeles, CA 90010
(213) 383-2322

Prima Model Mgmt., Inc.
832 N. La Brea Ave.
Los Angeles, CA 90038
(213) 465-8511

Privilege Talent
8170 Beverly Blvd.
Los Angeles, CA 90048
(213) 658-8781

Pro-Sport & Entertainment Co.
11661 San Vicente Blvd. #303
Los Angeles, CA 90049
(310) 207-0228

Progressive Artists
400 S. Beverly Drive
Beverly Hills, CA 90212
(310) 553-8561

Gordon Rael Company
1720 N. La Brea Ave.
Los Angeles, CA 90046
(213) 969-8493

Robinson / Weintraub & Gross
8428 Melose Place #C
Los Angeles, CA 90069
(213) 65305802

Stephanie Rogers & Assoc.
4855 Lankershim Blvd. #218
North Hollywood, CA 91604
(818) 509-1010

Gilla Roos West, Ltd.
9744 Wilshire Blvd. #203
Beverly Hills, CA 90212
(310) 274-9356

Marion Rosenberg Office
8428 Melrose Place #B
Los Angeles, CA 90069
(213) 653-7383

Natalie Rosson Agency
11712 Moorpark St. #204
Studio City, CA 91604
(818) 508-1445

The Sanders Agency
8831 Sunset Blvd. #304
Los Angeles, CA 90069
(310) 652-1119

The Sarnoff Company
12001 Ventura Place #311
Studio City, CA 91604
(818) 761-4495

The Savage Agency
6212 Banner Ave.
Los Angeles, CA 0038
(213) 461-83216

Jack Scagnetti Talent Agency
5330 Lankershim Blvd. #210
North Hollywood, CA 91601
(818) 762-3871

Irv Schechter Company
9300 Wilshire Blvd. #410
Beverly Hills, CA 90212
(310) 278-8070

Schiowitz / Clay / Rose
8228 Sunset Blvd. #212
Los Angeles, CA 90046
(213) 650-7300

Sandie Schnarr
8281 Melrose Ave. #200
Los Angeles, CA 90046
(213) 653-9479

Judy Schoen & Assoiates
606 N. Larchmont Blvd. #309
Los Angeles, CA 90004
(213) 962-1950

Booh Schut Agency
11350 Ventura Blvd. #206
Studio City, CA 91604
(818) 760-6669

Don Schwartz Associates
8749 Sunset Blvd.
Los Angeles, CA 90069
(310) 657-8910

Screen Children's Agency
12444 Ventura Blvd.
Studio City, CA 91604
(818) 985-6131

John Sekura / A Talent Agency
1680 N. Vine St. #1003
Hollywood, Ca 90028
(213) 962-6290

Selected Artists Agency
3575 Cahuenga Blvd. West, 2nd Fl
Hollywood, CA 90068
(818) 905-5744

David Shapira & Associates
15301 Ventura Blvd. #345
Sherman Oaks, CA 91403
(818) 906-0322

Shapiro-Lichtman
8827 Beverly Blvd.
Los Angeles, CA 90048
(310) 859-8877

Showbiz Entertainment
6922 Hollywood Blvd. #207
Hollywood, CA 90028
(213) 469-9931

The Shumaker Agency
6533 Hollywood Blvd. #301
Hollywood, Ca 90028
(213) 464-0745

Jerome Siegel Associates
7551 Sunset Blvd. #203
Los Angeles, CA 90046
(213) 850-1275

Silver, Kass & Massetti Agency Ltd.
8730 Sunset Blvd. #480
Los Angeles, CA 90069
(310) 289-0909

Silver Screen Artists Agcy / Model
Team, 8222 Melrose Ave. #302
Los Angeles, CA 90046
(213) 653-3296

Sindell & Elliott, Ltd.
8721 Sunset Blvd. #210
Los Angeles, CA 90069
(310) 659-9352

Michael Slessinger & Associates
8730 Sunset Blvd. #220
Los Angeles, CA 90069
(310) 657-7113

Susan Smith & Associates
121 N. San Vicente Blvd.
Beverly Hills, CA 90211
(213) 852-4777

Camille Sorice Agency
7540 Balboa Blvd. #1
Van Nuys, CA 91406
(818) 995-1775

Special Artists Agency
335 N. Maple Drive #360
Beverly Hills, CA 90210
(310) 859-9688

Specialty Models, Talent Agency
885 Westbourne Drive
West Hollywood, CA 90069
(310) 657-5367

Sportscasting Period
9230 Olympic Blvd. #201
Beverly Hills, CA 90212
(213) 653-0186

Spotlite Enterprises
8665 Wilshire Blvd. #208
Beverly Hills, CA 90211
(310) 657-8004

Star Talent
1050 N. Maple St.
Burbank, CA 91505
(818) 841-3317

STE Representation, Ltd.
9301 Wilshire Blvd. #312
Beverly Hills, CA 90210
(310) 550-3982

Charles H. Stern Agency
11755 Wilshire Blvd. #2320
Los Angeles, CA 90025
(310) 479-1788

Stone Manners Agency
8091 Selma Avenue
Los Angeles, CA 90046
(213) 654-7575

Elisabeth Sturm Talent Agency
19725 Sherman Way #200
Canoga Park, CA 91306
(818) 703-1805

Style Models & Artists
12377 Lewis St. #101
Garden Grove, CA 92640
(714) 750-4445

Sutton, Barth & Vennari, Inc.
145 S. Fairfax Ave. #310
Los Angeles, CA 90036
(213) 938-6000

Talent Bank
1680 N. Vine St. #721
Hollywood, CA 90028
(213) 466-7618

Talent Group, Inc.
9250 Wilshire Blvd.
Beverly Hills, CA 90212
(310)273-9559

Herb Tannen & Associates
1800 N. Vine St. #120
Los Angeles, Ca 90028
(212) 466-6191

Willie Thompson Agency
6381 Hollywood Blvd. #450
Los Angeles, CA 90028
(213) 461-6594

Arlene Thornton & Associates
5657 Wilshire Blvd. #290
Los Angeles, CA 90036
(213) 939-5757

Tisherman Agency
6767 Forest Lawn Drive
Hollywood, Ca 90068
(213) 850-6767

Tobias-Skouras & Assoc. Inc.
1015 Gayley Ave. #300
Los Angeles, CA 90024
(310) 208-2100

Triad Artists
10100 Santa Monica Blvd., 16th Flr.
Los Angeles, CA 90067
(310) 556-2727

The Turtle Agency
12456 Ventura Blvd. #1
Studio City, CA 91604
(818) 506-6898

United Talent Agency, Inc.
9560 Wilshire Blvd., 5th Flr.
Bevrly Hills, CA 90212
(310) 273-6700

Van Cleef Talent Agency
7319 Beverly Blvd. #7
Los Angeles, CA 90036
(213) 954-1965

Erika Wain Agency
1418 N. Highland Ave. #102
Los Angeles, CA 90028
(213) 460-4224

Sandra Watt & Associates
7551 Melose #5
Los Angeles, CA 90046
(213) 653-1229

Ann Waugh
4731 Laurel Canyon Road#5
North Hollywood, CA 91607
(818) 980-0141

Ruth Webb Enterprises, Inc.
7500 Devista Drive
Los Angeles, CA 90046
(213) 874-1700

West Model Management
7276-1/2 Melrose Ave.
Los Angeles, Ca 90046
(213) 525-3355

The Whitaker Agency
12725 Ventura Blvd. #F
Studio City, CA 91604
(818) 766-4441

Wilhelmina Artists' Representatives
8383 Wilshire Blvd. #650
Beverly Hills, CA 90211
(310) 655-0909

Shirley Wilson & Associates
5410 Wilshire Blvd. #227
Los Angeles, Ca 90036
(213) 857-6977

Ted Witzer
6310 San Vicente, Ste. 407
Los Angeles, CA 90048
(310) 552-9521

World Class Sports
9171 Wilshire Blvd. #404
Beverly Hills, CA 90210
(310) 278-2010

World Wide Acts
7226 Leota Lane
Canoga Park, CA 91304
(818) 340-8151

Carter Wright Talent Agency
6533 Hollywood Blvd. #201
Hollywood, CA 90028
(213) 469-0944

Writers & Artists
924 Westwood Blvd., Ste. 900
Los Angeles, CA 90024
(310) 824-6300

Stella Zadeh & Associates
11759 Iowa Avnue
Los Angeles CA 90025
(310) 207-4114

Other Southern California Cities

Agency II Model & Talent (SAG)
2425 San Diego Ave. #209
San Diego, CA 92110
(619) 291-9556

Artists Mgmt. Company (SAG)
835 5th Ave. #411
San Diego, CA 92101
(619) 233-6655

Liana Fields Talent Agency (SAG)
2181 El Camino Real #206
Oceanside, CA 92054
(619) 433-6429

Moya Lani Talent Agency
1589 East Date St.
San Bernardino, CA 92412
(714) 882-5215

Beatrice Lily Talent Agency (SAG)
1258 Prospect St.
La Jolla, CA 92037
(619) 454-3579

Janice Patterson Agency (SAG)
2247 San Diego Ave. #A136
San Diego, CA 92110
(619 295-9477

Cindy Romano Model / Talent Agcy.
266 S. Palm Canyon Dr.
Palm Springs, CA 92262
(619) 323-3333

Lew Sherrell Agency, Ltd.
1354 Los Robles
Palm Springs, CA 92262
(619) 323-9514

Dorothy Shreve Talent Agency
2665 N. Palm Canyon Drive
Palm Springs, CA 92262
(619) 327-5855

Shamon Freitas & Co. (SAG)
2400 Kettner Blvd. #212
San Diego, CA 92101
(619) 234-3043

Northern California

Actors Exchange
582 Market St., Ste. 302
San Francisco, CA 94104
(415) 433-3920

Actors Phantasy Company
744 San Antonio Rd., Ste. 23
Palo Alto, CA 94303
(415) 961-6546

Bay Area Talent
11750 Dublin Blvd. #113
Dublin, CA 94568
(510) 833-6014

Best Model & Talent Agcy. (SAG)
150 Powell St. #307
San Francisco, CA 94102
(415) 391-2378

Marla Dell Talent (SAG)
1996 Union St. #303
San Francisco, CA 94123
(415) 563-9213

Dorie Talent Agency (SAG)
11750 Dublin Blvd. #100
Dublin, CA 94568
(415) 551-7810

Film Theatre Actors Exch. (SAG)
582 Market St. #302
San Francisco, CA 94104
(415) 433-3920

Frazer Agency (SAG)
4300 Stevens Creek Blvd. #126
San Jose, CA 95129
(408) 554-1055

Grimme Agency (SAG)
207 Powell St., 6th Floor
San Francisco, CA 94102
(415) 421-8726

Look Model & Talent (SAG)
166 Geary Blvd. #106
San Francisco, CA 94108
(415) 781-2841

Look Talent (SAG)
166 Geary St.
San Francisco, CA 94108
(415) 781-2841

Los Latinos Talent Agency (SAG)
2801 Moorpark Ave. #11
San Jose, CA 95128
(408) 296-2213

Panda Talent Agency (SAG)
3721 Hoen Ave.
Santa Rosa, CA 95405
(707) 576-0711

Claudia Quinn Associates (SAG)
533 Airport Blvd. #400
Burlingame, CA 94010
(415) 615-9950

Quinn-Tonry Talent Agency (SAG)
601 Brannan St.
San Francisco, CA 94107
(415) 543-3797

Stars, The Agency (SAG)
777 Davis St.
San Francisco, CA 94111
(415) 421-6272

Super Talent Agency Resources
35 Mitchell Blvd., Ste. 8
San Rafael, CA 94903
(415) 479-7827

Talent Plus Agency (SAG)
2801 Moorpark Ave. #11
San Jose, CA 95128
(408) 296-2213

COLORADO

Aspen Talent & Production Services
PO Box 216
Aspen, CO 81612
(303) 928-2526

Donna Baldwin Talent (SAG)
50 S. Steele #260
Denver, CO 80209
(303) 320-0067

The Barbizon Agency (SAG)
7535 E. Hampton #108
Denver, CO 80231
(303) 337-6952

Big Fish Talent Representatives
312 W. 1st Avenue
Denver, CO 80223
(303) 744-7170

Carolyn Hodges Agency
1980 Glenwood Drive
Bouleder, CO 80304
(303) 443-4636

J. F. Talent Inc. (SAG)
5161 E. Arapahoe Rd. #400
Littleton, CO 80121
(303) 779-8888

Kristi's Agency (SAG)
10555 E. Dartmouth #100
Aurora, CO 80014
(303) 695-0123

Looks Agency (SAG)
3600 S. Beeler #310
Denver, CO 80237
(303) 740-2224

M. T. A. (SAG)
1026 W. Colorado Ave.
Colorado Springs, CO 80904
(719) 577-4704

CONNECTICUT

Several attempts to obtain Connecticut's listings from its Film Office and, those failing, even the Mayors of some Connecticut cities were asked to provide information. All attempts being unsuccessful, with regret we must suggest that for Connecticut actors perhaps any listings there may be can be obtained direct from the Director of the Connecticut Film Commission at 203-258-4301 or in area telephone directories under "Theatrical Agencies" or "Talent Agencies".

DELAWARE

The May Studio
234 Forrestal Drive
Bear, DE 19701
(302) 834-3048

R. McKinney Entmt.
203 Wellington Rd., Fairfax
Wilmington, DE 19803
(302) 652-0532

FLORIDA

A-1 Peg's Modeling & Talent (SAG)
133 E. Lauren Court
Fern Park, FL 32730
(407) 834-0406

Act One Talent Agency (SAG)
1220 Collins Ave. #200
Miami Beach, FL 33139
(305) 672-0200

Act 1 Model & Talent Agency, Inc.
Address not avail. (Miami Beach)
(305) 672-0200

Ariza Talent Agency
2180 W. State Road #434
Longwood, GL 32779
(407) 862-5454

Artists' Network Talent Agency
Address not avail. (Ft. Lauderdale)
(305) 524-4311

Azuree Modeling & Talent (SAG)

140 N. Orlando Ave. #120
Winter Park, FL 32789
(407) 629-5025

Barbizon Of Orlando
Street Address not available, in
Altamore Springs
(407) 774-3110

Bob Barnes Creative Services Inc.
Address not available (Orlando)
(407) 422-2035

Berg Talent & Model Agency (SAG)
1115 N. Himes Ave.
Tampa, FL 33607
(813) 877-5533

Jay Biro Entertainment Agency
Address not available (DeLand)
(904) 734-9446

Blade Agency
Address not available (Gainesville)
(904) 372-8158

Brevard Talent Group (SAG)
405 Palm Springs Blvd.
Indian Harbo Beach, FL 32937
(407) 773-1355

Dott Burns Talent
478 Severn, Davis Island
Tampa, FL 33606
(813) 251-5882

John Casablancas Model / Talent
329 Park Avenue South, Ste. 200
Winter Park, FL 32789
(407) 740-6697

Cassandra & Bailey Talent (SAG)
513 W. Colonial Drive #6
Olando, FL 32804
(407) 423-7872

Charmette Modeling Agency, Inc.
Address not avail. (Miami Springs)
(305) 885-2685

The Christensen Group (SAG)
114 D Park Ave. South
Winter Park, FL 32789
(407) 628-8803

Coconut Grove Talent (SAG)
3525 Vista Court
Coconut Grove, FL 33133
(305) 858-3002

Darlene's Artist / Model Agency
Address not avail. (Punta Gorda)
(813) 639-6115

Dimensions III Model & Talent (SAG)
5205 S. Orange Ave. #209
Orlando, FL 32809
(407) 851-3575

Famous Faces Entmt. Co. (SAG)
2013 Harding St.
Hollywood, FL 33020
(305) 922-0700

Firestone Modeling / Talent Agcy.
Address not available (Ft. Myers)
(813) 939-3880

Flick East-West Talents Inc. (SAG)
919 Collins Ave.
Miami Beach, FL 33139
(305) 674-9900

Florida Model Center & Agency
12421 N. Florida Avenue, Ste. 205
Tampa, FL 33613
(813) 935-2208

Ford Models, Inc. / Florida
Address not avail. (Miami Beach)
(305) 534-7200

Fun Makers, Inc.
Address not avail. (Tampa)
(813) 254-9207

The Gig Mart, Inc.
Address not avail. (Ft. Lauderdale)
(305) 525-9802

Judith Gindy Talent Agency
Address not avail. (Miami)
(305, 666-3470

Gold Coast Talent Agency
Address not avail. (Miami)
(305) 592-1130

Green & Green (SAG)
12550 Biscayne Blvd. #403
North Miami, FL 33181
(305) 899-9953

Susanne Haley Talent (SAG)
618 Wymore Rd. #2
Winter Park, FL 3279
(407) 644-0600

Hamilton-Hall Talent (SAG)
13700 58th St. N. #201
Clearwater, FL 34620
(813) 538-3838

Hollander-Lustig Entertainment
Address not avail. (N. Palm Beach)
(407) 863-5800

Hurt-Garver Talent (SAG)
400 N. New York Ave. #207
Winter Park, FL 32789
(407) 740-5700

International Artists Group (SAG)
420 Lincoln Road #382
Miami Beach, FL 331l39
(305) 538-6100

June 2 Modeling
249 W. State Road #436
Altamonte Spriongs, FL 32714
(407) 869-1144

Just For Kids / Gordon Talent (SAG)
1995 NE 150th St. #C
North Miami, FL 33181
(305) 940-1311

Jerry Kane Talent Agency (SAG)
117 South 10th St.
Haines City, FL 33844
(813) 422-5500

Longshot Talent Agency
Address not avail. (Cape Coral)
(813) 549-8854

Marbea (SAG)
6100 Hollywood Blvd. #201
Hollywood, FL 33024
(305) 964-7401

Irene Marie Inc. (SAG)
728 Ocean Drive
Miami Beach, FL 33139
(305) 672-2929

Irene Marie Inc.
1413 S. Howard Ave. #101
Tampa, FL 33629
(813) 251-5221

Syd Martin Talent Agency
Address not avail. (Hallandale)
(305) 932-4041

MGM Talent Agency, Inc.
Address not avail. (Boca Raton)
(407) 395-8881

The Modele Agency
Address not avail. (Miami)
(305) 255-3713

Montage Models & Talent Inc. (SAG)
1165 First St. South
Winter Haven, FL 33880
(813) 293-5363

Sarah Parker Modeling & Talent
Address not avail. (W. Palm Beach)
(407) 686-7201

Page Parkes Models (SAG)
660 Ocean Drive
Miami Beach, FL 33139
(305) 672-4869

Marian Polan Talent (SAG)
10 NE 11th Avenue
Fort Lauderdale, FL 33301
(305) 525-8351

Michele Pommier Models (SAG)
1126 Ocean Drive
Miami Beach, FL 33139
(305) 667-8710

Rasberry Model & Talent Mgmt.
Address not avail. (Naples)
(813) 262-6607

Smarter Image, Inc.
Address not avail. (Stuart)
(407-288-1188

Stars Talent Agency Inc.
11804A North 56th St.
Tampa, FL 33617
(813) 988-9393

Stellar Talent (SAG)
1234 Washington Ave. #204
Miami Beach, FL 33139
(305) 672-2217

Evelyn Stewart Model / Talent (SAG)
12421 N. Florida Ave. #D-218
Tampa, FL 33612
(813) 935-2208

Jimmy Stowe
Address not avail. (Margate)
(305) 974-4853

Strictly Speaking, Inc.
711 Executive Drive
Winter Park, FL
(407) 645-2111

Take 1 Employment Guild Inc (SAG)
2838 S. Tamiami Trail
Sarasota, FL 34239
(813) 364-9285

Talent Network
Address not avail. (N. Miami)
(305) 895-4480

The Talent Brokers (SAG)
420 Lincoln Road #202
Miami Beach, FL 33139
(305) 538-3939

Universal Entertainment
Address not avail. (Orlando)
(407) 351-5399

Wellington Models & Talent (SAG)
821-D E. Las Olas Blvd.
Fort Lauderdale, FL 33301
(305) 728-8003

Robert Wood Productions, Inc.
Address not avail. (Fort Myers)
(813, 540-0001

Zoli Management South, Inc.
Address not avail. (Miami Beach)
(305) 532-5960

GEORGIA

Atlanta Models & Talent, Inc. (SAG)
3030 Peachtree Rd. NW, #308
Atlanta, GA 30305
(404) 261-9627

AW / Atlanta (SAG)
887 W. Marietta St. #N-101
Atlanta, GA 30318
(404) 876-8555

Axtell Productions Int'l.
1800 Century Blvd., Ste. 950
Atlanta, GA 30345
(404) 325-8656

Babes 'N' Beaus Model/Talent Agcy.
4757 Canton Rd., Ste. 107
Marietta, GA 30066
(404) 928-5832

Elaine Barthé Talent Agency
6500 McDonough Drive, Ste. E-1
Norcross, GA 30093
(404) 263-0991

Ted Borden & Associates (SAG)
3098 Piedmont Road NE #320
Atlanta, GA 30305
(404) 266-0664

The Burns Agency (SAG)
3210 Peachtree Road, Ste. 9
Atlanta, GA 30305
(404) 233-3230

The Casting Connection
PO Box 1165
Atlanta, GA 30301
(404) 333-7517

Chadz Model & Talent Agency
3166 Maple Drive
Atlanta, GA 30305
(404) 261-4969

Ebony Empire / Black Stage
5891 New Peachtree Rd., Ste 106
Doraville, GA 30340
(404)458-0341

Elite Talent (SAG)
3060 Peachtree Rd., Ste. 1465
Atlanta, GA 30305
(404) 262-3422

Genesis Models & Talent Inc. (SAG)
1465 Northside Drive, Ste. 120
Atlanta, GA 30318
(404) 350-9212

Glyn Kennedy Talent (SAG)
200 Carnegie, 122 Carnegie Way
Atlanta, GA 30303
(404) 524-6120

The Houghton Agency Inc.
2400 Herodian Way, Ste. 147
Smyrma, GA 30080
(404) 850-0888

L'Agence Models & Talent (SAG)
5901-C Peachtee Dunwoody #60
Atlanta, GA 30328
(404) 396-9015, 391-0928

Modeling Images Talent Agency
2100 Roswell Road, Ste. 200-L
Marietta, GA 30061
(404) 565-4581

The People Store Inc. (SAG)
1776 Peachtree Road NW #336-S
Atlanta, GA 30309
(404) 874-6448

Real People Models & Talent
482 Armour Circle
Atlanta, GA 30324
(404) 872-4007

Starlite USA Models & Talent
1702 Anderson Drive
Jonesboro, GA 30236
(404) 477-1917

Donna Summers Talent (SAG)
8950 Laurel Way, Ste. 200
Atlanta, GA 30202
(404) 518-9855

Talent Source Talent Agency
PO Box 14120
Savannah, GA 31416
(912) 232-6639

Tara Modeling & Talent Agency
650 Morrow Industrial Blvd., Ste. 1
Jonesboro, GA 30236
(404) 968-7700

John F. Templeton Talent Agency
73 Waddell St. NE
Atlanta, GA 30307
(404) 688-4103

TMA Talents
1702 Dunwoody Place
Atlanta, GA 30324
(404) 231-1778

The William Reynolds Agency
2025 Monroe Drive
Atlanta, GA 30324
(404) 872-2270

HAWAII

ADR Model & Talent Agency (SAG)
431 Kuwili St.
Honolulu, HI 96817
(808) 524-4777

Kotomori Agent Service (SAG)
1018A Hoawa Lane
Honolulu, HI 96826
(808) 955-6511

Kathy Muller Agency (SAG)
619 Kapahulu Ave. (Penthouse)
Honolulu, HI 96815
(8089) 737-7917

Ruth Woodhall Talent Agcy. (SAG)
2003 Kalia Road #71
Honolulu, HI 96815
(808) 947-3307

IDAHO

Blanche Evans Agency
205 N. 10th, Ste. 500
Boise, ID 83702
(208) 344-5380

The Total Modeling Agency
103 S. Main
Pocatello, ID 83204
(208) 234-2456

ILLINOIS

Allied Artists Agency (SAG)
811 W. Evergreen
Chicago, IL 60622
(312) 482-8488

Ambassador Talent Agents (SAG)
203 N. Wabash Ave. #2212
Chicago, IL 60601
(312) 641-3491

Aria Model & Talent Mgt. (SAG)
1017 W. Washington #2A
Chicago, IL 60607
(312) 243-9400

Mary Boncher Talent Agency
575 W. Madison, Ste. 810
Chicago, IL 60661
(312) 902-2400

David & Lee Commercial
70 W. Hubbard, Ste. 200
Chicago, IL 60610
(312) 670-4444

Harrise Davidson & Assoc. (SAG)
65 East Wacker Place #2401
Chicago, IL 60601
(312) 782-4480

Durkin Agency
27 E. Monroe, Ste. 518
Chicago, IL 60603
(312) 943-3226

Elite Model Management
212 W. Superior
Chicago, IL 60610
(312) 943-3226

ETA, Inc. (SAG)
7558 S. Chicago Ave.
Chicago, IL 60619
(312) 752-3955

Geddes Agency (SAG)
1925 N. Clybourn #402
Chicago, IL 60614
(312) 348-3333

Shirley Hamilton Inc. (SAG)
333 E. Ontario #B
Chicago, IL 60611
(312) 787-4700

Jefferson & Associates Inc. (SAG)
1050 N. State
Chicago, IL 60610
(312) 337-1930

Lily's & Company (SAG)
5962 North Elston
Chicago, IL 60646
(312) 792-3456

Emilia Lorence Ltd. (SAG)
619 N. Wabash Ave.
Chicago, IL 60611
(312) 787-2033

North Shore Talent (SAG)
450 Peterson Road
Libertyville, IL 60040
(708) 816-1811

Nouvelle Talent Mgmt. (SAG)
15 W. Hubbard St., 3rd Floor
Chicago, IL 60610
(312) 944-1133

Philbin Talent Agency (SAG)
6301 N. Kedvale
Chicago, IL 60646
(312) 777-5394

Phoenix Talent (SAG)
1020 S. Wabash #301
Chicago, IL 60605
(312) 786-2024

Res Les
PO Box 1245
North Riverside, IL 60546
(708) 656-2256

Salazar & Navas (SAG)
367 W. Chicago Ave.
Chhicago, IL 60610
(312) 751-3419

Sa-Rah Talent Agency (SAG)
1935 S. Halsted #301
Chicago, IL 60600
(312) 733-2822

Norman Schucart Enterprises (SAG)
1417 Green Bay Road
Highland Park, IL 60035
(708) 433-1113

Stavins Enterprises
155 N. Michigan, Ste. 544
Chicago, IL 60601
(312) 938-1140

Stewart Talent Mgmt. (SAG)
212 W. Superior #406
Chicago, IL 60610
(312) 943-3131

Susanne's / A-Plus Talent (SAG)
108 W. Oak St.
Chicago, IL 60610
(312) 943-8315

Voices Unlimited (SAG)
680 N. Lake Shore Drive #1330
Chicago, IL 60611
(312) 642-3262

Arlene Wilson Talent Inc. (SAG)
430 W. Erie #210
Chicago, IL 60610
(312) 573-0200

INDIANA

Act 1 Model & Talent Agency
3843 N. Meridian St.
Indianapolis, IN 46208
(317) 926-2324

Charmaine Model Agency
3538 Stellhorn Road
Fort Wayne, IN 46815
(219-485-8421

Indiana Talent
727 Cardinal Drive
Evansville, IN 47711
(812) 425-0304

Kristle of Chicago, Inc.
8900 Keystone at Crossing, #320
Indianapolis, IN 46240
(317) 846-9656

C. J. Mercury, Inc. (SAG)
1330 Lake Ave.
Whiting, IN 46394
(219) 659-2701

Union Street Modeling & Talent
9 E. Union St.
Liberty, IN 47353
(317) 458-6466

Helen Wells Agency, Inc.
11711 N. Meridian St., Ste. 640
Carmel, IN 46032
(317) 843-5363

IOWA

All Star Attractions
321 Mount Vernon Road
Iowa City, IA 52244
(319) 338-0000

Corrine Shover Agency
326 N. Walnut
Monticello, IA 52310
(319) 395-7772

Iowa Casting & Production Service
282 Kellys Bluff
Dubuque, IA 52001
(319) 556-4367

Mid-Coast Talent Group
1454 30th St., Ste. 205
West Des Moines, IA 50265
(515) 223-9892

Shari Vail Talent
656 SE Bloomfield Road
Des Moines, IA 50320
(515) 285-1209

Talent / Iowa
6546 SE Bloomfield Road
Des Moines, IA 50320
(515) 285-1209

David Michael's Talent Agency
4th & Jackson Sts., Ste. 903
Sioux City, IA 51101
(712) 252-1974

KANSAS

The Agency Models & Talent
4711 Lamar Ave.
Mission, KS 66202
(913) 362-8382

All StAr Casting Company
9418 W. 87th Terrace
Overland Park, KS 66212
(913) 642-2278

Career Images
8519 Lathrop Ave.
Kansas City, KS 66109
(913) 334-2200

Crown Uptown Theatre
3207 E. Douglas
Wichita, KS 67218
(316) 681-1566

Empire Entmt. & Artist Mgmt.
6001 Stearns
Shawnee Mission, KS 66203
(913) 631-5685, (816) 968-9590

Hoffman International (SAG)
10540 Marty, Ste. 100
Overland Park, KS 66212
(913) 642-1060

Jackson Artists Corp. (SAG)
7251 Lowell Dr., Ste. 200
Overland Park, KS 66204
(913) 384-6688

KENTUCKY

Alix Adams Agency
333 Guthrie, Speed Building
Louisville, KY 40202
(502) 587-0765

Cosmo / Casablancas
Norwood Office Park, Ste. 204
7410 La Grange Road
Louisville, KY 40222
(502) 425-8000

Lorraine Doss
314-1 Wendover Ave.
Louisville, KY 40207
(502) 896-1394

Images Model Agency
163 East Reynolds Road
Lexington, KY 40503
(606) 273-2301

K Casting
P O Box 22927
Louisville, KY 40222
(502) 426-7008

Terri Pulley
3229 Pepperhill Drive
Lexington, KY 40502
(606) 266-0789

Vogue of Lexington Inc.
3347 Tates Creek Road, Ste. 8
Lexington, KY 40502
(606) 269-8407

LOUISIANA

Acadian Music & Dance Co.
PO Box 15908
New Orleans, LA 70175
(504) 899-0615

Acclaim Model & Talent Agency
PO Box 80438
Baton Rouge, LA 70898
(504) 922-7750

The Agency
PO Box 714
Metairie, LA 70004
(504) 288-8085

The Cole Agency, Inc.
PO Box 640697
Kenner, LA 70064
(504) 464-9389

del Corral Model & Talent
101 W. Robert E. Lee Blvd
New Orleans, LA 70124
(504) 288-8963

Fame Model & Talent Agency
220 Julia St.
New Orleans, LA 70130
(840) 458-9112

Glamour Modeling
2626 Charles Drive
Chalmette, LA 70043
(504) 279-7313

Model & Talent Management
3535 S. Sherwood Forest Blvd.
Baton Rouge, LA 70815
504-292-2424

Models & Talents Plus
1 Galleria Row, Ste. 825
Metaire, LA 70001
(504) 831-8118

New Orleans Model & Talent
1347 Magazine St.
New Orleans, LA 70130
(504) 525-0100

Renaissance Entertainment
PO Box 57505
New Orleans, LA 70157
(504) 893-7046

Jack Snowdy Modeling & Talent
PO Drawer BA
205 W 4th St.,
Reserve, LA 70084
(504) 288-8963

MAINE

Carol Scott Casting Agency
41 Fillmore Ave.
South Portland, ME 04106
(207) 774-6328

Gibson Modeling & Casting
650 Forest Ave.
Portland, ME 04105
(207) 772-2638

Mid Maine Models
RR 1, Box 162
Belgrade, ME 04917
(207) 495-2446

Murielle, Inc.
410 Hammond St.
Bangor, ME 04401
(207) 942-3463

Portland Models Group & Talent
10 Moulton St.
Portland, ME (207) 775-0414

MARYLAND

Accurate Casting & Talent
1889 Grempler Way
Edgewood, MD 21040
(410) 679-2116

Baldy More's Hardcore & Look-
Alike Casting
P O Box 241, Sunshine at US #1
Kingsville, MD 21087
(410) 335-2270

Central Agency (SAG)
2229 N. Charles St.
Baltimore, MD 21218
(301) 889-3200

Flair Models & Talent
1008 Mondawmin Mall
Baltimore, MD 21215
(410) 669-5365

Powell Talent Agency
P O Box 1677
Waldorf, MD 20604
(301) 843-6550

USA International Studios
516 Allegheny Ave.
Towson, MD 21204
(410) 296-2326

WilMarc Casting, Baltimore
107 Warren Ave. (Federal Hill)
Baltimore, MD 21230
(410) 339-2882

Adrienne's Star Casting Inc.
14415 Hoyles Mill Road
Boyds, MD 20841
(301) 428-0046

Camera Ready Kids
11421 Lockwood Drive, Ste. 410
Silver Spring, MD 20904
(301) 589-4864

The Central Agency
2229 N. Charles St.
Baltimore, MD 21218
(301) 889-3200

S.A.M.S. Universal Talent Mgmt.
11207 Chantilly Lane
Mitchellville, MD 20721
(301) 805-2985

Taylor Royall Agency
2308 South Road
Baltimore, MD 21209
(301) 466-5959

Linda Townsend Management
1611 Birchwood Drive
Oxon Hill, MD 20745
(301) 567-0531

MASSACHUSETTS

Cameo Kids and Teens / Adults
437 Boylston St.
Boston, MA 02116
(617) 536-6004

Collings-Pickman Casting
138 Mt. Auburn St.
Cambridge, MA 02138
(617) 491-4212

Ford Model Mgmt Inc. (SAG)
297 Newbury St.
Boston, MA 02116
(617) 266-6939

Image
137 North St., Ste. 202
Pittsfield, MA 01201
(413) 443-2773

Image Makers (SAG)
210 Lincoln St., Ste. 210
Boston, MA 02111
(617) 482-3622

Maggie, Inc. (SAG)
35 Newbury St.
Boston, MA 02116
(617) 536-2639

John McGee Casting
P O Box 1930
Brookline, MA 02159
(617) 964-2607

Michaelangelo Casting (SAG)
JFK P O Box 8888
Boston, MA 02114
(617) 864-9749

The Models Group (SAG)
374 Congress St. #305
Boston, MA 02210
(617) 426-4711

Raquel Osborne Casting (SAG)
P O Box 616, Kenmore State
Boston, MA 02215
(617) 749-8923

Outcasting, Inc. (SAG)
27 Harvard St.
Brookline, MA 02146
(617) 738-6322

Rose Agency
2A Mt. Auburn St.
Watertown, MA 02172
(617) 926-7673

Maura Tighe Casting
478 California St.
Newton, MA 02160
(617) 332-7506

Tom Elliott Productions
14R Russell St.
Waltham, MA 01730
(617) 647-2825

MICHIGAN

Affiliated Models Inc. (SAG)
1680 Crooks Road, Ste. 200
Troy, MI 48084
(313) 244-8770

Clervi Productions
PO Box 2127
Farmington Hills, MI 48333
(313) 442-8888

Michael Jeffrey Model /Talent (SAG
122 S. Main #270
Ann Arbor (48104)
(313) 663-6398

Pastiche Models / Talent (SAG)
1514 Wealthy St. SE, #280
Grand Rapids, MI 49506
(616) 451-2181

Production-Plus (SAG)
30600 Telegraph Road #2181
Birmingham, MI 48010
(313) 644-5566

Talent Shop (SAG)
30100 Telegraph Road #116
Birmingham, MI 48010
(313) 644-4877

The Wayman Agency (SAG)
1959 E. Jefferson #4C
Detroit, MI 48207
(313) 393-8300

MINNESOTA

Action Casting (SAG)
8337 Penn Ave. S.
Bloomington, MN 55431
(612) 884-5870

Actors Plus / Voice Plus
1564 54th St.
White Bear Lake, MN 55110
(612) 426-9400

Caryn Model & Talent
63 S. 9th St., Ste. 201
Minneapolis, MN 55402
(612) 338-0102

Lilly Chorolec (SAG)
4231 Irving Ave. N.
Minneapolis, MN 55412
(612) 522-2422

Creative Casting, Inc. (SAG)
10 S. 5th St., Ste. 860
Minneapolis, MN 55402
(612) 375-0525

Eleanor Moore Agency, Inc. (SAG)
1610 W. Lake St.
Minneapolis, MN 55408
(612) 827-3823

Kimberly Franson
4620 W. 77th St., Ste. 219
Edina, MN 55435
(612) 830-0111

Lipservice, Inc. (SAG)
400 1st Ave. N., Ste. 318
Minneapolis, MN 55401
(612) 338-5477

Meredith Model (SAG)
555 Fort Road, Ste. 300
St. Paul, MN 55102
(612) 298-9555

Paramount Models & Talent
126 N. 3rd St., Ste. 502
Minneapolis, MN 55401
(612) 338-4450

Portfolio 1
15 S. 5th St., Ste. 380
Minneapolis, MN 55402
(612) 338-5800

Richter Casting
112 N. 3rd St., Ste. 305
Minneapolis, MN 55401
(612) 338-8223

Susan Wehmann Talent (SAG)
1128 Hamon Place #205
Minneapolis, MN 55402
(612) 333-6393

MISSOURI

Backstage Workshop Talent (SAG)
8025 Ward Parkway Plaza
Kansas City, MO 64114
(816) 363-8088

Celebrity Plus, Inc. (SAG)
55 Maryland Plaza
St. Louis, MO 63108
(314) 367-5588

The Delcia Agency
7201 Delmar #202
St. Louis, MO 53130
(314) 726-3223

First Class, Inc.
209 Jefferson
St. Charles, MO 63301
(314) 947-1400

Kids Pix
35 N. Brentwood
St. Louis, MO 63105
(314) 727-7007

Korliss Management Corporation
199 Northport Hills Drive
St. Louis, MO 63033
(314) 253-1637

The Louis Michael Agency
306 East Walnut #202
Springfield, MO 65806
(417) 869-7827

The Model & Talent Network
6523 Hadley
Raytown, MO 64133
(816) 737-1033

Model Talent Management
11815 Manchester Road
St. Louis, MO 63131
(314) 965-3264

MTC
4043 Broadway
Kansas City, MO 64111
(816) 531-FACE

Norma's Modeling & Talent Agency
1253 E. Republic Road
Springfield, MO 65804
(417) 882-2436

Poise Professionals
2905 East Stanford
Springfield, MO 65804
(417) 882-3076

Professional Images
PO Box 3852
Springfield, MO 65808
(417) 886-8171

Betty Riccardi
P O Box 5398
Kansas City, MO 64131
(816) 941-9512

Patricia Stevens Model Agency
4638 J. C. Nichols Parkway
Kansas City, MO 64112
(816) 531-3800

Talent Plus, Inc. (SAG)
4049 Pennsylvania, Ste. 300
Kansas City, MO 64111
(816) 561-9040

Talent Plus Inc. (SAG)
55 Maryland Plaza
St. Louis, MO 63108
(314) 367-5588

The Talent Source
14 S. Euclid Ave., Ste. D
St. Louis, MO 63108
(314) 367-8585

Top Of The Line
1602 Locust, 3rd Floor
St. Louis, MO 63103
(314) 241-7791

Voices, Inc. (SAG)
3725 Broadway #201
Kansas City, MO 64111

MISSISSIPPI

In Mississippi, actors should contact Casting Directors Direct . . . See Casting Directors Listings. The following agency is the only one that couldbe located here.

Opportunity Knocks Talent Agcy.
931 Hwy. 80 West, Box 48
Jackson, MS 39204
(601) 354-3811

MONTANA

Marianne Adams
Adams / O'Connell Casting
Helena address not furnished
(406) 449-8767

Sunny Adams
Sunny Adams Casting
Helena address not furnished
(406) 933-8461

Lynette C. Michael
Creative World, Inc.
Billings address not furnished
(406) 259-9540

Linda Pabst
Entertainment Connection, Inc.
Billings address not furnished
(406) 656-9678

Jennie Sax
Montana Mystique Talent Agency
Bozeman address not furnished
(406) 586-6099

Cal Sorenson
Cal Sorenson Talent Agency
Livingston address not furnished
(406) 222-7736

Belle Gard
Take V Talent Studio
Helena address not furnished
(406) 449-2561

NEBRASKA

Actors, Etc., Limited
16812 "N" Circle
Omaha, NE 68135
(402)-896-9908

Nancy Bounds International
4803 Davenport St.
Omaha, NE 68132
(402) 558-9292

Liz Craig
3105 Maplewood Blvd., Apt. #78
Omaha, NE 68134
(402) 330-0110

Talent Pool, Inc.
9246 Mormon Bridge Road
Omaha, NE 68152
(402) 455-3000

Vision Quest
7529 Washington St.
Omaha, NE 68127
(402) 592-2536

NEW HAMPSHIRE

*New Hampshire does not have
any known Talent Agencies; only a
few Casting Services (See Casting
Director listings).*

NEW JERSEY

Jo Anderson Models
999 Route 70 West
Cherry Hill, NJ 08002
(609) 428-5700

Bal-Zac & Misty Morn Performers
263 Main St.
West Orange, NJ 07052
(201) 736-5072

Barbizon Modeling
377 Route 17 South (Penthouse)
Hasbrouk Heights, NJ 07604
(201) 845-4606

Barbizon School & Agency
300 Raritan Ave.
Highland Park, NJ 07402
(201) 783-4030

Ralph Borzi Productions
616 Florence Road
River Vale, NJ 07675
(201) 666-9286

California Models & Talent
937 Brunswick Ave.
Trenton, NJ 08638
(609) 393-3323

Ben Cattano Agency
30 Coral Drive
Hazlet, NJ 07730
(201) 739-1339

Rox Clancy
937 Brunswick Ave.
Trenton, NJ 08638
(609) 393-3323

Joyce Conover Agency
33 Gallowae
Westfield, NJ 07090
(201) 232-0908

Dee Management
PO Box 2350
Ventnor, NJ 08406
(609) 652-0350

The Dell Center
RR 1, Box 312, Ganttown Road
Sewell, NJ 08080
(609) 589-4099

Robert Donatelli Agency
3 Sleepy Hollow Road
Edison, NJ 08817
(201) 548-5169

Adine Duron
62 Beverley Road
Upper Montclair, NJ 07043
(201) 744-5698

Giraldi Modeling & Talent Agency
42 Harmon Place
North Haledon, NJ 07508
(201) 423-5115

Shirley Grant Management
PO Box 866
Teaneck, NJ 07666
(201) 692-1653

Sharon S. Hillegas
23B Holly Cove
Mount Laurel, NJ 08054
(609) 778-4935

Eddie Howard Agency
91 Monmouth St.
Red Bank, NJ 07701
(201) 747-8228

Jerry Leopaldi Enterprises
358 Bloomfield Ave.
Montclair, NJ 07042
(201) 746-3755

McCullough's Agency
8 S. Hanover Ave.
Margate, NJ 08402
(609) 822-2222

Meredith Agency
10 Furler St.
Totowa, NJ 07512
(201) 812-0122

National Casting Network
30 Two Bridges Road
Fairfield, NJ 07006
(201) 882-9150

National Talent Associates
186 Fairfield Road
Fairfield, NJ 07006
(201) 575-7300

New Jersey Talentworks
PO Box 6580
Fair Haven, NJ 07701
(201) 530-2945

New Talent Management
590 Route 70
Bricktown, NJ 08712
(201) 477-3366

Prime Time Casting Associates
91 Monmouth St.
Red Bank, NJ 07701
(201) 219-0422

Special Artists Management Inc.
12 Broad St., PO Box 8637
Red Bank, NJ 07701
(201) 758-9393

Tiffany Talent Agency
Blackwood-Clementon Road
Clementon, NJ 08021
(609) 784-2256

West Models & Talent Inc.
1969 Morris Ave.
Union, NJ 07083
(201) 688-0077

Blanche Zeller
28 Chestnut Road
Verona, NJ 07044
(201) 239-1545

NEW MEXICO

Aesthetics Inc. (SAG)
489 Camino Don Miguel
Santa Fe, NM 87501
(505) 982-5883

Applause Talent Agency (SAG)
1415-B University Blvd. NE
Albuquerque, NM 87102
(505) 2l47-9333

Asoke Talent Agency
1336 Wyoming NE
Albuquerque, NM 87112
(505) 296-7531

Aspen Productions in Taos
44 Melaringa
Taos, NM 87571
(505) 758-2280

Cimarron Talent Agency (SAG)
10605 Casador Del Oso
Albuquerque, NM 87111
(505) 292-2314

The Eaton Agency (SAG)
3636 High St. NE
Albuquerque, NM 87107
(505) 344-3149

Flair Talent Agency
8900 Menaul NE
Albuquerque, NM 87112
(505) 296-5571

Hooser World Enterprises
SRS B 940
Alamagordo, NM 88310
(505) 437-2669

The Mannequin Agency (SAG)
2021 San Mateo NE
Albuquerque, NM 87110
(505) 266-6823

The Phoenix Agency (SAG)
6400 Uptown Blvd. #481W
Albuquerque, NM 87110
(505) 881-1209

Southwest Models Inc.
PO Box 64
Farmington, NM 87499
(505) 525-5449

NEVADA

Aviance Profile Model & Talent
100 Washington St. #104
Reno, NV 89503
(702) 322-4332

J. Baskow & Assoc. (SAG)
4503 Paradise Road # I
Las Vegas, NV 89109
(702) 733-7818

Classic Models
3305 Spring Mountain Rd #12
Las Vegas, NV 89102
(702) 367-1444

Convention Ease
2300 Paseo Del Prado #C-306
Las Vegas, NV 89102
(702) 365-1057

Dale Production Services
PO Box 4102
Incline Village, NV 89450
(702) 831-2122

Farington Productions
4350 Arville #27
Las Vegas, NV 89103
(702) 362-3000

Holiday Models & Talent
1909 Weldon Place
Las Vegas, NV 89104
(702) 735-7353

Las Vegas Models
3625 S. Mojave #9
Las Vegas, NV 89104
(702) 737-1800

Lear Casting
1112 S. 3rd St.
Las Vegas, NV 89104
(702) 459-2090

Lear Casting
421 Hill St.
Reno, NV 89501
(702) 322-8187

Lenz Agency
1591 E. Desert Inn #100
Las Vegas, NV 89109
(702) 733-6888

Reno Barbizon Agency
4600 Kietzke Lane #A-104
Reno, NV 89502
(702) 825-4644

Sandy Dobritch Enterprises
3430 E. Flamingo #218
Las Vegas, NV 89119
(702) 451-0701

Spectrum Services
810 S. 7th St.
Las Vegas, NV 89101
(702) 388-7557

Supreme Agency (SAG)
3750 S. Jones Blvd.
Las Vegas, NV 89103
(702) 221-8851

Unique Entertainment Agency
1555 E. Flamingo #252
Las Vegas, NV 89119
(702) 731-1202

Vegas Entertainment International
101 Convention Ctr., Dr. #1202
Las Vegas, NV 89109
(702) 794-0052

NEW YORK

Most of the main York talent agencies are located in New York City. We are providing all agency lists for other parts of New York State that could be obtained from the cities themselves, since the State Offices could not provide them.

With regard to New York City:
Readers will find a less receptive response, as might be expected, in most of the agencies located in Manhattan (NYC), since they serve the far more demanding talent requirements and are for that reason more selective as to actor clients. Many represent almost exclusively stars and top players with offices on both coasts, some even in Europe. Also, since talent agencies in the major production centers open and close from time to time we do not warrant that the following list will be either current or complete when the reader is using this book. In fact, there are hundreds more agencies in Manhattan that are not franchised by the Screen Actors Guild & AFTRA, representing only for theatre. But this book is concerned with film and television, so the New York City list is limited to those agencies that are SAG-franchised. We do warrant that most of those agencies listed are generally

among the best known, longest established and most effective in film and television. A new, inexperienced talent might find those agencies that are not SAG-franchised more receptive and willing to represent them, but for film and television representation, in this major industry center, even newcomers should seek SAG agency representation.

New York City:

About Talent (SAG)
37 E. 28th St.
New York, NY 10016
(212) 889-8284

Abrams Artists & Assoc., Inc. (SAG)
420 Madison Ave.
New York, NY 10017
(212) 935-8980

The Actors Group Agency (SAG)
157 W. 57th St., Ste. 604
New York, NY 10019
(212) 245-2930

Bret Adams Ltd. (SAG)
448 W. 44th St.
New York, NY
(212) 765-5630

Agency For Performing Arts (SAG)
888 Seventh Ave.
New York, NY 10106
(212) 582-1500

Agents For The Arts, Inc. (SAG)
203 W. 23rd St., 3rd Flt.
New York, NY 10011
(212) 229-2562

Michael Amato Agency (SAG)
1650 Broadway
New York, NY 10019
(212) 247-4456

Ambrosio / Mortimer & Assoc. (SAG)
165 W. 46th St. #1109
New York, NY 10036
(212) 719-1677

American International Talent (SAG)
303 W. 42nd St. #608
New York, NY 10036
(212) 245-8888

Beverly Anderson Agency (SAG)
1501 Broadway #2008
New York, NY 10036
(212) 944-7773

Andreadis Talent Agency (SAG)
119 W. 57th St. #711
New York, NY 10019
(212) 315-0303

Artist's Agency (SAG)
230 W. 55th St. #29D
New York, NY 10019
(212) 245-6960

Artists Group East (SAG)
1650 Broadway #711
NewYork, NY 10019
(212) 586-1452

Associated Booking (SAG)
1995 Broadway
New York, NY 10023
(212) 874-2400

Richard Astor Agency (SAG)
1697 Broadway
New York, NY 10019
(212) 581-1970

Avenue Talent Ltd. (SAG)
295 Madison Ave.
New York, NY 10017
(212) 972-9040

Barry, Haft, Brown Agency (SAG)
165 W. 46th St.
New York, NY 10036
(212) 859-9310

Bauman, Hiller & Associates (SAG)
250 W. 57th St. #2223
New York, NY 10107
(212) 757-0098

Peter Beilin Agency (SAG)
230 Park Ave.
New York, NY 10169
(212) 949-9119

The Bethel Agency (SAG)
641 W. 59th St. #16
New York, NY 10019
(212) 6564-0455

J. Michael Bloom & Assoc. (SAG)
233 Park Ave. So., 10th Flr.
New York, NY 10003
(212) 529-6500

Bookers Inc. (SAG)
150 Fifth Ave. #834
New York, NY 10011
(212) 645-9706

Don Buchwald & Associates (SAG)
10 E. 44th St.
New York, NY 10017
(212) 867-1070

Carry Company (SAG)
1501 Broadway #1408
New York, NY 10036
(212) 768-2793

Carson-Adler Agency, Inc. (SAG)
250 W. 57th St.
New York, NY 10107
(212) 307-1882

Richard Cataldi Agency (SAG)
180 Seventh Ave. #1C
New York, NY 10011
(212) 741-7450

Celebrity Talent Inc. (SAG)
247 Grand St., 2nd Flr.
New York, NY 10002
(212) 925-3050

Coleman-Rosenberg (SAG)
210E. 58th St. #2F
New York, NY 10022
(212) 838-0734

Bill Cooper Assoc. (SAG)
224 W. 49th St. #411
New York, NY 10019
(212) 307-1100

Cunningham, Escott, Dipene (SAG)
118 E. 25th St.
New York, NY 10010
(212) 477-1666

Diamond Artists, Ltd. (SAG)
170 West End Ave. #3K
New York, NY 10023
(212) 247-3025

Ginger Dicce Talent (SAG)
1650 Broadway #714
New York, NY 10019
(212) 307-1100

Douglas, Gorman, Rothacker
& Wilhelm (SAG), 1501 Broadway
New York, NY 10036
(212) 355-6617

David Drummond Talent (SAG)
102 W. 75th St.
New York, NY 10023
(212) 877-6753

Dulcina Eisen Assoc. (SAG)
154 E. 61st St.
New York, NY 10021
(212) 355-6617

Eisenberg / Aqua / Hart (SAG)
145 Ave. of the Americas #200
New York, NY 10013
(212) 929-8472

Epstein / Wyckoff & Assoc. (SAG)
311 W. 43rd St. #401
New York, NY 10036
(212) 586-9110

Elite Model Agency
111 E. 22nd St.
New York, NY 10010
(212) 529-9800

Marje Fields, Inc. (SAG)
165 W. 46tth St., Rm. 909
New York, NY 10036
(212) 764-5740

Allen Flannagan Agency (SAG)
1501 Broadway #404
New York, NY 10036
(212) 840-6868

Flick East-West Talents, inc. (SAG)
881 Seventh Ave. #1110
New York, NY 10019
(212) 207-1850

Ford Talent Group
344 E. 59th St.
New York, NY 10022
(212) 688-8628

Foster-Fell Inc. (SAG)
42 E. 23rd St., 4th Flr.
New York, NY 10010
(212) 353-0300\

Frontier Booking Int'l. (SAG)
1560 Broadway #1110
New York, NY 10036
(212) 221-0220

The Gage Group (SAG)
315 W. 57th St. #4H
New York, NY 10019
(212) 541-5250

The Gersh Agency / N.Y. (SAG)
130 W. 42nd St. #2400
New York, NY 10036
(212) 997-1818

Gilchrist Talent Group (SAG)
310 Madison Ave. #1003
New York, NY 10017
(212) 692-9166

Peggy Hadley Enterprises (SAG)
250 W. 57th St.
New York, NY 10019
(212) 246-2166

Harter / Manning / Woo (SAG)
111 E. 22nd St.
New York, NY 10010
(212) 529-4555

Michael Hartig Agency, Ltd. (SAG)
114 E. 28th St.
New York, NY 10016
(212) 684-0010

Henderson / Hogan Agency (SAG)
840 Seventh Ave. #1003
New York, NY 10019
(212) 765-5190

H. V. Talents (SAG)
18 E. 53rd St.
New York, NY 10022
(212) 228-0300

Innovative Artists Talent (SAG)
130 W. 57th St.
New York, NY 10019
(212) 315-4455

International Creative Mgt. (ICM)
40 W. 57th St.
New York, NY 10019
(212) 556-5600

It Models / Omar's Men (SAG)
251 Fifth Ave., 7th Flr. Penthouse
New York, NY 10016
(212) 481-7220

Jan J. Agency, Inc. (SAG)
213 E. 38th St. #3F
New York, NY 10016
(212) 682-0202

Joe Jordan Talent Agency (SAG)
156 5th Ave.
New York, NY 10010
(212) 463-8344

Jordan, Gill & Dornbaum (SAG)
156 5th Avenue #711
New York, NY 10010
(212) 463-8455

Jerry Kahn, Inc. (SAG)
853 Seventh Ave.
New York, NY 10019
(212) 245-7317

Charles Kerin Associates (SAG)
360 E. 65th St. #11J
New York, NY 10021
(212) 288-6111

Archer King, Ltd. (SAG)
10 Columbus Circle #1492
New York, NY 10019
(212) 765-3103

Roseanne Kirk Artists (SAG)
730 Fifth Ave.
New York, NY 10019
(212) 315-3487

KMA Associates (SAG)
211 W. 56th St., Ste. 17D
New York, NY 10019
(212) 581-4610

The Krasny Office (SAG)
1501 Broadway #1510
New York, NY 10036
(212) 730-8160

Lucy Kroll Agency (SAG)
390 West End Ave.
New York, NY 10024
(212) 877-0627

Kronick, Kelly & Lauren Agcy (SAG)
420 Madison Ave.
New York, NY 10017
(212) 935-8980

Lally Talent Agency (SAG)
630 Ninth Ave.
New York, NY 10036
(212) 974-8718

The Lantz Office (SAG)
888 Seventh Ave.
New York, NY 10106
(212) 586-0200

Lionel Larner, Ltd. (SAG)
130 W. 57th St.
New York, NY 10019
(212) 246-3105

Lure Int'l. Talent Group Inc. (SAG)
156 5th Ave. #1210
New York, NY 10010
(212) 675-5454

LW2 (SAG)
9 E. 37th St.
New York, NY 10016
(212) 889-9450

John Martinelli Attractions (SAG)
888 Eighth Ave.
New York, NY 1003
(212) 586-0963

Marge McDermott (Children) (SAG)
216 E. 39th St.
New York, NY 10016
(212) 889-1583

Meredith Model Mgmt. (SAG)
10 Furler St.
Totowa, NJ 07512
(201) 812-0122

William Morris Agency
1350 Avenue of the Americas
New York, NY 10019
(212) 586-5100

The News & Entmt. Corp. (SAG)
650 First Ave., 8th Flr.
New York, NY 10016
(212) 889-8555

The New York Agency (SAG)
1501 Broadway #308
New York, NY 10036
(212) 391-2110

Nouvelle Talent Management (SAG)
20 Bethune St. #3B
New York, NY 10014
(212) 645-0940

Omnipop, Inc. (SAG)
55 West Old Country Rd.
Hicksville (LI), NY 11801
(516) 937-6011

Oppenheim Christie Assoc. (SAG)
13 E. 37th St.
New York, NY 10016
(212) 213-4330

Fifi Oscard Agency (SAG)
24 W. 40th St. #1700
New York, NY 10018
(212) 764-1100

Harry Packwood Talent (SAG)
250 W. 57th St. #2012
New York, NY 10107
(212) 596-8900

Dorothy Palmer Talent Agcy. (SAG)
235 W. 56th St. #24K
New York, NY 10019
(212) 765-4280

Pauline's Talent Corp. (SAG)
379 W. Broadway #502
New York, NY 10012
(212) 941-6000

Premier Talent Associates (SAG)
3 E. 54th St.
New York, NY 10022
(212) 758-4900

Professional Artists Unltd. (SAG)
513 W. 54th St.
New York, NY 10019
(212) 247-8770

Pyramid Entertainment Group (SAG)
89 Fifth Ave.
New York, NY 10003
(212) 242-7274

Radioactive Talent, Inc. (SAG)
240-03 Linden Blvd.
Elmont, NY 11003
(212) 315-1919

Rascals Unlimited (SAG)
135 E. 65th St.
New York, NY 10021
(212) 517-6500

Norman Reich Agency (SAG)
65 W. 55th St. #4D
New York, NY 10019
(212) 399-2881

Gilla Roos, Ltd. (SAG)
16 W. 22nd St., 7th Flr.
New York, NY 10010
(212) 727-7820

Charles Vernon Ryan Ent. (SAG)
1841 Broadway #907
New York, NY 10023
(212) 245-2225

Sames & Rollnick Assoc. (SAG)
250 W. 57th St. #703
New York, NY 10107
(212) 315-4434

Sanders Agency, Ltd. (SAG)
1204 Broadway #306
New York, NY 10001
(212) 779-3737

Schiffman/Ekman/Morrison/Marx
(SAG) 22 W. 19th St., 8th Flr.
New York, NY 10011
(212) 627-5500

William Schill Agency (SAG)
250 W. 57th St. #1429
New York, NY 10107
(212) 315-5919

Schuller Talent Inc. (SAG)
276 Fifth Ave.
New York, NY 10001
(212) 532-6005

Select Artists Representatives(SAG)
337 W. 43rd St.
New York, NY 10036
(212) 586-4300

Silver, Kass & Massetti / East (SAG)
145 W. 45th St. #1204
New York, NY 10036
(212) 391-4545

Susan Smith & Assoc. (SAG)
192 Lexington Ave., 12th Flr.
New York, NY 10016
(212) 545-0500

The Starkman Agency (SAG)
1501 Broadway
New York, NY 10036
(212) 921-9191

STE Representation Ltd. (SAG)
888 7th Ave.
New York, NY 10019
(212) 246-1030

Stewart Artists Corporation (SAG)
215 E. 81st St.
New York, NY 10028
(212) 249-5540

Peter Strain & Assoc. (SAG)
1500 Broadway   #2001
New York, NY 10036
(212) 391-0380

Stroud Management (SAG)
1040 First Ave. #273
New York, NY 10022
(212) 750-3035

Talent East (SAG)
152 Ninth Ave.
New York, NY 10011
(212) 838-1392

Talent Representatives, Inc. (SAG)
20 East 53rd St.
New York, NY 10022
(212) 752-1835

Talentswest, Inc. (SAG)
38 Chatham Road
Short Hills, NJ 07078
(201) 379-3887

Michael Thomas Agency, Inc. (SAG)
305 Madison Ave.
New York, NY 10165
(212) 867-0303

Tranum, Robertson, Hughes (SAG)
2 Dag Hammarskjold Plaza
New York, NY 10017
(212) 371-7500

Triad Artists (SAG)
888 Seventh Ave. #1602
New York, NY 10106
(212) 489-8100

Unique Sports Entmt. Mktg. (SAG)
541 Lexington Ave.
New York, NY 10022
(212) 888-0333

Universal Talent Agency (SAG)
1501 Broadway #1304
New York, NY 10036
(212) 302-0680

Van Der Veer People (SAG)
401 E. 57th St.
New York, NY 10022
(212) 688-2880

Bob Waters Agency (SAG)
1501 Broadway #705
New York, NY 10036
(212) 302-8787

Ruth Webb Enterprises (SAG)
701 Seventh Ave. #9W
New York, NY 10036
(212) 757-6300

Hanns Wolters Theat. Agcy. (SAG)
10 W. 37th St.
New York, NY 10018
(212) 714-0100

Ann Wright Representatives (SAG)
136 E. 56th St. #2C
New York, NY 10022
(212) 832-0110

Writers & Artists Agency (SAG)
19 W. 44th St. #1000
New York, NY 10036
(212) 391-1112

Zoli Management, Inc. (SAG)
3 W. 18th St., 5th Flr.
New York, NY 10011
(212) 242-7490

Other New York State Cities:

Barbizon Agency
1980 Central Avenue
Albany, NY 12205
(518) 456-6713

Famous Atist Series, Ltd.
Hotels At Syracuse Square
Syracuse, NY 13202
(315) 424-8210

Daniel F. Rubado Prods. Agency
114 Revere Avenue
East Syracuse, NY 13202
(315) 475-7280

Barbara Thomas Agency
469 Albany-Shaker Road
Loudonville, NY 12211
(508) 458-7849

Trade Winds Talent Agency
429 N. Salina St.
Syracuse, NY 13202
(315) 422-2795

NORTH CAROLINA

Actors Unlimited
5607 Shadowbrook Drive
Raleigh, NC 27612
(919) 781-4524

Amron Casting & Talent Agency
1315 Medlin Road
Monroe, NC 28112
(704) 283-4290

Bizon Talent management Int'l.
4109 Wake Forest Road, Ste. 400
Raleigh, NC 27609
(919) 876-8201

Bontalent
146 Great Oak Drive
Hampstead, NC 28443
(919) 270-9413

Carolina Talent Inc.
119 E. 8th St., Studio D
Charlotte, NC 28202
(704) 332-3218

Commercial Talents, Inc.
721 Wachovia St.
Winston-Salem, NC 27101
(919) 723-4397

Diections Talent Agency
119 E. 7th St.
Charlotte, NC 28202
(703) 377-3151

Directions Talent Agency
3717D West Market St.
Greensboro, NC 27403
(919) 292-2800

Dancer and Company
1068 West 4th St.
Winston-Salem, NC 27284
(919) 725-3281

Enterprise Models Talent Mgmt.
2719 Westport Road
Charlotte, NC 28208
(704) 393-8886

Fashion Circle Model & Talent Mgt.
PO Box 7494
Asheville, NC 28802
(704) 257-1983

JTA, Inc.
820 East Blvd.
Charlotte, NC 28203
(704) 377-5987

Kimberly's Models & Talent
6508 Falls of Neuse Road, Ste. 120
Raleigh, NC 27615
(919) 876-8482

Linx, Inc.
620 S. Elm St., Ste. 335
Greensboro, NC 27406
(919) 691-1705

Marilyn's, Inc.
601 Norwalk St.
Greensboro, NC 27407
(919) 292-5950

Marquette Talent Management
403 Furman Road #7
Boone, NC 28607
(704) 262-3923

MCM Model & Talent Agency
134 Johnston Blvd.
Asheville, NC 28806
(704) 252-9449

MLM Model & Talent Agency
203 W. View Ct.
Morgantown, NC 28655
(704) 584-1551

Metropolitan Modeling & Talent
313-100 Blount St., Ste. A
Raleigh, NC 27601
(919) 834-2469

Mountain Casting & Talent
PO Box 969
Newland, NC 28657
(704) 733-4051

North Carolina Models' Assoc. Inc.
2660 Yonkers Road, Ste. R
Raleigh, NC 27604
(919) 836-8848

William Pettit Agency
632 West Summit Avenue
Charlotte, NC 28203
(704)343-4922

Professional Talent Management
PO Box 856
Swannonoa, NC 28778
(704) 686-8117

Raleighwood Casting & Talent
117 S. West St.
Raleigh, NC 27603
(919) 829-3637

Rick's Talent & Modeling Agency
643 W. Lee St., Ste. 203
Greensboro, NC 27403
(919) 379-0033

Robert Roth Entertainment Agency
PO Drawer 3387
Greensboro, NC 27402
(919) 273-7271

Talent Associates International
418 Star Hill Drive
Cape Carteret, NC 28584
(919) 393-2723

Tamre Modeling & Acting Agency
PO Box 65
Connelly Springs, NC 28612
(704) 874-3849

Touch of Class Models & Talent
1152 Executive Circle
Cary, NC 27511
(919) 460-9911

Touch of Class Models & Talent
401 W. First St.
Greenville, NC 27834
(919) 752-0509

Touch of Class Models & Talent
213 NE Main St.
Rocky Mount, NC
(919) 446-4758

Touch of Class Models & Talent
PO Box 434
Snow Hill, NC 28580
(919) 747-8661

Touch of Class Models & Talent
805 S. Tarboro St.
Wilson, NC 27893
(919) 291-6888

Unique Modeling & Talent Agency
PO Box 9115
Asheville, NC 28815
(704) 686-3156

Unlimited Impressions
PO Box 946
Apex, NC 27502
(919) 460-1626

The Nancy Watson Agency
PO Box 557
Waxhaw, NC 28173
(704) 843-1219

Wilmington Talent Productions
PO Box 1526
Wilmington, NC 28402
(919) 343-9911

Wordwide Talent & Productions
209-A S. Gurney St.
Burlington, NC 27215
(919) 227-1326

NORTH DAKOTA

Academie Modeling & Talent Agcy.
220-1/4 Broadway
Fargo, ND 58102
(701) 235-8132

The Acting Studio
824 Main
Fargo, ND 58102
(701) 232-7313

92

OHIO

American Performing Arts Network
17113 Neff Road
Cleveland, OH 44119
(216) 481-0523

Ashley Talent Agency
128 E. 6th St.
Cincinnati, OH 45202
(513) 381-6996

Barbara Proffitt/Bette Massie Agcy.
3563 Columbia Parkway
Cincinnati, OH 45226
(513) 533-1144, (512) 435-3477

Casablancas Model & Talent Mgmt.
10680 McSwain Drive
Cincinnati, OH 45241
(513) 733-8998

Cline & Mosic Talent Agency Inc
369 W. 3rd Ave.
Columbus, OH 43201
(614) 297-1711, (513) 421-1711

Colleen Shannon Talent Agency
1384 Grandview Ave., Ste. 200
Columbus, OH 43212
(614) 486-0529

Creative Talent Company
1102 Neil Ave.
Columbus, OH 43201
(614) 294-7827

Creative Talent Company
700 W. Pete Rose Way
Cincinnati, OH 45203
(513) 241-7827

David & Lee Talent Agency
1127 Euclid Ave. (Penthouse)
Cleveland, OH 44115
(216) 522-1300

Gloria Sustar Agency, Inc.
35 E. 7th St., Ste. 401
Cincinnati, OH 45202
(513) 721-3737

Heyman / Halper Talent Group
7280 Meadowbrook Drive
Cincinnati, OH 45237
(513) 631-4646

Lemodeln, Inc.
7536 Market St.
Boardman, OH 44512
(216) 758-0076

L'Esprit Models & Talent, Inc.
4807 Evanswood Dr., Ste. 204
Columbus, OH 43229
(614) 885-9752

Jack Moran All Star Talent Agency
5714 Scarborough Drive
Cincinnati, OH 45238
(513) 922-0621, (800) 354-2284

Mac Worthington Agency
844 N. High St.
Columbus, OH 43215
(614) 294-0100

The Miller Group (SAG)
1001 Eastwind Drive, Ste. 302
Westerville, OH 43081
(614) 891-6161

Powers Models & Talent
2101 Richmond Road
Beachwood, OH 44122
(216) 464-1600

Protocol Model & Talent Agency
1969 N. Cleveland-Massillon Rd.
Akron, OH 44333
(216) 666-6066

Send Me Talent Casting
PO Box 563
Swanton, OH 43558
(419) 826-8417

Sierra Vista Entertainment Ltd.
3362 Ormond Road
Cleveland Heights, OH 44118
(216) 779-6597, (216) 932-1123

Taxi Models, Inc.
2044 Euclid Ave., Ste. 202
Cleveland, OH 44115
(216) 781-8294

OKLAHOMA

American Indian Casting
Box 32329
Oklahoma City, OK 73123
(405) 789-4300, (405) 787-5131

Barbizon Modeling Agency
8137 E. 63rd Place, Ste. B
Tulsa, OK 74133
(918) 250-5514

John Casablancas Model & Talent
6520 N.Western, Ste. 201
Oklahoma City, OK 73116
(405) 842-0000

Cast
P O Box 60744
Oklahoma City, OK 73146
(405) 840-1187

Fullerton Modeling & Casting Agcy.
8138 S. Harvard
Tulsa, OK 74137
(918) 488-9246

Fullerton Modeling & Casting Agcy.
1432 W. Britton
Oklahoma City, OK 73114
(405) 848-4839

Hammon And Associates
P O Box 2356
Norman, OK 73070
(405) 329-8111

Harrison Gers Model & Talent Agcy.,
2624 West Britton Road
Oklahoma City, OK 73120
(405) 840-4515

Kandid Kids Theatre
6209 NW Expressway
Oklahoma City, OK 73172
(405) 722-4383

Linda Layman Agency Ltd.
3546 E. 51st St.
Tulsa, OK 74135
(918) 744-0888

Donna Leird Talent Agency
4147 Cove Drive
Yukon, OK 73099
(405) 789-4938

Regina McCally Talent Agency
7140 S. Lewis, #140
Tulsa, OK 74136

Native American Registry of
Performing Arts
407 S. Muskogee
Tahlequah, OK 74464
(918) 458-5199

Network Modeling & Talent Agency
1718 S. Kelly
Edmond, OK 73013
(405) 348-7004

Oklahoma Talent & Models Assn.
P O Box 25593
Oklahoma City, OK 73125
(405) 732-2212

Production Associates (SAG)
5530 S. 79th E. Place
Tulsa, OK 74145
(918) 622-7038

Lloyd Riddles Talent Agency
518 N. James St.
Guymon, OK 73942
(405) 338-7735

OREGON

ABC Kids-N-Teens Model / Talent
3829 NE Tillamook
Portland, OR 97212
(503) 249-2945

American Talent Professionals
835 Bennett
Medford, OR 97504
(503) 773-8888

Barbizon Modeling & Talent Agency
104 SW Clay
Portland, OR 97201
(503) 223-3265

Cinderella Models Agency
317 Court NE, Ste. 300
Salem, OR 97301
(503) 581-1073

Cusick's Talent Agency, Inc. (SAG)
1515 SW 5th Ave. #560
Portland, OR 97201
(503) 274-8555

Feathers & Fur Talent Agency
PO Box 20816
Portland, OR 97220
(503) 255-1422

Holly Agency
PO Box 4703
Medford, OR 97501
(503) 776-3032

John Casablanca Model Talent Mgt.
5440 SW Westgate Drive, Ste. 350
Portland, OR 97221
(503) 297-7730

Multicultural Media
PO Box 374
Eugene, OR 97440
(503) 485-6647

Perfect Image International, Inc.
535 E. 11th, Ste. 2
Eugene, OR 97401
(503) 485-1340

Silverwing Productions
485 West Centennial, Ste. 8
Springfield, OR 97477
(503) 741-2867

TMNW Talent Mgmt NW (SAG)
935 NW 19th Ave.
Portland, OR 97209
(503) 223-1931

The Troutman / Downey Group Inc.
3906 SW Kelly
Portland, OR 97201
(503) 243-5000

Wilson Entertainment Inc. (SAG)
1915 NE 39th Ave.
Portland, OR 97212
(503) 282-6028

PENNSYLVANIA

Denise Askins Talent Agency (SAG)
New Market #200, Head House Sq.
Philadelphia, PA 19147
(215) 925-7795

Bravo Talent
7 Parkway Center, Ste. 320
Pittsbugh, PA 15228
(412) 922-8354

The Claro Agency (SAG)
1513 West Passyunk Ave.
Philadelphia, PA 19145
(215) 465-7788

Donatelli Model-Talent Mgmt.
700 Lancaster Ave.
Reading, PA 19607
(215) 372-8051

Expressions Modeling / Talent(SAG)
104 Church St.
Philadelphia, PA 19106
(215) 923-4420

Fashion Mystique Modeling, Talent
451 Hockersville Road
Hershey, PA 17033
(717) 534-2750

Hot Foot Agency
73 Academy Road
Bala Cynwyd, PA 19004
(215) 55309921

Kane Model / Talent Mgmt.
1022 N. Main St.
Butler, PA 16001
(412) 287-05676

Greer Lange (SAG)
18 Great Valley Parkway, Ste. 180
Malvern, PA 19355
(215) 647-5515

Plaza 3 (SAG)
160 King of Prussia Pl.
King of Prussia, PA 19306
(215) 565-5445

Reinhard Agency (SAG)
2021 Arch St., 4th Floor
Philadelphia, PA 19103
(215) 567-2008

Vincent Stefanelli & Associates
P O Box 8163
Erie, PA 16505
(814) 453-2722

Van Enterprises Theatrical &
Modeling Agency
400 Stanwix St.
Pittsburgh, PA 15222
(412) 366-0412

RHODE ISLAND

The Rhode Island Film Commission did not furnish a list of talent agencies. The Mayor's Office in Providence was also asked for any listings. We must assume there are no talent agencies in Rhode Island. Perhaps a few can be located at some future time through the Rhode Island Film Commission. Its telephone number is (401) 277-3456.

SOUTH CAROLINA

Amur Entmt. & Film Group
419 Green St.
Orangeburg, SC 29115
(803) 533-7401

Changes of Charleston
18 Linbach Drive, Ste. G
Charleston, SC 29407
(803) 571-2117

Boots Ewing Crowder Talent Group
175 Corey Blvd., Ste. 15
Summerville, SC 29483
(803) 871-4335

Harvest Talent
PO Box 50505
Columbia, SC 29250
(804) 798-4840

Identity Modeling & Talent Agency
15 S. Main St., Ste. 613
Greenville, SC 29602
(803) 239-0500

Kross Talent
PO Box 21731
Charleston, SC 29413
(803) 577-4169

Millie Lewis Agency
1901 Ashley River Rd., Ste. 6A
Charleston, SC 29407
(803) 571-7781

MCM Model & Talent
PO Box 1265
Fort Mill, SC 28716
(803) 366-7039

William Pettit Talent Agency
1237 Gadsden St.
Columbia, SC 29201
(803) 256-6325

Show People Talent Agency
PO Drawer 2859
Myrtle Beach, SC 29578
(803) 448-6684

South Carolina Casting
3031 Kline St.
Columbia, SC 29205
(803) 252-8811

Stepping Stones
326 Laurel St.
Conway, SC 29527
(803) 248-5867

Jenny Trussell Modeling Agency
1030 St. Andrews Rd.
Columbia, SC 29210
(803) 798-0553

Upstart Talent Agency
131 Vallejo Circle
Columbia, SC 29206
(803) 736-3313

Carolina Winds
141 Gladsden St.
Chester, SC 29706
(803) 581-2278

SOUTH DAKOTA

Bernice Johnson Modeling Agency
1320 S. Minnesota Ave.
Sioux Falls, SD 57105
(No telephone no. supplied)

Haute Models, Inc.
109 S. Main Ave.
Sioux Falls, SD 57105
(No telephone no. supplied)

Professional Image Modeling Agcy.
1118 S. Minnesota Ave.
Sioux Falls, SD 57105

TENNESSEE

Aim Model & Talent Agency
Belle Meade Plaza, Ste. 205
4552 Harding Road
Nashville, TN 37205
(615) 292-0246

Ambiance Modeling & Career Ctr.
6925 Shallowford Rd., Ste. 208
Chattanooga, TN 37421
(615) 499-1994

Artist Management Agency
163 Cumberland Dr.
Henderson, TN 37075
(615) 822-6023

Baker Communications
5204 Kingston Pike
Knoxville, TN 37919
(615) 584-1395

Achie Campbell Talent Services
PO Box 335
Brentwood, TN 37027
(615-329-4939

Carvel Model and Talent Agency
7075 Poplar Park
Memphis, TN 38138
(901) 324-1122

Chaparral Talent Agency
PO Box 25
Ooltewah, TN 37363
(615) 238-9790

Circuit Rider Talent
123 Walton Ferry Rd.
Hendersonville, TN 37075
(615) 824-1947

Billy Deaton Talent Agency
1300 Division, Ste. 102
Nashville, TN 37203
(615) 244-4259

Faces Model & Talent Agency
408 Cedar Bluff Rd., Ste. 362
Knoxville, TN 37923
(Telephone was not available.)

Flair Models
PO Box 17372
Nashville, TN 37217
(615) 361-3737

Lancaster Models, Inc.
785 Crossover Lane, Ste. 149
Memphis, TN 38117
(901) 761-1046

Buddy Lee Attractions (SAG)
38 Music Square East
Nashville, TN 37203
(615) 244-4336

Miller Talent Group
11 Music Circle South, Ste. 1
Nashville, TN 37203
(615) 255-4620

William Morris Agency (SAG)
2325 Crestmoor
NAshville, TN 37215
(615) 385-0310

Nouveau Model & Talent Agency
2400 Crestmoor Rd.
Nashville, TN 37215
(615) 386-7090

Take 1 Talent
2003 Blair Blvd., Ste. 200
Nashville, TN 37212
(615) 383-6339

Talent & Model Land (SAG)
705 18th Ave. South #3202
Nashville, TN 37203
(615) 321-5596

Talent Trek Agency
544 E. Broadway, Walnut Square
Maryville, TN 37801
(615) 977-8735

T.M.L. Talent Agency
1501 12th Ave. So.
Nashville, TN 37203
(615) 385-2723

Trends, Inc.
1213 Park Place Mall, #246
Memphis, TN 38119
(901) 761-0211

World Class Talent, Inc.
111 Free Hill Road
Hendersonville, TN 37075
(615) 244-1964

Jackie Wright
3522 Midland
Memphis, TN 38111
(Telephone no. was not available.)

TEXAS

Actors, Etc., Inc. (SAG)
2630 Fountainview #211
Houston, TX 77057
(713) 785-4495

Actors Clearinghouse
501 N. I-35
Austin, TX 78702
(512) 476-3412

Donna Adams Talent Agency
7729 Northcross Drive, Ste. D
Austin, TX 78747
(512) 451-CAST

Artista Talent Agency
8531 N. New Braunfels, Ste. 200
San Antonio, TX 78217
(512) 829-1715

BLVD Co.
4621 Twin Valley Drive
Austin, TX 78731
(512) 458-2583

The Campbell Agency (SAG)
3906 Lemmon Ave. #200
Dallas, TX 75219
(214) 522-8991

Mary Collins Agency (SAG)
5956 Sherry Lane #506
Dallas, TX 75225
(214) 369-0900

Condra & Company Talent Agency
13300 Old Blanco Rd., Ste. 201
San Antonio, TX 78216
(512) 492-9947

Dallas Classic Talent Agency
P O Box 585060
Dallas, TX 75258
(214) 528-9960

D B Talent
P O Box 3778
Austin, TX 78764
(512) 892-7814

Kim Dawson Agency (SAG)
6309 N. O'Connor Rd. #113-LB22
Irving, TX 75039
(214) 556-0891

Durrett Talent Agency
3310 Jamaica Way
Mesquite, TX 75150
(214) 270-5256

Cherie Eaton Ltd.
P O Box 181660
Dallas, TX 75218
(214) 644-5744

Corpus Christi Reflections
3817 S. Alameda, Ste. C
Corpus Christi, TX 78411
(512) 857-5414

Phyllis Dumont Agency
P O Box 701248
San Antonio, TX 78270
(512) 366-0096

Vicki Eisenberg Agency
4514 Travis St. #217
Dallas, TX 75205
(214) 521-8430

Entourage Model & Talent
2101 S. I-25, Ste. 211
Austin, TX 78741
(512) 447-5000

Elite / Dallas (SAG)
3100 McKinnon, # 900
Dallas, TX 75201
(214) 720-4550

K. Hall Agency
101 W. 6th St., Ste. 518
Austin, TX 78701
(512) 476-7523

Neal Hamil Agency (SAG)
7887 San Felipe #227
Houston, TX 77063
(713) 622-8282

Ingamells Modeling & Talent
9622 Circle S Drive
Helotes, TX 78205
(512) 695-8511

Intermedia Talent Agency (SAG)
5353 W. Alabama #222
Houston, TX 77056
(713) 622-8282

J & D Talent (SAG)
1825 Market Center Blvd. #320
Dallas, TX 75207
(214) 744-4411

Mad Hatter TalentAgency (SAG)
10101 Harin #100
Houston, TX 77036
(713) 988-3900

Models & Talent Plus
3201 Cherry Ridge, Ste. C323A
San Antonio, TX 78230
(512) 366-9558

The Anne O'Briant Agency Inc.
3100 Carlisle, Ste. 120
Dallas, TX 75204
(214) 871-7568

Pastorini-Bosby Agency (SAG)
3013 Fountainview Drive #240
Houston, TX 77057
(713) 266-4488

Plaza 3 Talent Agency
9434 Viscount, Ste. 234
El Paso, TX 79925
(915) 593-8333

Select Talent
313 S. Congress Ave., Ste. 200
Austin, TX 78704
(512) 326-8585

Sinclair Modeling & Talent Agency
I9311 San Pedro
San Antonio, TX 78216
(512) 524-7740

Ivett Stone Agency (SAG)
6309 N. O'Connor Rd #116-LB123
Irving, TX 75039
(324) 506-9962

Stone / Campbell (SAG)
3906 Lemmon Agve.., Ste. 200
Dallas, TX 75219
(214) 522-8991

Talent Express
602 College
Grand Prairie, TX 75050
(214) 642-3201

Talento Hispano Agency
8204 Elmbook, Ste. 117-A
Dallas, TX 75240
(214) 638-5727

Peggy Taylor Agency (SAG)
1825 Market Center Blvd. #430A
Dallas, TX 75207
(214) 651-7884

Tiba Inc.
4528 McKinney Ave. #107
Dallas, TX 75205
(214) 622-9750

Sherry Young Agency, Inc. (SAG)
6620 Harwin #270
Houston, TX 77036
(713) 266-5800

Zoom Model & Talent Management
10723 Composite Drive
Dallas, TX 75220
(214) 362-6702

UTAH

Act- 1 Agency
4120 Highland Drive, Ste. 101
Salt Lake City, UT 84124
(801) 277-9127

Barbizon
1363 South State St.
Salt Lake City, UT 84115
(801) 487-7591

Burton & Perkins Agency (SAG)
1800 SW Temple #103
Salt Lake City, UT 84115
(801) 485-9253

John Casablancas Models / Talent
2797 S. Main St.
Salt Lake City, UT 84115
(801) 484-2402

Casting Talent Agency
4646 S. Highland Dr., Ste. 203
Salt Lake City, UT 84117
(801) 272-9543

Cover Agncy
240 W. 300 North, #103
Salt Lake City, UT 84103
(801) 364-9706

Eastman Agency
560 W. 200 South, Ste. 2002
Salt Lake City, UH 84101
(801) 364-8434

Ethnic Extras
PO Box 1201
Provo, UT 84603
(801) 377-3339

Galaxy Talent Agency
24 W. 2000 North
Sunset, UT 84015
(801) 544-4682

Hotshotz Talent Promotion
921 E. 900 South
Salt Lake City, UT 84105
(801) 355-7468

KLC Talent Inc. (SAG)
174 W. 300 South
Salt Lake City, UT 84101
(801) 364-7447

Lasting Impressions
62 W. 940 North
Orem, UT 84057
(801) 224-1837

The McCarty Agency (SAG)
1326 S. Foothill Blvd. #D
Salt Lake City, UT 84108
(801) 581-9292

Models International
8188 S. Highland D., Ste. D4
Salt Lake City, UT 84093
(801) 942-8485

Premiere Media Artists Agency
3067 Comanche Lane, Ste. 111
Provo, UT 84064
(801) 377-9705

Premiere Modeling & Talent
250 W. Center St. #111
Provo, UT 84601
(801) 377-9855

Right Side Production Services
5835 S. Waterbury Drive, Ste. H
Salt Lake City, UT 84121
(801) 272-5060

S. I. E.
2403 Washington Blvd.
Ogden, UT 84401
(801) 393-3936

Universal Talent Management
2611 South State
Salt Lake City, UT 84115
(801) 467-4921

Utah Talent Find
148 E. 5065 South, Ste. 1
Murray, UT 84107
(801) 268-1199

VERMONT

Classic Age
266 Pine St.
Burlington, VT 05401
(802) 863-1770

Monica Farrington
4 Green Dolphin Drive
S. Burlington, VT 05402
(802) 862-4882

Parlato Productions
13 Kilburn St.
Burlington, VT 05401
(802) 862-3517

Promark Models & Promotions
2 Church St., Richardson Place
Burlington, VT 05401
(802) 862-2749

Resources
187 St. Paul St.
Burlington, VT 05401
(802) 862-0550

Curtis Wright
Box 34
Waitsfield, VT 05673
(802) 496-2030

VIRGINIA

Carnes International
5770 Hopkins Road
Richmond, VA 23234
(804) 271-7522

Charm Associates, Inc.
831 St. Lawrence Drive
Chesapeake, VA 23325
(804) 545-5105

The Erickson Agency
1483 Chain Bridge Rd., Ste. 105
McLean, VA 22101
(703) 356-0040

The Gardner Agency
8644 Aldeburgh Drive
Richmond, VA 23229
(804) 270-0066

Glamour Modeling & Talent Ltd.
1115 Independence, Stes. 110-111
Virginia Beach, VA 23455
(804) 363-8844

Just Faces, Inc. (SAG)
P O Box 1027
Colonial Heights, VA 23834
(804) 768-0483

Margaret B, Kimmel
10605 Railroad Ct.
Fairfax, VA 22030
(703) 385-1713

Evie Mansfield Modeling & Talent
505 S. Independence, Ste. 205
Virginia Beach, VA 23452
(804) 490-5990

Marilyn Professional Talent Agency
2721 Chartstone Drive
Midlothian, VA 23113
(804) 379-1946

New Faces Model Mgmt.
813 Diligence Drive
Newport News, VA 23606
(804) 873-1402

Personality Plus Talent Agency
8 E. Main St.
Richmond, VA 23219
(804) 788-6800

S. R. Eubanks & Company
2828 Emissary Drive NW
Roanoke, VA 24019
(703) 562-2101

Steinhart-Norton Talent Mgt. (SAG)
312 Arctic Crescent
Virginia Beach, VA 23451
(804) 422-8535

Kathleen Stuart, Inc. (SAG)
PO Box 7271
Richmond, VA 23221
(804) 359-0999

Talent Connection, Inc. (SAG)
809 Brandon Av., Ste. 300
Norfolk, VA 23501
(804) 624-1975

The Talent Image, Inc.
110 N. Jefferson St.
Richmond, VA 23220
(804) 644-7700

Talent One, Inc.
813 Woodhaven Drive
Richmond, VA 23224
(804) 233-0934

TMT Agency
2708 Royster Court
Virginia Beach, VA 23454
(804) 481-7851

Uptown Talent, Inc.
4156 Laurel Oak Road
Richmond, VA 23237
(804) 275-7337

WASHINGTON

Actors &Walker
114 Alaskan Way S
Seattle, WA 98104
(206) 682-4368

The Actors Group (SAG)
219 Ist Ave. S #205
Seattle, WA 98104
(206) 624-9465

D&R (SAG)
3220 118th Ave. SE #105
Bellevue, WA 98004
(206) 644-1039

Lola Hallowell Talent Agency (SAG)
1700 Westlake Ave. N. #436
Seattle, WA 98109
(206) 281-4646

Jean Hill Models & Talent Inc.
40 Lake Bellevue #115
Bellevue, WA 98005
(206) 635-1103

Carol James Talent Agency (SAG)
117 S. Main St.
Seattle, WA 98104
(206) 447-9191

McBreen Model Talent Mgmt.
2215 70th Ave. W
Tacoma, WA 98466
(206) 565-4790

Eileen Seals International (SAG)
Plaza 600 Bldg., 600 Stewart St.
Seattle, WA 98101
(206) 449-2040

Terry Terry Talent Mgmt.
13751 Lake City Way NE #212
Seattle, WA 98125
(206) 261-6713

WASHINGTON D.C.

Central Agency (SAG)
623 Pennsylvania Ave. SE
Washington D.C. 20003
(202) 547-6300

The Characters Agency (SAG)
PO Box 73643
Washington D.C. 20056
(202) 232-2230

WEST VIRGINIA

Image Associates
2108 Stratford Road
South Charleston, WV 25303
(304) 345-4429

McHugh Management Co.
5010 Ridgecross
Charleston, WV 25313
(304) 776-6768

WISCONSION

Cameron Casting
247 Langdon St., Ste. 4
Madison, WI 53703
(608) 251-3907

Emerald Talent Inc.
130 E. Franklin St.
Appleton, WI 54911
(414) 735-8999

Michelle Olson Productions
1821 Wood Lane
Green Bay, WI 54304
(414) 476-5980

Thallis & Associates
3055 N. Gordon Circle
Milwaukee, WI 53212
(414) 264-8796

WYOMING

*Wyoming, while furnishing its list
of Casting Directors, appears to
have no talent agencies per se.
You could check the Wyoming Film
Office, at telephone number (307)
777-7777, also local telephone
directories, under "Theatrical
Agencies" and "Talent Agencies".*

CASTING DIRECTORS & CASTING SERVICES IN ALL U. S. STATES

ALABAMA

Donna Clark
120 Trafalgar Square
Birmingham, AL 35215
(205) 856-0605

Shirley Crumley
1825 Molly Lane
Birmingham, AL 35235
(205) 854-7382

Elizabeth Dano Fischer
2940 Old Farm Road
Montgomery, AL 36111
(205) 263-4658

Mary Gaffney
Route 4, 5021 Cole Drive West
Mobile, AL 36619
(205) 661-0599

Michael Howley
3349 S. Hull St.
Montgomery, AL 36105
(205) 262-1155

Marie Prater
2642 O'Neal Circle
Birmingham, AL 35206
(205) 822-8135

Lloyd Riley
2600 Woodland Hills Road
Tuscaloosa, AL 36405
(205) 553-3345

Doris Rogers
c/o Somar Fleming
Route 2, Box 462
Hamilton, AL 35570
(205) 921-3275

Octavia Spencer
12942 US Hwy 80 East
Pike Road, AL 36064
(205) 270-9856

Tonya Suzanne
Route 1, Box 159
Sheffield, AL 35881
(205) 766-9885

ALASKA

Carlson's Co. of Models & Talent
4011 Arctic Blvd., Ste. 206
Anchorage, AK 99503
(907 561-2454

Thompson Media Talent
11522 24th Ave. NE
Seattle, WA 98125
(206) 363-5555

ARIZONA

Buffalo Rick's Wild West, Inc.
P O Box 255
Cave Creek, AZ 85331
(602) 992-4578

Cochise Casting Co.
12 Hawthorne St.
Huachuca City, AZ 85616
(602) 456-9348

Casting Calls Unlimited
4020 E. Alvernon Circle
Tucson, AZ 85718
(602) 577-6229

Casting Unlimited
PO Box 31970
Phoenix, AZ 85046
(602) 493-0973

Holly Hire Casting
PO Box 37137
Tucson, AZ 85740
(602) 743-7886

Irene Levitt
9707 E. Mountain View #2407
Scottsdale, AZ 85258
(602) 860-4188

Sunny Seibel Casting
8778 E. Via De Sereno
Scottsdale, AZ 85258
(602) 956-7700

White Hawk Amer. Indian Casting
222 W. Brown Rd., #116
Mesa, AZ 85201
(602) 827-1628

Doug Worcheck Casting
19007 Camino Del Sol
Sun City West, AZ 85375
(602) 584-4643

Darlene Wyatt
1138 E. Highland
Phoenix, AZ 85014
(602) 263-8650

CALIFORNIA

The Hollywood Casting Directors Lists are not that important for our readers until this book's contents no longer apply from a career standpoint; however, the list of current members of the Casting Society of America as this book goes to press are included because our title "Wherever You Are" can apply to those in the Greater Los Angeles Area as well as in other areas. Those casting people who get their mail at the Society may be addressed c/o CSA, 6565 Sunset Blvd., #306, Los Angeles, CA 90028. Casting Director lists change from time to time. Up to date lists are available from Samuel French Bookstores in Hollywood when the reader is ready to relocate there.

Hollywood & Southern California

Robin Joy Allan
c/o CSA
(213) 653-7501

Julie Alter Casting
8721 Sunset Blvd. #210
West Hollywood, CA 90069
(310) 652-7373

Donna Anderson
c/o CSA
(213) 463-1925

Maureen Arata
100 Universal Studios, Bldg. 466
Universal City, CA 91608
(818) 777-3036

Simon Ayer
4063 Radford Ave. #203A
Studio City, CA 91604
(818) 505-6696

Barbara Baldavin
c/o CSA
(No tel. no. available at this time)

Deborah Barylski
c/o CSA
(818) 560-2896

Fran Bascom
3400 Riverside Drive #1075
Burbank, CA 91505
(818) 972-8332

Pamela Basker
c/o CSA
(213) 851-6475

Cheryl Bayer
c/o CSA
(818) 760-5278

Lisa Beach
1157 Horn Ave., Ste. 2
Los Angeles, CA 90069
(213) 854-0206

Annette Benson
c/o CSA
(213) 463-1925

Chemin Sylvia Bernard
20th Cent.-Fox, 10101 W. Pico Blvd
Los Angeles, Ca 90035
(310) 281-8558

Sharyn Bialy
1680 N. Vine St. #904
Los Angeles, CA 90028
(213) 871-0051

Tammara Billik Casting
1438 N. Gower St. #2407
Los Angeles, CA 90028
(213) 460-7266

Susan Bluestein Casting
4063 Radford Ave. #1-5
Studio City, CA 91604
(818) 505-6636

Deedee Bradley
Warner Bros., 4000 Warner Blvd.
North Admin. Bldg., Rm. 27
Burbank, Ca 91522
(818) 954-2015

Risa Bramon
3110 Main St., 3rd Flr.
Santa Monica, CA 90405
(310) 450-1333

Megan Branman
100 Universal City Studios
Bldg. 463, Rm. 112
Universal City, CA 91608

Jackie Briskey
c/o CSA
(310) 453-1542

Mary V. Buck
4051 Radford Ave., Bungalow B
Studio City, CA 91604
(818) 506-7328

Perry Bullington
6930 Sunset Blvd, 2nd Flr.
Los Angeles, CA 90028
(213) 957-0091

Jackie Burch
c/o CSA
(213) 463-1925

Victoria Burrows
Green/Epstein Productions
4400 Coldwater Cyn., #300
Studio City, CA 91604
(818) 753-9086

Irene Cagen
Liberman/Hirschfeld Casting
1438 N. Gower St. #1410
Los Angeles, CA 90028
(213) 460-7258

Anne Capizzi
c/o CSA
(818)763-3452

AliceCassidy
20th Century-Fox Studios
10201 W. Pico Blvd, Pico Apts. #5
Los Angeles, CA 90035
(310) 203-1127

Lucy Cavallo
Stephen J. Cannell Prods.
7083 Hollywood Blvd.
Hollywood, CA 90028
(213) 856-7573

Denise Chamian
c/o CSA
(213) 850-3599

Fern Champion Casting
7060 Hollywood Blvd. #808
Los Angeles, CA 90028
(213) 466-1884

Brian Chavanne Casting
c/o CSA
(310) 306-7182

Ellen Chenoweth
c/o CSA
(No tel. no. available at this time)

Barbara Claman
6565 Sunset Blvd. #412
Los Angeles, CA 90028
(213) 466-3943

Lori Cobe Casting
10351 Santa Monica Blvd. #410
Los Angeles, CA 90025
(310) 277-5777

Andrew Cohen
Warner Bros., 4000 Warner Blvd.
No. Admin. Bldg., #17
Burbank, CA 91522
(818) 954-1621

David Cohn
c/o CSA
(818) 377-9677

Annelise Collins Casting
Centre Films, 1103 N. El Centro Av.
Los Angeles, CA 90038
(213) 962-9561

Ruth Conforte Casting
5300 Laurel Canyon Blvd. #168
North Hollywood, CA 91607
(818) 760-8220

Glenn Daniels
c/o CSA
(213) 851-0164

Anita Dann Casting
P O Box 2041
Beverly Hills, CA 90213
(310) 278-7765

Patricia De Oliveira
6702 Moeser Lane
El Cerrito, CA 94530
(510) 527-0509

Pam Dixon Casting
P O Box 672
Beverly Hills, CA 90213
(310) 271-8064

Donna Dockstader
100 Universal City Plaza, Bldg. 463
Universal City, CA 91608
(818) 777-1961

Kim Dorr
100 Univ. City Plaza, Bldg. 447
Universal City, CA 91608
(818) 505-1200

Nan Dutton & Associates
12001 Ventura Place #305
Studio City, CA 91604
(818) 508-9683

Susan Edelman
4051 Radford Ave., Bungalow B
Studio City, CA 91604
(818) 506-7328

Penny Ellers Casting
8228 Sunset Blvd. #312
Los Angeles, CA 90046
(213) 656-9511

Cody Ewell Casting
c/o CSA
(FAX # only: (213) 657-6243

Rachelle Farberman
The Kushner-Locke Company
11601 Wilshire Blvd., 21st Flr.
Los Angeles, CA 90025
(310) 445-1111

Mike Fenton & Associates
100 Universal City Plaza, Trlr. 78
Universal City, CA 91608
(818) 777-4610

Nancy Foy
Paramount, Dressing Rm. Bldg 330
5555 Melrose Ave.
Los Angeles, CA 90038
(213) 956-5444

Jerold Franks
c/o CSA
(213) 468-8833

Carrie Frazier (Sony Pictures)
10202 W. Washington Blvd.
Culver City, CA 90232
(310) 247-0370

Jean Frost
c/o CSA
(213) 463-1925

Melinda Gartzman
Paramount, Clara Bow Bldg. #219
5555 Melrose Ave.
Los Angeles, CA 90038
(213) 956-4373

Shani Ginsberg
Sony Pictures Entertainment
10202 W. Washington Blvd.
Culver City, CA 90232
(310) 247-0370

Jan Glaser / Slater Casting
10000 W. Washington Blvd #7118
Culver City, CA 90232
(310) 280-6238

Laura Gleason
c/o CSA
(213) 463-1925

Susan Glicksman Casting
5433 Bethoven St.
Los Angeles, CA 90066
(310) 302-9149

Pat Golden
303 N. Glen Oaks Blvd., Ste. 540
Burbank, CA 91502
(818) 768-2003

Peter Golden (Cannell Prods.)
7083 Hollywood Blvd.
Los Angeles, CA 90028
(213) 856-7576

Lisa Goodman
P O Box 67217
Los Angeles, CA 90067
(310-317-1299

Lynda Gordon
PO Box 46118
Los Angeles, CA 90046
(213) 656-997`

David Graham
590 N. Rossmore Ave. #2
Los Angeles, CA 90004
(213) 871-2012

Jeff Greenberg
Marx Brothers Bldg. #102
5555 Melrose Ave.
Los angeles, CA 90038
(213) 956-4886

Milt Hamerman
c/o CSA
(213) 463-1925

Theodore Hann (Lorimar Casting)
300 S. Lorimar Plaza, Bldg. 140
Burbank, CA 91505
(818) 954-7642

Bob Harbin (Fox Bcstg.)
0201 W. Pico, Bldg 325
Los Angeles, CA 90035
(310) 203-3847

Karen Hendel
2049 Centry Park East #4100
Los Angeles, CA 90067
(310) 201-9402

Cathy Henderson
4307 Coldwater Canyon
Studio City, CA 91604
(818) 763-6659

Paula Herold
c/o CSA
(213) 463-1925

Marc Hirschfeld
1438 N. Gower St. (#1410)
Los Angeles, CA 90028
(213) 460-7258

Janet Hirshenson (The Casting Co.
8925 Venice Blvd.
Los Angeles, CA 90034
(310) 842-7551

Bobby Hoffman Casting
c/o CSA
(213) 463-7986

Judith Holstra Casting
4043 Radford Ave.
Studio City, CA 91604
(818) 761-9420

Vicki Huff
962 N. LaCienega Blvd.
West Hollywood, CA 90069
(310) 659-8557

Beth JHymson
Warner / Hollyw2ood Studios
1041 N. Formosa Blvd.
Los Angeles, CA 90046
(213) 850-2607

Justine Jacoby
Aurora Prods.
8642 Melrose Ave. #2
Los Angeles, CA 90027
(213) 854-6900

Jane Jenkins, The Casting Co.
8925 Venice Blvd.
Los Angeles, CA 90034
(310) 842-7551

Caro Jones Casting
5858 Hollywood Blvd. #220
Los Angeles, CA 90028
(213) 464-9216

Darlene Kaplan
P O Box 261160
Encino, CA 91426
(818) 981-3527

Marsha Kleinman
704 N. Gardner St. #2
Los Angeles, Ca 90046
(213) 852-1521

Eileen Knight, CBS / MTM Studios
4063 Radfcord Ave., Ste. 109
Studio City, CA 91604
(818) 752-1994

AnnaMarie Kostura (NBC Entmt.)
3000 W. Alameda #233
Burbank, CA 91523
(818) 840-4410

Wendy Kurtzman
c/o CSA
(213) 463-1925

Kathleen Letterie
761 N. Cahuenga Blvd.
Los Angeles, CA 90038
(213) 465-7132

Elisabeth Leustig
c/o CSA
(213) 463-1925

John Levey
Warner Bros., 4000 Warner Blvd.
No. Administration Bldg. #17
Burbank, CA 91522

Meg Liberman
1438 N. Gower St. #1410
Los Angeles, CA 90028
(213) 460-7258

Terry Liebling Casting
c/o CSA
(213) 463-1925

Tracy Lilienfield
c/o CSA
(818) 784-3901

Shawn Linahan
c/o CSA
(213) 463-1925

Robin Lippin
c/o CSA
(213-463-1925

Lisa London
c/o CSA
(818) 506-0692

Molly Lopata Casting
4043 Radford Ave.
Studio City, CA 91604
(818) 753-8086

Junie Lowry-Johnson
20th Century-Fox, Bldg. 26, Stg. 2
10201 W. Pico Blvd.
Los Angeles, CA 90035
(310) 203-1296

Bob MacDonald
6930 Sunset Blvd., 2nd Flr.
Los Angeles, CA 90028
(213) 957-0091

Francine Maisler Casting
c/o CSA
(213) 462-1925

Mindy Marin, Casting Artists Inc.
P O Box 1731
Pacific Palisades, CA 90272
(310) 454-1065

Rick Millikan (Columbia Pictures)
3400 Riverside Drive #853
Burbank, CA 915405
(818) 972-8344

Lisa Mionie
c/o CSA
(213) 463-1925

Patricia Mock
8489 W. 3rd St.
Los Angeles, CA 90048
(310) 276-5814

Helen Mossler
Paramount, Bluhdorn Bldg #128
5555 Melrose Ave.
Los Angeles, CA 90038
(213) 956-5578

Roger Mussenden
CBS
7800 Beverly Blvd.
Los Angeles, CA 90036
(310) 852-2975

Robin Stoltz Nassif
ABC
2040 Ave. of The Stars #500
Los Angeles, CA 90067
(213) 557-6423

Nancy Nayor, Universal Studios
100 Universal City Plaza, Bldg 500
Universal City, CA 91608
(818) 777-3566

Meryl O'Loughlin
c/o CSA
(213) 444-8345

Al Onorato
1717 N. Highl;and Ave. #812
Los Angeles, CA 90028
(213) 468-8833

Lori Openden (NBC)
3000 Alameda Ave.
Burbank, CA 91523
(818) 840-3774

Pat Orseth Casting
c/o CSA
(310) 372-8411

Jeff Oshen & Adssociates
Disney Studios
500 S. Buena Vista Blvd, Zorro Bldg
Burbank, CA 91521
(818) 560-6930

Marvin Paige Casting
P O Box 69964
West Hollywood, CA 90069
(818) 760-3040

Linda Phillips Palo & Assoc.
650 N. Bronson #144
Los Angeles, CA 90004
(213) 461-0982

Jennifer Jackson Part, Universal
100 Universal City Plaza, Bldg. 507
Universal City, CA 91608
(818) 777-5013

Camille H. Patton Casting
c/o CSA
(818) 344-3264

Don Pemrick Casting
3939 Lankershim Blvd.
Universal City, CA 91604
(818) 505-0555

Pam Polifroni
New World Television
3000 W. Alameda Av., Studio 11
Burbank, CA 91523
(818) 840-4641

Holly Powell Casting
c/o CSA
(213) 655-2970

Sally Powes Casting
c/o CSA
(213) 463-1925

Johanna Ray Casting
Propaganda Films
940 N. Mansfield
Los Angeles, CA 90038
(213) 463-9451

Robi Reed & Associates
8036 Wilshire Blvd. #429
Beverly Hills, CA 90211
(213) 281-8302

Joe Reich & Friends Casting
Glendale Studios
1239 S. Glendale Ave.
Glendale, CA 91206
(818) 502-5536

Barbara Remsen & Associates
Raleigh Studios
650 N. Bronson Ave. #124
Los Angeles, CA 90004
(213) 464-7968

Gretchen Rennell Casting
c/o CSA
(213) 462-1925

Vicki Rosenberg & Assoc.
Sunset Gower Studios
1438 N. Gower St.
Los Angeles, CA 90028
(213) 460-7593

Marcia Ross
Time / Warner Inc.
4000 Warner Blvd.
Burbank, CA 91522
(818) 954-1123

Renee Rousselot Casting
c/o CSA
(213) 463-1925

Stu Rosen & Associates
c/o CSA
(213) 463-1925

Ben Rubin Casting
5750 Wilshire Blvd. #222
Los Angeles, Ca 90036
(213) 965-1500

David Rubin Casting
c/o CSA
(213) 463-1925

Debra Rubinstein Casting
c/o CSA
(213) 463-1925

Mark Saks (Lorimar Casting)
300 S. Lorimar Plaza, Bldg. 140
Burbank, CA 91505
(818) 954-7326

Susan Scudder Casting
4765 Bellflower
North Hollywood, CA 91602
(818) 761-7917

Joe Scully
c/o CSA
(818) 705-0620

Tony Sepulveda (Lorimar Casting)
300 S. Lorimar Plaza, Bldg. 140
Burbank, CA 91505
(818) 954-7639

Gary Shaffer Casting
1502 Queens Road
Los Angeles, CA 90069
(213) 656-9498

Bill Shepard Casting
c/o CSA
(818) 789-4776

Jennifer Shull Casting
c/o CSA
(No tel. no. available at this time)

Melissa Skoff Casting
11684 Ventura Blvd. #5141
Studio City, CA 91604
(818) 760-2058

Mary Jo Slater
10000 W. Washington Blvd. #7118
Culver City, CA 90232
(310) 280-6238

Stanley Soble (Taper / Ahmanson)
601 W. Temple St.
Los Angeles, CA 90012
(213) 972-7374

Dawn Steinberg
c/o CSA
(No tel. no. available at this time)

Ron Stephenson (Universal)
100 Univ. City Plaza, Bldg 463 #100
Universal City, CA 91608
(818) 777-3498

Sally Stiner Casting
12228 Venice Blvd. #503
Los Angeles, CA 90066
(310) 827-9796

Stanzi Stokes (Universal)
100 Univ. City Plaza, Bldg. 133
Universal City, CA 91608
(818) 777-3446

Randy Stone
9336 W. Washington Blvd, , Rm 200
Culver City, CA 90232
(310) 202-3393

Gilda Stratton & Assoc.
Warner Studios,
4000 Warner Blvd., Bldg 3A #18
Burbank, CA 91522
(818) 954-2843

Monica Swann Casting
Von Sternberg Bldg. #209
5555 Melose Ave.
Los Angeles, CA 90038
(213) 956-4703

Judy Taylor
P O Box 461198
Los Angeles, CA 90046
(213) 656-9971

Mark Teschner Casting
ABC, 4151 Prospect Ave.
Hollywood, Ca 90027
(213) 557-5542

Rosemay Welden Casting
c/o CSA
(213) 463-1925

Megan Whitaker Casting
c/o CSA
(213) 463-1925

Geri Windsor-Fischer
4500 Forman Ave. #1
Toluca Lake, CA 91602
(818) 509-9993

Ronnie Yeskel
Pico Apartments, #6
20th Century-Fox Studios
10201 W. Pico Blvd.
Los Angeles, CA 90035
(310) 203-2662

Dianne Young
14955 Calvert St.
Van Nuys, CA 91411
(818) 778-2324

Joanne Zaluski
9348 Civic Center Drive #407
Beverly Hills, Ca 90210
(310) 456-5160

Gary Zuckerbrod
c/o CSA
(213) 463-1925

Northern California

Judy Berlin (for children)
240 Steuart St.
San Francisco, VA 94105
(415) 882-9878
        (and)
PO Box 293
Mill Valley, CA 94942
(415) 883-5315

California Casting
744 San Antonio Rd., Ste. 23
Palo Alto, CA 94303
(415) 961-6546

California North Network
PO Box 4657
Davis, CA 95617
(707) 448-3439

Casting Works
1045 Sansome St., Ste. 100
San Francisco, CA 94111
(415) 922-6218

Central Coast Production Services
140 W. Franklin, Ste. 307
Monterey, CA 93940
(408) 656-9191

Dorothy Desrosiers
The Corporate Video
111 New Montgomery St. #405
San Francisco, CA 94105
(415) 543-3118

Patricia De Oliveira
PO Box 9462
Berkeley, CA 94709
(510) 527-0509

Steve Dobbins Casting
650 Geary St.
San Franc isco, CA 94102
(415) 861-6655

Laura Folger
2245 17th Ave.
San Francisco, CA 94116

Scott Fortier / Richard Carreon
240 Steuart St.
San Francisco, CA 94105
(4l5) 777-1142

Scott Globus Casting
833 Market St., Ste. 809
San Francisco, CA 94103
(4125) 495-0915

Goodman-Edelman Casting
16170 Kennedy Rd.
Los Gatos, CA 95032
(408) 367-2804

Nancy Hayes Casting
2124 Union St.
San Francisco, CA 94123
(415) 567-2278

Yvonne Israel Productions
PO Box 590724
San Francisco, CA 94159
(415) 346-2979

Johnson-Mansour Agency
2941 Sunrise Blvd., Ste. 105
Rancho Cordova, CA 95742
(916) 535-6100

Oriental Horizons, Inc.
1474 Washington St.
San Francisco, CA 94109
(415) 441-2411

Annette Pirone
PO Box 591419
San Francisco, CA 94159
(415) 221-4118

Reel Talent Of Santa Barbara
1214 Coast Village Rd., Ste. 14
Santa Barbara, CA 93108
(804) 959-9555

S. F. Casting
842 Folsom St., Ste. 153
San Francisco, CA 94107
(415, 255-0113

Sammis Associates Casting
PO Box J
San Rafael, CA 94913
(415) 492-9872

Talent Source Central
PO Box 99214
Stockton, CA 95209
(209) 464-1387

Barbara Tengeri
PO Box 20591
Oakland, CA 94620
(510) 832-2349

Steven Thompson
PO Box 5017
Santa Rosa, CA 95404
(707) 579-8619

Up Image Company
429 Johnson St.
Sausalito, CA 94965
(415) 331-3246

Samuel Warren & Associates
5563 Dream St.
San Diego, CA 92114
(619) 264-4136

COLORADO

Colorado Casting Associates
1441 York St., #102
Denver, CO 80206
(303) 355-5888

Conifer Production Company
13131 W. Cedar Drive
Lakewood, CO 80228
(303) 988-9277

Emphasis, Inc.
PO Box 3630
Vail, CO 81658
(303) 476-2619

Flynn Entertainment
PO Box 7F
Arvada, CO 80001
(303) 420-8840

CONNECTICUT

We are not aware of any Independent Casting Directors in Connecticut, being so close to New York City, and no listings were supplied to us by Conn. Film Commission or by the Mayors' offices of several Connecticut cities that we contacted. Perhaps Connecticut ac-

107

tors can obtain any listings there may be at a later time by contacting the Conn. Film Commission or looking under "Agencies" in local telephone directories.

DELAWARE

DeSantos-Hedges Casting
234 Forrestal Drive
Bear, DE 19701
(302) 834-3048

S/FX Network
2204 Millers Rd., Ardentown
Wilmington, DE 19810
(302) 529-1232

FLORIDA

Casting By Reel People
Address not avail. (Palm Harbor)
(813) 785-5418

The Casting Crew, Inc.
Address not avail. (Hollywood)
(305) 927-2329

Christensen Talent Group
114-D Park Avenue South
Winter Park, FL 32790
(407) 628-8803

Coast to Coast Casting, Inc.
524 Still Meadows Circle N.
Palm Harbor, FL 34683
(813) 789-4545

Creative Casting
Address not avail. (Jacksonville)
(904) 346-0540

Evors Casting Connection
9720 N. Armenia, Ste. G
Tampa, FL 33612
(803) 935-7793

Extra Express
2000 Universal Studios Plaza
Orlando, FL 32819
(407) 363-0024

Extras Only, Inc.
7566 Southland Blvd., Ste. 101
Orlando, FL 32859
(407) 240-5200

Katrin Fechler
Address not avail. (Miami Beach)
(305) 532-7900

Florida Casting Group
Address Not Avail. (Miami)
(305) 594-7600

Florida Extras's Registry, Inc.
933 Lee Road, Ste. 400
Orlando, FL 32810
(407) 644-1277

Lillian Gordon - A Production Svc.
8313 W. Hillsborough Av. #4
Tampa, FL 33615
(813) 884-8335

Hollywood Casting Group
Address not avail. (North Miami)
(305) 981-7225

Heitz McLean Casting, Inc.
112 Ammoe St.
Orlando, FL 32806
(407) 649-8686

Hollywood East Casting Group
Address not avail. (Olando)
(407) 380-3658

Independent Castings, Inc.
8313 Hillsborough Ave.
Tampa, FL 33615
(813) 884-8335

Jody Jackson Casting
1607 West Kennedy Blvd.
Tampa, FL 33606
(813) 254-4236

Ellen Jacoby Casting International
420 Lincoln Road, Ste. 210
Miami Beach, FL 33139
(305) 531-5300

Jan & Company
4630 S. Kirkman Road, Ste. 160
Orlando, FL 32811
(407) 294-1692

Melvin Johnson & Associates
7061 Grand National Drive #131
Orlando, FL 32861
(407) 646-0490

Lynne and Buz Kramer
Address not avail. (Orlando)
(407) 295-3864

Veronica Krupski
2663 Tuscarora Trail
Maitland, FL 32751

James Ross Lee
Address not avail. (Orlando)
(407) 380-3655

Herb Mandell Casting
9460 Delegates Drive, Ste. 104
Orlando, FL 32821
(407) 855-3400

Beverly McDermott Casting
Address not avail.
(305) 625-5111

MCV Casting
300 Crown Oak Centre Drive
Longwood, FL 32750
(407) 834-5000

Dee Miller
The Casting Directors Inc.
1524 NE 147th St.
North Miami, FL 33161
(305) 944-8559

Sandra Milliner-Watters
Address not avail. (Venice)
(813) 488-5186

Lynne Presley
Address not avail. (Treasure Island)
(813) 397-7403

Reel People
3505 Tarpon Woods Blvd., # L405
Palm Harb or, FL 34685
(813) 785-5418

Rose Rosen Casting
4706 Country Hills Drive
Tampa, FL 33624
(813) 968-9399

Turnbull / Landis Assoc iates
1441 E. Fletcher Ave., Bldg. 2200
Tampa, FL 33612
(813) 975-0251

Unique Casting Co., Inc.
540 NW 165th Road #110
Miami, FL 33169
(305) 947-9339

Lori Wyman Casting
16499 NE 19th Ave. #203
North Miami Beach, FL 33162
(305) 354-3901

Zachary Casting Associates
PO Box 617108
Orlando, FL 32861
(407) 648-2400

GEORGIA

Joann Smith
650 Morrow Industrial Blvd., Ste. 2
Jonesboro, GA 30236
(404) 968-5500

Kay Allison Casting
210 Interstate North Pkwy., Ste. 700
Atlanta, GA 30339

Shay Griffin
572 Armour Circle
Atlanta, GA 30324
(404) 873-1215

Len Hunt, The Casting Network
4203 Harvest Grove
Conyers, GA 30208
(404) 760-7331

Michael Colford
1969 Mendenhall St.
Chamblee, GA 30341
(404) 452-8744

Dee Voigt
2517 Stanford Drive
Ellenwood, GA 30049
(404) 361-5651

Evelyn Dysart
3815 Old Waynesboro Road
Augusta, GA 30906
(404) 793-5091

Sylvia D. Mays
3317 Old Salem Road
Conyers, GA 30208
(404) 441-6351

Don Slaton Casting
572 Armour Circle NE
Atlanta, GA 30324
(404) 885-1498

Lillie Benitez
Stage Left
963 Gresham Ave. SE
Atlanta, GA 30316
(404) 622-0682

Jackson Bailey
Star Time Production Co.
178 Fairplay St.
Rutledge, GA 30662
(404) 557-2937

Cynthia F. Stillwell
Stillwell Promotions
PO Box 2862
Savannah, GA 31402
(912) 234-5994, (404) 808-0766

Barbara M. Clark
The Talent X'Press
PO Box 56481
Atlanta, GA 30343
(404) 808-7035

Tom Webb Castings, Inc.
1655 Peachtree St., Ste. 1102
Atlanta, GA 30309
(404) 607-8475

Elyn S. Wright
PO Box 1996
Douglasville, GA 30133
(404) 920-8249

HAWAII

No list furnished; None known.

IDAHO

*Idaho's Casting Directors'
addresses were not made
available, but via their telephone
numbers actors can locate their
addresses in the applicable (by
telephone number) cities.*

Lynn Bishop
Address not available.
(208) 344-1948

Larry Burke
Address not furnished.
(208) 385-1577

Doug Ford
Address not furnished.
(818) 882-0900

Michel Goddard
Address not furnished.
(307) 73301517

Victoria Golden
Address not furnished.
(208) 726-2251

109

Idaho Casting
Address not furnished.
(208) 634-8335

Suzanne Jordan
Address not furnished.
(307) 733-8857

Jean Medley Casting
Address not furnished.
(503-223-4520

Jennifer Rahr
Address not furnished.
(208) 774-3369

Tamara Thomson
Address not furnished.
(208) 345-0038

Joseph Weisnewski
Address not furnished.
(208) 336-9221

ILLINOIS

Alderman Casting
190 N. State, 7th Floor
Chicago, IL 60601
(312) 899-4250

Alert Casting
253 E. Delaware, Ste. 7-A
Chicago, IL 60611
(312) 944-7319

An Extra Hand Casting
PO Box 4519
Chicago, IL 60680
(312) 235-1826

Jeffrey Brandon Post Casting
528 W. Addison, Ste. 119
Chicago, IL 60613
(312) 528-8468

Jane Brody Casting
20 W. Hubbard, Ste. 2-E
Chicago, IL 60610
(312) 527-0665

Casting by McLean
PO Box 10569
Chicago, IL 60610
(312) 336-0100

Casting Eye Chicago
405 N. Wabash, Ste. 3709
Chicago, IL 60611
(312) 661-1128

Heitz Casting
920 N. Franklin, Ste. 205
Chicago, IL 60610
(312) 664-0601

Judith Jacobs Casting
33 E. Cedar, Ste. 3-E
Chicago, IL 60611
(312) 649-9585

K.T.'s Casting
PO Box 4958
Chicago, IL 60680
(312) 525-1126

Kordos & Charbonneau
430 Hibbard Road
Wilmette, IL 60091
(708) 251-2072

Cherie Mann Casting
1540 N. LaSalle, Ste. 1004
Chicago, IL 60610
(312) 751-2927

Rabedeau Casting
225 W. Ohio, Ste. 400
Chicago, IL 60610
(312) 222-0181

Lawrence Santoro
3313 N. Clark, 2nd Floor
Chicago, IL 60657
(312) 327-9377

Soozan Todd Casting
1357 W. Fullerton
Chicago, IL 60657
(312) 975-5015

Carol Verblen Casting
2408 North Burling
Chicago, IL 60614
(312) 348-0047

Susan Wieder c/o Alderman
190 N. State St.
Chicago, IL 60601
(312) 899-4250

INDIANA

Artistic Enterprises Casting
8537 Bash St., Ste. 1
Indianapolis, IN 46250
(317) 577-1717

Indiana Talent
727 Carinal Drive
Evansville, IN 47711
(812) 425-0304

Kristle of Chicago, Inc.
8900 Keystone at Crossing, #320
Indianapolis, IN 46240
(317) 846-9655

Union Street Modeling & Talent
9 E. Union St.
Liberty, IN 46240
(317) 458-5466

IOWA

Maria Bennett
Mid-Coast Talent Group
1454 30th St., Ste. 205
West Des Moines, IA 50265
(515) 223-9892

Art Breese
1940 68th St.
Des Moines, IA 50322
(515) 276-0170

Neil Brooks
Cuningham Phase One Prods.
406 W. Depot St.
Fairfield, IA 52556
(515) 472-4499

Ryan Case
206 South Main
Oakland, IA 51560
(712) 482-3154

Jay Edelnant
Univ. of Northern Iowa
Cedar Falls, IA 50614
(319) 273-6386

Rodney Franz
PO Box 1842
Fairfield, IA 52556
(515) 462-8384

Dennis Hitchcock
PO Box 3784
Rock Island, IA 61204
(309) 786-2667

Thomas Jacobs, Marycrest Comms.
1607 W. 12th St.
Davenport, IA 52804
(3I9) 326-9343

David McMaster, Gan Network
612 E. Buchanan
Fairfield, IA 52556
(515) 472-7012

Sue Riedel
Iowa Casting Service
282 Kellys Bluff
Dubuque, IA 52001
(319) 556-4367

KANSAS

Action Casting
3156 Woodview Ridge Dr., 10-205
Kansas City, KS 66103
(913) 262-0030

All Star Casting Company
9418 W. 87th Terrace
Overland Park, KS 66212
(913) 642-2278

Stacey A. Boothe
3444 E. Douglas #7
Wichita, KS 67208
(316) 683-2644

Joyce Cavarozzi
1544 Matlock Drive
Wichita, KS 67208
(316) 683-4896

Terry Alan Jones
999 N. Silver Springs Blvd #715
Wichita, KS 67212
(316) 943-6544

Jack Wright
317 Murphy Hall
Univ. of Kansas
Lawrence, KS 66045

KENTUCKY

Jennifer Carroll
1537 Wessels Drive #10
Fort Wright, KY 41011
(606) 261-8750

Mina Davis
1120 Julia Ave.
Louisville, KY 40204
(502) 459-2807

Jeni Lee Dinkel
877 Squire Lake Court
Villa Hills, KY 41017
(606) 331-0552

Juanita Everman
435 Schollsville Road
Winchester, KY 40391
(606) 842-4441

Hammond Productions, Inc.
173 Trade St.
Lexington, KY 40510
(606) 254-1878

K Casting
PO BVox 22927
Louisville, KY 40222
(502) 416-7008

Mindy Marchal
1708 Calder Court
Louisville, KY 40205
(502) 458-9657

Pioneer Playhouse (Eben Henson)
Winderness Road
Danville, KY 40422
(606) 237-2747

Terri Pulley
3229 Pepperhill Road
Lexington, KY 40501
(606) 266-0789

Tascam Communications, Inc.
PO Box 3082
Louisville, KY 40201
(502) 776-4681

Vanir Productions
517 Broadway, Ste. 220
Paducah, KY 42001
(502) 442-4463

LOUISIANA

Castleman Production Services
20230 5th Avenue
Covington, LA 70433
(504) 892-2628

Cynthia Cohen
2514 Pinehurst
Shreveport, LA 71104
(318) 226-1146

Dacotah Promotions
1629 Washington Ave. #14
New Orleans, LA 70130
(504) 895-0297

Dixieland Studios
PO Box 71782
New Orleans, LA 70172
(504) 889-8719

Miriam L. Fontenot
200 Arceneaux St.
Lafayette, LA 70506
(318) 981-7386

Sam Glynn
420 Orange Drive
Plaquemine, LA 70764
(504) 687-8648

Shirley Harrison
2840 Jefferson Ave.
New Orleans, LA 70115

Rick Landry Casting
PO Box 51244
New Orleans, LA 70151
(504) 454-8000

Fern Griswold LaRoach
10920 Airline Highway, #150
Baton Rouge, LA 70816
(504) 291-5707

Ann Massey Casting
2601 Iowa Ave.
Kenner, LA 70062
(504) 737-3742

Jennifer B. Rivas
2014 Prytania St.
New Orleans, LA 70130
(504) 523-6273

Rockit Productions, Inc.
PO Box 533
Kenner, LA 70063
(504) 464-6335

Stephanie Brett Samuel
2008 Camp Street
New Orleans, LA 70115
(504) 895-5666

Melinda Walsh
PO Box 202
Bayou Goala, LA 70716
(800) 933-1077

Paul Yacich Productions
7364 Beryl St.
New Orleans, LA 70124
(504) 282-2384

MAINE

Carol Scott Casting
41 Fillmore Ave.
South Portland, ME 04106
(207) 774-6328

Ruth Gibson Casting
650 Forest Avenue
Portland, ME 04105
(207) 772-2638

Dee Cooke Casting
RR 1, Box 162
Belgrade, ME 04917
(207) 495-2446

Murielle Wood
410 Hammond St.
Bangor, ME 04401
(207) 942-3463

Laura Butterworth
Portland Talent Group
10 Moulton St.
Portland, ME 04101
(207) 775-0414

MARYLAND

Baldy Moore's Casting
PO Box 241
Sunshine at US 1
Kingsville, MD 21087
(410) 335-2270

The Baltimore Casting Company
PO Box 66463
Baltimore, MD 21239
(410) 882-4098

Susan Marya Baronoff
PO Box 215
Bozman, MD 21612
(410) 745-3550

Central Casting, Baltimore
2229 N. Charles St.
Baltimore, MD 21218
(410) 889-3200

Central Casting, D. C.
623 Pennsylvania Ave. SE
Washington, D.C. 20003
(202) 547-6300

Alice Dalton
4 Acorn Drive
Annapolis, MD 21401
(410) 266-6180

The Erickson Agency (Casting)
1483 Chain Bridge Rd., #105
McLean, VA 22101
(703) 356-0040

Lindsey Evans
1722 Westmoreland Trail
Annapolis, MD 21401
(410) 841-5353

Fatima's Productions
PO Box 28075
Baltimore, MD 21239
(410) 444-5444

Greg Mason
1237 Ashland Ave.
Baltimore, MD 21202
(410) 563-4327

Pat Moran
805 Park Avenue
Baltimore, MD 21201
(410) 244-0237

King Productions
6377 Old Branch Ave.
Camp Springs, MD 20748
(301) 449-1277

Steele Casting
PO Box 1621
Glen Burnie, MD 21060
(410) 544-8444

Taylor Royall Casting
2308 South Road
Baltimore, MD 21209
(410) 466-5959

Techniques Unlimited Casting
PO Box 22880
Baltimore, MD 21203
(410) 752-7969

3 West Casting Inc.
3 West 23rd St.
Baltimore, MD 21218
(410) 366-7727

Urban Faces Casting Agency
2047 Division St.
Baltimore, MD 21217
(410) 669-0069

WilMarc Casting, Baltimore
107 Warren Ave. (Federal Hill)
Baltimore, MD 21230
(410) 339-2882

MASSAC HUSETTS

Collinge-Pickman Casting
138 Mt. Auburn St.
Cambridge, MA 02138
(617) 492-4212

John McGee Casting
PO Box 1930
Brookline, MA 02159
(617) 964-2607

Michelangelo Casting
JFK PO Box 8888
Boston, MA 02114
(617) 864-9749

Raquel Osborne Casting
PO Box 616, Kenmore State
Boston, MA 02215
(617) 749-8923

Outcasting, Inc.
27 Harvard St.
Brookline, MA 02146
(617) 738-6322

Maura Tighe Casting
478 California St.
Newton, MA 02160
(617) 332-7506

Tom Elliott Productions
Box 247
Bedford, MA 01730
(617) 647-2825

MICHIGAN

Affiliated Talent & Casting Service
1680 Crooks Road
Troy, MI 48084
(313) 244-8770

Clervi Productions
PO Box 2127
Farmington Hills, MI 48333
(313) 442-8888

Locker / Hurd Casting
12653 McDougall
Detroit, MI 48212
(313) 366-4942

Judith A. Strow
6915 Evershed Terrace
West Bloomfield, MI 48323
(313) 360-2488

MINNESOTA

Action Casting
8337 Penn Ave. S.
Bloomington, MN 55431
(612) 884-5870

Akerland Steele Casting
312 Washington Ave. N., Ste. C
Minneapolis, MN 55408
(612) 339-6141

Carrie Almaer
14500 34th Ave. N. #220
Plymouth, MN 55447
(612) 550-0835

Bab's Casting
420 N. 5th St. #1158
Minneapolis, MN 55401
(612) 332-6858

Lynn Blumenthal Casting
410 N. 3rd St., Ste. 660
Minneapolis, MN 55401
(612) 338-0369

Lilly Chorolec
4231 Irving Ave. N.
Minneapolis, MN 55412
(612) 522-2422

Creative Casting, Inc.
10 S. 5th St., Ste. 860
Minneapolis, MN 55402
(612) 375-0525

Debra Dahlberg
3440 St. Paul Ave. S.
Minneapolis, MN 55412
(612) 925-5391

Anne Healy
4304 Zenith Ave. S.
Minneapolis, MN 55410
(612) 922-6702

Meighan McGuire
3617 39th Ave. S.
Minneapolis, MN 55406
(612) 724-4386

Midwest Connections, Inc.
394 Lake Ave. S. #405
Duluth, MN 55802
(218) 727-0997

Kate O'Toole
1992 Jefferson Ave.
St. Paul, MN 55105
(612) 698-3842

Richter Casting
112 N. 3rd St., Ste. 305
Minneapolis, MN 55401
(612) 338-8223

Jenee Schmidt
3849 Aldrich Ave. S.
Minneapolis, MN 55409
(612) 825-8234

MISSOURI

Jennifer Barnes
3156 Woodview Ridge
Building 10, #205
Kansas City, MO 66103
(913) 262-0030

Wendy Gray
5009 Grand Avenue
Kansas City, MO 64112
(816) 931-5828

Carrie Houk Casting
6300 Northwood
St. Louis, MO 53105
(314) 862-1236

Laura Nelson Casting
PO Box 30157
Kansas City, MO 64112
(816) 444-2254

MISSISSIPPI

Margaret E. Anderson
1887 Clinton-Raymond Road
Bolton, MS 39041
(601) 924-6544

Mark Franks
PO Box 1602
Oxford, MS 38655
(601) 234-0056

W. Brunson Green
2065 Heritage Hill Drive
Jackson, MS 39211
(601) 982-8144

Gloia B. Hancock
222 St. Charles St.
Gulfport, MS 39503
(601) 832-8819

Ramsay King's Heartland Casting
13904 Washington Ave.
PO Box 6025
Gulfport, MS 39057
(601) 864-5193

Brenda Varner Judin
PO Box 10988
Jackson, MS 39289
(601) 922-3635

Jack Stevens
PO Box 4380
Jackson, MS 39296
(601) 355-75235

Georgia Wise
106 Dogwood Drive
Hazlehurst, MS 39083

MONTANA

Marianne Adams
Adams / O'Connell Casting
Helena address not furnished
(406) 449-8767

Sunny Anderson
Sunny Anderson Casting
Helena address not furnished
(406) 933-8461

Lynette C. Michael
Creative World, Inc.
Billings address not furnished
(406) 259-9540

NEBRASKA

Actors, Etc., Ltd.
16812 "N" Circle
Omaha, NE 68136
(402) 896-9908

Nancy Bounds International
4803 Davenport St.
Omaha, NE 68132
(402) 558-9292

Lyn Donovan
1817 N. 53rd St.
Omaha, NE 68104
(402) 551-1816

Talent Pool, Inc.
9236 Mormon Bridge Road
Omaha, NE 68152
(402) 455-8269

NEW HAMPSHIRE

Airwaves Audio Productions
Box 1021
Manchester, NH 03105
(603) 627-2774

Mimi Bergere
New Hampshire Theatre Project
PO Box 6507
Portsmouth, NH 03801
(603) 433-4793

Sean Tracey Associates Casting
126 Daniel Street
Portsmouth, NH 03801
(603) 427-2800

NEW JERSEY

New Jersey has few Casting Directors, being situated so close to New York City.

Gail Walton Casting
c/o Weist Barron
2921 Atlantic Avenue
Atlantic City, NJ 08401
(609) 347-0074

MiShar Productions
23B Holly Cove
Mount Laurel, NJ 08054
(609) 778-4935

NEW MEXICO

Ellen Blake Casting
635 N. Chavez Place
Santa Fe, NM 87501
(505) 982-9281

Harold Service Casting
2100 Isaacks Lane #5
Las Cruces, NM 88005
(505) 523-5010

Irene Levitt Casting
PO Box 9460
Santa Fe, NM 87504
(505) 983-2330

Lisa Law Casting
310 Ojo de la Vaca
Santa Fe, NM 87505
(505) 984-8194

Mary Simons Casting
PO Box 2
Santa Fe, NM 87504
(505) 989-1276

Carmen Martinez Casting
928 Avenida Manana NE
Albuquerque, NM 87110
(505) 265-0396

Teresa Neptune
Rainbow Casting Service
160 Washington Se, Ste. 119
Albuquerque, NM 87108
(505) 268-9315

Sally Jackson Casting
286 Calle Loma Norte
Santa Fe, NM 87501

Santa Fe Casting
PO Box 9550
Santa Fe, NM 87504
(505) 988-7374

Therese Schoeppner
1901 Tijeras Rd.
Santa Fe, NM 87501
(505) 982-1061

NEVADA

Shirley Dale
Dale Production Services
PO Box 4102
Incline Village, NV 89450
(702) 831-2122

Sally Lear Casting
1112 S. 3rd St.
Las Vegas, NV 89104
(702) 459-2090

Sally Lear Casting
421 Hill St.
Reno, NV 89501
(702) 322-8187

Christine O'Rourke
Spectrum Services
810 S. 7th St.
Las Vegas, NV 89101
(702) 388-7557

NEW YORK

The listings of New York City's hundreds of Casting Directors are available in many publications on newsstands and in bookstores in New York City. A selected list of them appears here. The letters (CSA) following their names means that they are members of the Casting Society of America, the organization of the "casting elite" with stringent qualifications for membership.

As for other cities and areas of New York State, the N.Y. State Govt. Office, due to stringent budget cuts, could not provide any listings. The following have been obtained directly from the individual cities themselves where possible. Perhaps some nearer to the actor's location can be found in area telephone directories, listed under either "Theatrical Agencies" or "Talent Agencies."

New York City

Joseph Abaldo Casting (CSA)
450 W. 42nd St., Ste. 2F
New York, NY 10036
(212) 947-3697

ABC / Cap Cities (CSA)
40 W. 66th St., 3rd Flr.
New York, NY 10023
(212) 887-3631

Deborah Aquila Casting (CSA)
333 W. 52nd St., Ste. 1008
New York, NY 10019
(212) 664-5049

115

Marta Carlson Casting (CSA)
c/o CSA, 311 W. 43rd St., #700
New York, NY 10036
(212) 533-3776

Aleta Helena Chappelle (CSA)
c/o CSA, 311 W. 43rd St. #700
New York, NY 10036
(212) 333-4552

Joan D'Incecco
c/o CSA, 311 W. 43rd St., #700
New York, NY 10036
(212) 333-4552

Deborah Brown Casting (CSA)
250 W. 57th St., Ste. 2608
New York, NY 10107

Complete Casting
45 W. 45th St.
New York, NY 10023
(212) 944-5724

Donna Deseta Casting
424 W. 33rd St.
New York, NY 10001
(212) 239-0988

Lou DiGiaimo
869 3rd Ave.
New York, NY 10022
(212) 753-3590

Howard Feuer (CSA)
c/o CSA, 311 W. 43rd St. #700
New York, NY 10036
(212) 333-4552

Bonnie Finnegan Casting (CSA)
175 W. 93rd St., #17D
New York, NY 10025
(212) 316-2863

Alixe Gordin (CSA)
129 W. 12th St.
New York, NY 10011
(212) 627-0472

Maria Greco Casting
630 Ninth Ave.
New York, NY 10036
(212) 247-2011

Judy Henderson (CSA)
330 W. 89th St.
New York, NY 10024
(212) 877-0225

Hispanocast
39 W. 19th St., 12th Flr.
New York, NY 10011
(212) 691-7366

Stuart Howard (CSA)
22 W. 27th St., 10th Flr.
New York, NY 10001
(212) 725-7770

Julie Hughes (CSA)
c/o CSA, 311 W. 43rd St. #700
New York, NY 10036

Phyllis Huffman (CSA)
1325 6th Ave.
New York, NY 10010
(212) 636-5023

Donna Isaacson Casting (CSA)
453 W. 16th St.
New York, NY 10011
(212) 691-8555

Geoffrey Johnson (CSA)
1501 Broadway, Ste. 1400
New York, NY 10036
(212) 391-2680

Johnson-Liff Casting Assn. (CSA)
1501 Broadway, Ste. 1400
New York, NY 10036
(212) 391-2680

Rosalie Joseph (CSA)
1501 Broadway, Ste. 2605
New York, NY 10036
(212) 921-5781

Avy Kaufman Casting (CSA)
c/o CSA, 311 W. 43rd St. #700
New York, NY 10036
(212) 206-0315

Lynn Kressel Casting (CSA)
445 Park Ave., 7th Flr.
New York, NY 10022
(212) 605-9122

Vince Liebhart (CSA)
524 W. 57th St., #5329
New York, NY 10019

John Lyons Casting (CSA)
311 W. 43rd St., #700
New York, NY 10036
(212) 799-8695

McCorkle Casting, Ltd. (CSA)
264 W. 40th St., 9th Flr.
New York, NY 10018
(212) 840-0992

Joanna Merlin Casting (CSA)
221 W. 82nd St., #15F
New York, NY 10024
(212) 724-8575

Barry Moss (CSA)
c/o CSA, 311 W. 43rd St. #700
New York, NY 10036
(212) 307-6690

Elissa Myers Casting (CSA)
333 W. 52nd St. #1008
New York, NY 10010
(212) 315-4777

Ellen Novack Casting (CSA)
20 Jay St.
New York, NY 10013
(212) 431-3939

Carole Pfeffer
79 Madson Ave.
New York, NY
(212) 689-6587

116

Betty Rea (CSA)
222 E. 44th St.
New York, NY 10017
(212) 982-1610

Shirley Rich (CSA)
200 E. 66th St. #1202
New York, NY 10021
(212) 688-9540

Barbara Shapiro Casting
111 W. 57th St.
New York, NY 10107
(212) 582-8228

Susan Shaw Casting (CSA)
35 E. 10th St., Ste. 7E
New York, NY 10003

Meg Simon (CSA)
1600 Boadway, Ste. 1005
New York, NY 10019
(212) 245-7670

Bernie Styles Central Casting
200 W. 54th St.
New York, NY 10019
(212) 582-4933

Juliet Taylor (CSA)
130 W. 57th St.
New York, NY 10019
(212) 245-4635

Bonnie Timmermann (CSA)
c/o CSA, 311 W. 43rd St. #700
New York, NY 10036
(Telephone not available)

Joy Todd (CSA)
37 E. 28th St., #700
New York, NY 10016
(212) 685-3537

Joy Weber Casting
250 W. 57th St.
New York, NY 10107
(212) 245-5220

Susan Willett (CSA)
1170 Broadway, Ste. 1008
New York, NY 10001
(212) 725-3588

Bill Williams Casting
1501 Broadway
New York, NY 10036
(212) 221-7111

Andrew Zerman (CSA)
1501 Broadway #1400
New York, NY 10036
(212) 391-2680

Other New York State Cities

The New York State Film Commission couldn't furnish Casting Director lists for any New York State cities other than New York City and since even those cities' Mayors' Offices didn't respond it's believed that---like Connecticut and Rhode Island---most New York State cities probably use the enormous talent resources of New York City's casting people for their needs.

NORTH CAROLINA

Action Casting of the Southeast
2002 Eastwood Road, Ste. 101
Wilmington, NC 28403
(919) 256-9650

Fincannon & Assoiates, Inc.
201 N. Front St., Ste. 107
Wilmington, NC 28401
(919) 261-1500

NORTH DAKOTA

North Dakota's film casting is apparently handled in the main by its talent agencies, listed under "Talent Agencies".

OHIO

Although Ohio's Casting Directors' addresses are not available, their locations by City areas have been included in their listings so actors can locate them in their cities' local telephone directories .

Anita Daugherty
Address not available (Cincinnati)
(513) 961-7607

Charlene Duncan
Address not available (Cleveland)
(216) 241-6000

Mary S. Evans
Address not available (Columbus)
(614) 261-6459

Thomas Fant
Address not available (Cincinnati)
(513) 732-4700

Anita M. Ferris
Address not available (Cleveland)
(216) 867-7501

Jo Goenner
Address not available (Cincinnati)
(513) 885-2595

Stacey Herman
Address not available (Cleveland)
(216) 777-3235

Annie H. Hoffman
Address not available (Cleveland
(216) 491-1776

Carol Inskeep
Address not available (Cincinnati)
(513) 984-3541

Anne McDermott Jones (Columbus)
Address not available
(614) 488-3548

Julie Matthews
Address not available (Cleveland)
(216) 481-0523

Nicole McMillan
Address not available (Cincinnati)
(606) 356-8222

Laurie McSwain
Address not available (Cincinnati)
(513-738-2265

Nancy Paul
Address not available (Columbus)
(614) 486-1643

Richard B. Sauer
Address not available (Columbus)
(614) 274-4946

Denise L. Waldman (Cleveland)
Address not available
(216) 455-7220

Linda Weaver
Address not available (Cleveland)
(216) 758-4417

Lisa Weaver
Addess not available (Cleveland)
(216) 777-6117

Lee Wiser
Address not available (Toledo vic.)
(419) 243-5900

OKLAHOMA

American Indian Casting
Box 32329
Oklahoma City, OK 73123
(405) 789-4300

Elizabeth Anderson
12367 St. Andrews Drive, Apt. D
Oklahoma City, OK 73120
(405) 755-9504

Roger W. Branson
1000 Cheyenne Drive
Edmonton, OK 73013
(405) 340-1237

Mary Jane Colbert
11010 E. 44th St. So., Apt. 3106
Tulsa, OK 74146
(908) 663-4812

Steven Fuller
2218 NW 16th
Oklahoma City, OK 73107
(405) 521-1161

Fullerton Casting Agency
8138 S. Harvard
Tulsa, OK 74137
(918) 488-9246

Fullerton Casting Agency
1432 W. Britton
Oklahoma City, OK 73114
(405) 848-4839

Becky Grantham
2429 NW 55th Place
Oklahoma City, OK 73112
(405) 840-9166

Ricki G. Maslar
1432 W. Britton Rd.
Oklahoma City, OK 73114
(405) 848-4839

Marilyn Morris
4921-A S. 72nd E. Ave
Tulsa, OK 74145
(918) 664-0808

Laura M. Moxley
1626 Village Drive
Norman, OK 73071
(405) 321-0708

Oklahoma Reenactors Association
2100 N. Lincoln Blvd.
Oklahoma City, OK 73105
(405) 521-2491

Southwest Casting Service
PO Box 32329
Oklahoma City, OK 73123
(405) 789-4300

OREGON

A/M Casting Associates
3829 NE Tillamook
Portland, OR 97212
(503) 249-2945

Central Xtras Casting
935 NW 19th Ave.
Portland, OR 97209
(503) 223-1931

Freedom Productions
200 W Jackson St.
Medford, OR 97501
(503) 779-9161

L&M Casting
PO Box 86861
Portland, OR 97286
(503) 230-8813

Wilshire Casting
1436 SW Montgomery
Portland, OR 97201
(503) 274-1717

PENNSYLVANIA

Joanne P. Alexis
100 Conway St.
Carlisle, PA 17013
(717) 243-2000

Donna Belajac & Company, Inc.
1 Bigelow Square, Ste. 1924
Pittsburgh, PA 15219
(412) 391-1005

Bravo Talent
7 Parkway Center, Ste.320
Pittsburgh, PA 15228
(412) 922-8354

Constance Rankin Crowder
4289 Beaufort Hunt Drive
Harrisburg, PA 17110
(717) 652-4607

Cynmar Talent Locators
PO Box 1530
Harrisburg, PA 17105
(717) 234-2994

Randall DiNinni Productions
435 N. 69th St.
Harrisburg, PA 17111
(717) 564-1103

Carol McClenahan
319 Woodland Road
Sewickley, PA 15143
(412) 741-0275

MiShar Productions
724 Carol St.
New Cumberland, PA 17070
(717) 774-4315

Nancy A. Mosser
1739 E. Carson St., Ste. 360
Pittsburgh, PA 15203
(412) 381-9994

Susan Leigh Primm
276 Ewing Road
Pittsburgh, PA 15205
(412) 921-7202

Renaissance Entertainment Prods.
2441 Waverly St.
Pittsburgh, PA 15218
(412) 271-8388

Walton-Wickline Casting
447 Fairmount Ave.
Philadelphia, PA 19123
(215) 629-1114

Heidi H. Williams
118 Merimac
Pittsburgh, PA 15211
(412) 481-0767

Rich Wilson Creative Services
PO Box 30199
Philadelphia, PA 19103
(215) 557-7550

RHODE ISLAND

The Rhode Island Film Commission did not furnish its list of Casting Directors. Perhaps the list may be obtained by actors from the Commission at telephone number (401) 277-3456.

SOUTH CAROLINA

Sandra M. Ballard
PO Box 11001
Charleston, SC 29411

Cheryle A. Bourgeois
2182 Spoleto Lane
North Charleston, SC 29418

CHC Associates Casting
3704 Verner St.
Columbia, SC 292304
(803) 787-7777

Boots Ewing Crowder
175 Corey Blvd., Ste. 15
Summerville, SC 29483
(803) 871-4335

Charlotte A. Dobyns
PO Box 2450
Beaufort, SC I29901
(803) 522-9133

Richard Ganaway
2181 Dunlop St., #12-H
North Charleston, SC 29418
(803) 572-3444

Harvest Talent
PO Box 50505
Columbia, SC 29250
(803) 798-4840

Tona B. Dahlquest
314 Bakerton Rd.
Columbia, SC 29212
(803) 732-7590

Len Hunt
5835 Octavia Ave.
Ravenel, SC 29470
(803) 889-2789

Jeffrey Main
32 S. Battery
Charleston, SC 29401
(803) 722-1079

Keith Newland
15 Popular St.
Charleston, SC 29403
(803) 577-4169

Brenda Jean Schwarz
8A Harborside
Lexington, SC 29072
(803) 957-8701

South Carolina Casting
3031 Kline St.
Columbia, SC 29205
(803) 252-8811

Southeastern Talent Bank
3008 Millwood Ave.
Columbia, SC 29205
(803) 765-1001

D. S. Wright
244 President St.
Charleston, SC 29403
(803) 724-7785

Young / Yocum & Associates
PO Box 417
Summerville, SC 29484
(803) 556-3201

Jeff Zachary
4917 Long Bay Estates
Myrtle Beach, SC 238-2710

SOUTH DAKOTA

Melody Dennis, Mike Percevich
Black Hills Film
69 Forest Ave.
Deadwood, SD 57332
(605) 578-7581

Rosemary Savage
Professional Image by Rosemary
1118 S. Minnesota Ave.
Sioux Falls, SD 57105
(605) 334-0619

James J. Garrett
PO Box 1134
Eagle Butte, SD 57625
(605) 964-6559

Pam Gough
3903 W. Chicago
Rapid City, SD 57702
(605) 341-1961

Candy Hamilton
PO Box 151
Oglala, SD 57764
(605) 867-5807

TENNESSEE

Diane Boyte
787 High Point Rofdge
Franklin, TN 37064
(615) 790-0518

Tess Carrier
PO Box 11862
Memphis, TN 38118
(901) 278-7454

Jo Doster
PO Box 120641
Nashville, TN 37212
(615) 385-3850

Diane Gayden Casting
176 2nd Ave. North
Nashville, TN 37201
(615) 244-4179

G-Force Production Co.
PO Box 30296
Knoxville, TN 37930
(615) 691-9694

Jim Kup
PO Box 22748
Nashville, TN 37202
(615) 327-0181

Darilyn S. Mason
621 Albany
Hermitage, TN 37076
(615) 885-5122

Cynthia Phillips-Armonstrong
3746 Winderwood Circle
Memphis, TN 38128
(901) 377-1888

Bruce Ribble
5709 Lyons View Drive, Ste. 2103
Knoxville, TN 37919
(615) 588-3166

George Roberts
738 W. Hunt
Alcoa, TN 37701
(615) 983-3302

TEXAS

Shirley Abrams Casting
PO Box 29199
Dallas, TX 75229
(214) 484-6774, (213) 484-4995

Actors Clearinghouse
501 N. I-35
Austin, TX 78702
(512) 476-3412

Agencia de Talento Hispano
5761 Glen Falls Lane
Dallas, TX 75209
(214) 559-7956

Alexander
PO Box 66164
Houston, TX 77266
(713) 521-3059

Lynn Ambrose
6102 E. Mockingbird Lane, Ste. 343
Dallas, TX 75214
(214) 823-8702

Mary Anna Austin
1420 Dragon
Dallas, TX 75207
(214) 744-2278, (214) 369-2849

Kitty Blair
1505 Concordia Ave.
Austin, TX 78722
(512) 474-4334

B. M.Copeland
PO Box 12410
San Antonio, TX 78212
(512) 826-1719

Phyllis Dumont Agency
PO Box 701248
San Antonio, TX 78270
(512) 266-0096, (512) 366-0097

Caryn Gormé
2900 S. Gessner #2204
Houston, TX 77063
(712) 953-7825

Corina Harmon
PO Box 2084
Laredo, TX 78044
(512) 724-8737, (512) 726-2606

Penne Jennings
3519 Minglewood
Houston, TX 77023
(713) 644-5103

Rody Kent
PO Box 140857
Dallas, TX 75214
(214) 827-3418

Kris Nicolau
9817 Estacado
Dallas, TX 75228
(214) 328-0372

Pat Harrison Peraino
PO Box 7519
Corpus Christi, TX 78415
(512) 852-3203, (512) 852-2364

Third Coast Casting
313 S. Congress Ave., #200-A
Austin, TX 78704
(512) 443-5252

UTAH

Sarah Behrens
2424 Walken Lane
Salt Lake City, UT 84117
(801) 359-5834

Tama Condie
441 E. 500 North
Provo, UT 84606
(801) 374-4713

Linda Goudy
10551 Silver Mountain Drive
Sandy, UT 84070
(801) 572-4392

Debra Greenband
3450 S. Highland Drive
Salt Lake City, UT 84106
(801) 485-7399

Ron Griffith
4300 East Street
Moab, UT 84532
(801) 259-5141

Kimball Jacobs
1875 S. Orchard Drive
Bountiful, UT 84010
(801) 292-9762

Barry Johnson
P O Box 3452
Park City, UT 84060
(801) 649-4920

Joseph Kiffmeyer
1590 Murphy Lane
Moab, UT 84532
(801) 259-7263

Timothy Kindred
166 W. Main St.
Hyrum, UT 84319
(801) 245-3442

Suzanne Loritz
38 Santa Rosa Place
West Jordan, UT 84084
(801) 575-7470

Viola McGee
1526 Kensington
Salt Lake City, UT 84105
(801) 485-9438

Catrine McGregor
856 E. Cedar Pine Ct.
Salt Lake City, UT 84106
(801) 266-7621

Jack North
1144 E. 7625 South
Midvale, UT 84047
(801) 561-1163

Terri Pappas
1540 Kensington Ave.
Salt Lake City, UT 84105
(801) 467-4443

Cate Praggastis
5480S. Wood Crest Drive
Salt Lake City, UT 84117
(801) 461-5843

Rachel Rencher
148 N. Sandrun Road
Salt Lake City, UT 84103
(801) 531-8494

Irene Saxton
P O Box 271165
Salt Lake City, UT 84127
(801) 467-7544

Jaymelinn Saxton
2316 Tottenham Court Road
Salt Lake City, UT 84119
(801) 968-5531

Rosalind Soulam
554 Douglas St.
Salt Lake City, UT 84102
(801) 373-3315

Lynne Van Dam
1183 Herbert Ave.
Salt Lake City, UT 84105
(801) 583-0946

Sarah Vanwagenen
2230 E. 6015 South
Salt Lake City, UT 84121
(801) 278-0212

Karl Wesson
348 N. 1160 East
Orem, UT 84057
(801) 224-2020

VERMONT

Dayna & Robert Lisaius
Classic Age
266 Pine St.
Burlington, VT 05401
(802) 852-1770

Phil DiMaggio
RFD #3, Box 77
Barton, VT 05822
(802) 755-6232

Monica Farrington
4 Green Dolphin Drive
South Burlington, VT 05403
(802) 852-4882

Laura Megroz
Goodyville Productions
Goodyville Rd.
South Londonderry, VT 05155
(802) 297-2310, -1976

Sarah O'Brien
PO Box 387
Barre, VT 05641
(802) 379-5535

Curtis Wright
Box 34
Waitsfield, VT 05673
(802) 496-2030

VIRGINIA

Joe Cacciotti
2153 Old Indian Road
Richmond, VA 23235
(804) 272-8787

The Erickson Agency
1483 Chain Bridge Road, Ste. 105
McLean, VA 22101
(703) 356-0040

Margaret B. Kimmel
10605 Railroad Court
Fairfax, VA 22030
(702) 385-1713

Just Faces, Inc.
PO Box 1027
Colonial Heights, VA 23834
(804) 768-0483

Living History Assoc., Ltd.
PO Box 4914
1100 West Franklin St.
Richmond, VA 23220
(804) 264-9451

Type Casting, Inc.
3380 Jude's Ferry Road
Powhatan, VA 23139
(804) 794-5929

Uptown Talent, Inc.
4156 Laurel Oak Road
Richmond, VA 23237
(804) 271-6054

William Dean
728 Deerlake Drive
Virginia Beach, VA 23462
(804) 626-0156

Petrich Associates Casting
865 Monticello Ave., Ste. 201
Norfolk, VA 23510
(804) 625-CAST

Remae Productions
1409 Peabody Drive
Hampton, VA 23666
(804) 826-0755

BarbaraSimpson
3844 Old Forge Road
Virginia Beach, VA 23452
(804) 486-6705

S. R. Eubanks & Company
Full Casting Services
2828 Emissary Drive NW
Roanoke, VA 24019
(703) 562-2101

WASHINGTON

Douglas Byers
OI Box 3662
Portland, OR 97208
(503) 231-7654

Complete Casting by Stephen
Salamunovich
2226 3rd Ave. #205
Seattle, WA 98121
(206) 441-5058

Dixon / Walker Casting Associates
2114 Western Ave.
Seattle, WA 98121
(206) 448-7448

Kalles Casting
506 2nd Ave. #1525
Seattle, WA 98104
(206) 447-9318

L & M Casting
PO BVox 86861
Portland, OR 97286
(800) 834-7705

Northwest Productions Consortium
200W. Jackson St.
Medford, OR 97501
(800) 241-2113

ProduccionesPino
2609 198th Place SW
Lynwood, WA 98036
(206) 774-7772

Roth Casting Associates
1258 1st Ave. S. #9
Seattle, WA 98134
(206) 587-2468

White Light Casting
PO Box 70406
Bellevue, WA 98007
(818(252-1683

WEST VIRGINIA

Sharon Harms
Image Associates
2108 Stratford Road
South Charleston, WV 26303
(304) 345-4429, (304) 345-3134

Kellas-Grindley Productions
1329 National Road
Wheeling, WV 26003
(304) 242-5201

Lakeview Theatre
PO Box 4270
Morgantown, WV 26504
(304) 598-0144

David Wohl
729 Garvin Ave.
Charleston, WV 25302
(304) 766-3186, (304) 346-4808

WISCONSIN

Colin Cameron Casting
247 Langdon St., Apt. 4
Madison, WI 53703
(608) 251-3907

K C Talent
402 D. Bedford St., Ste. 3
Madison, WI 53703
(608) 271-1771

Michele Olson Productions
1821 Wood Lane
Green Bay, WI 54304
(414) 498-3453

WYOMING

Raine Hall
Extreme Locations & Real
Real People Casting
PO Box 279
Moose, WY 83012
(307) 733-8857

Annie Hamilton Casting
10699 Roundtop Road
Cheyenne, WY 82009
(307) 650-7403

THE TERMS ACTORS ARE EXPECTED TO KNOW IN FILM AND TELEVISION

Although there's no law that says actors must know all the technical terms used in the filming process, it often gives some feeling of security to know what all those technicians, the director, the cameraman and others are talking about in what might otherwise sound like a lot of mumbo-jumgo. The following terms aren't all, but they're probably the ones the actor will profit most from understanding and having available for use when they're helpful:

Added Scenes
Additional filming for which a cast member is called back to shoot ad - ditional (new) footage after a pic- ture is completed.

Assistant
The First Assistant Director---more often called "The First".

Atmosphere
The "extras" on the set.

Background
Either actors, extras or scenery behind foreground players.

Blues
Blue (usually first revision) pages of the script.

Boom
The sound crew member who con- trols the mike extended above the actors' heads; also the "boom" from which the mike is suspended.

Bouncing
Bouncing up and down by actors. A no-no quickly stopped!

Buzzer
The buzzer on a set that with a long single blast quiets all noise, either on a soundstage or on an exterior location; also the buzzer that with two short blasts signals "All clear", the shot is finished and noise is permissible.

CU
This, in a script, indicates "closeup" shot of the actor's face or something else.

Camera Car
The car that has a camera mounted on it for filming car chose and other traveling car shots.

Cameraman
The Director of Photography, or the Cinematographer. He sets up shots requested by the director, or shots of his own suggestion, checks light- ing, lenses and filters, operates the camera during rehearsals of shots and sometimes also during actual filming of the takes.

Call
The actor's work call, with details of when and where and to whom the actor is to report for filming.

Call Sheet
Published by the Production Dept., showing all work calls for cast and crew, planned filming locations, scenes to be shot and equipment needed.

Chalks
The marks made around the actor's feet during the rehearsal of a shot. His "marks".

Character Description
This is almost always found at the *very first appearance* of the character in the script.

Cheating
A slang expression for what actors playing foreground must do when playing a scene with actors standing behind them.

Check Authorization Form
What the actor signs for the agent to send to Payroll Departments that directs that the actor's pay check be mailed to the agency for deducting of the agent's 10% commission before issuing the actor the agency's own check for the balance.

Clapboards
Called "Slates". The two-boarded slates that are clapped loudly in front of the actor's face or an object just as a shot is starting.

Clean Entrance, Clean Exit
Being all the way out of a shot--- either before walking into it or when exiting a shot---"Clean" meaning all the way out or in.

Closeup
A shot including little more than the actor's face.

Commercial Composite
The usually two-sided photo print of actors seeking commercials, with one large photo on the front and several "in character" shots on the back with the actor in wardrobe, using props, in various locations that suggest what the actor is right for.

Continuity
The person who on some sets is responsible for the "matching" of all details in all sequences of shots.

Conversion Rate
A contract provision that can convert a day player's salary rate to a three-day or weekly rate which will not be as much as the same amount of work period at the daily rate would be.

Co-Star
The billing level which immediately follows "Starring" in opening or end credits of films and television.

Coverage
Additional takes of scenes from other angles; reaction shots; closeups; medium shots; closeups of hands doing something; a clock ticking, etc.

Covering
Accidentally covering another actor or something else by an actor.

Cut!
This is yelled to stop a shot in progress or finished.

Crew
The technicians of all kinds-- Cameramen, Sound or Lighting Crew, Grips, Drivers, Makeup, Hairdresser, etc.

Dailies
The previous day's "rushes" (all footage), synched up for early morning checking by the Director, the Producer and perhaps others.

Daily
The contract for an actor hired for either a single day of work or the contract for an actor who's to be paid at a "per day" rate rather than a weekly salary.

Day Player
An actor who customarily plays one-day engagements.

Deal Memo
The draft of a series player's contract sent by the Producer to the actor's agent, representing the still tentative terms of a series contract

Dialogue Director
The person who "runs scenes" with actors before time for their actual filming and reports to the Director if some problems are evident that the Director won't yet know about.

Downgrading
In a commercial, if someone hired as a "principal" (face recognizable in the finished commercial) is unrecognizable in the final version of the commercial.

Dupe Neg
What the actor asks a Photo Reproduction Lab to make up from which 8x10 prints can be duplicated.

Dissolve
A slow fading out of one shot and the slow emerging of another.

Dolly
The mount for the camera, or the action when the camera moves toward, away from or with the scene action.

Double
Does stunts and hazardous actions while made to appear to be the actor.

Drifting
An actor drifting from one side of a shot to the other, usually blocking something by doing so.

Drive On
Permission to drive the actor's own car onto the studio lot and park near to where shooting is planned rather than parking off the lot.

Drop-Pickup
A SAG concession that allows actors to work one day, be paid, then be called back after a period of time to resume a role.

Dry Run
A rehearsal before filming a shot.

Dubbing
The adding of music track, sound track and special sound effects in the post-production work on a film. Also refers to an actor "dubbing" of a different language over the original dialogue track.

Editor
The man or woman who cuts the film together in the "cutting room".

End Credits
The lists---usually the character names with the actors who played the roles; the production staff's names and titles; etc.

Episode
A single show segment of a continuing series.

Est. Shot
This is a suggestion to the Cameraman that a shot *establish* a place, a building or something else.

Executive Producer
The head honcho of a production company or one of the top producers for such a company. He or she plans projects, assigns them to Supervising Producers for handling, then rides herd on the projects from their inception to completion.

EXT:
In the scene description, means "Exterior".

Favored Nations
This is the standard phrase used to guarantee that no other player will receive a higher salary in a film or television series than the actor to whom "Favored Nations" is contractually promised.

Featured
This is the billing given to the less important roles in film and television. It normally follows the Co-Star billings in end credit listings.

Final Cut
This is what finally meets the approval of the producer, director and technicians before it's dubbed (with the adding of music track, special effects, etc.) and sent to the Lab for "answer printing".

Firming
The "setting" (official hiring) of the actor to definitely play the role.

Firm Start Date
The date a production company promises to an actor as the date of starting the actor's employment.

First
See "Assistant" and "First Assistant Director".

First Position
The position where an actor is directed to be located for the start of a shot.

First Team!
The call for the actors to return to the set for filming as the "Second Team" (their stand-ins) are retired after the setting of lighting for shots.

Fitting Fee
Extra fee for having to go to the Wardrobe Department or elsewhere to be fitted for wardrobe.

Force Majeure
The clause in a contract which allows the production company to halt production, whether expecting to resume or not, under certain unexpected or catastrophic conditions.

Foreground
Action closest to the camera.

Foreign Films
Films produced by production companies based in foreign countries, over which SAG has no jurisdiction.

Golden Time
That overtime which is still later than simple overtime, time-and-a-half and double-time hours used in figuring cast and crew pay.

Greens (or **Green Pages**)
Usually the set of third revision pages of the script, to be substituted for like-numbered pages previously received by the actor.

Grips
The crew members who move, hold and carry things on the set.

Guarantee
The minimum employment period guaranteed the actor in a contract.

Hairdresser
Combs out, touches up women's hair on the set.

Heads
What "closeups" are sometimes called.

Head Shots
Actors' professional photos, usually of just the head.

125

Holding Fee
A fee paid an actor to keep the actor available until something starts, resumes or airs on television.

Honey Wagon
The portable john truck on location.

Insert Stage
Where "cutaway" shots are made that involve things like a hand holding a note, a clock ticking, a hand ringing a doorbell, etc.

INT:
In the scene description in a script, means "Interior" shot.

Intermediate Cut
That working cut of a picture prepared when a director or producer wants to see some changes prior to "final cut" preparation.

Kill The Blowers!
The yell to turn off airconditioners on a soundstage just before a shot.

Lapel Mike
The small microphone hidden on an actor who doesn't speak loudly enough to be recorded ideally. Actors talking as they walk along outdoors are fitted with lapel mikes.

Left Frame
To your right when you're facing the camera.

Lines
The speeches of your role.

Lip-Sync
Actor lip-synching lines synchronously with silent footage running on a screen.

Location
Shooting that's anywhere outside the studio lot, either distant or just on a nearby streetcorner.

Location Casting Director
The person who calls in for interviews the actors and extras who are residents of the location areas.

Location Manager
When a film is preparing to shoot at a distant, usually out of state location, the Location Manager is in charge of the small cadre of personnel sent out to prepare everything---housing for staff, crew and cast members; use permits for shooting on private property; scouting of more locations in the area; rounding up local crew members, etc. During actual filming, the Location Manager is still in charge of such details.

Long Shot
When action is distant from camera.

Looping
Re-recording the actor's dialogue while he listens to a playback of his original dialogue recorded on the set, to produce better dialogue track. The actor is sent to the **Looping Stage** for this.

M.O.S.
In scene descriptions, means "Music or Sound" rather than dialogue track.

Makeup
Either the Studio Makeup Department or the man or woman on the set who does the job.

Marks
Chalk marks or tapes on the floor or sidewalk to mark feet positions the actor is expected to start on, to walk onto or stand on for a shot.

Master
A shot which usually includes large or moving action. One of the very first shots taken of a scene. Actors

must remember all details of movement, positions, etc., to duplicate them skillfully in the additional shots of portions of the same scene when they're done.

Matching
The art of duplicating all actions, positions, handling of props, etc., in additional shots of same scenes.

Meal Penalty
When meal breaks don't come after filming for periods specified by SAG, a meal penalty is assessed over and above the actor's salary for the day.

Medium Shot
Shows most of your body, sometimes with others in the shot also.

Merchandising
The actor's contracted share in items sold or licensed by production companies that bear his or her likeness and/or his or her character's likeness in the role.

Mileage
The amount paid an actor for gas mileage when he or she drives their own car to a location.

Minimum
The term used to indicate that the actor will receive only the SAG-regulated minimum salary. It's standard for actors to receive "minimum plus ten" (usually called "scale plus ten") so the agency can receive its ten percent commission.

Mini-Series
A program that is prepared to be aired on television in two or more segments.

Mixer
The Sound Crew member who controls the volume levels of sound recording---to maximize dialogue and minimize other sounds or noise.

Morals Clause
The clause that authorizes the firing of an actor if he or she does something during employment that offends public standards.

Multiple Contract
A not often used contract nowadays that employs an actor to appear in more than one film for a studio or production company over a given period of time.

Must Join
Station 12 at the Screen Actors Guild reports to casting people that a proposed cast member is a "Must Join", meaning that he or she must come to SAG and join before being allowed to work. Also, actors are called by SAG "Must Join" people if they've done their first film under the *Taft-Hartley Law* and must join prior to their next employment.

Number One Position (or **First Position**) The "marks" position where the actor is to start in a shot.

(O.S.)
When this appears with a character's speech it indicates that the speech is heard "off screen". The actor should anticipate, however, that the speech will probably be filmed on-camera anyhow.

On A Bell!
Called out when ready to make a take. Then comes the long buzzer sound signaling "Quiet!"

On Or About
This phrase is used to offer the production, when setting an actor for a role, a little more flexibility as to actual working date in case of some problem delaying the actor's scene or scenes by a day or so.

Opening Credits
The credits---usually Producers, Director, Stars' Names---at the start of a film or television program.

Operator
The Assistant Cameraman, who usually rides the camera dolly and does the actual filming after the setup is set up by the Cameraman.

Option
The production company's option to use the actor within a contracted period of time.

Out Takes
The extra prints of shots which were filmed but which aren't cut into the film in final editing.

Outgrading
Removing an actor totally from a commercial in the final version.

Over The Shoulder Shot
A shot in which most of the frame is devoted to an actor's face or something else while perhaps part of a head and shoulder of someone frames the edge of the shot in the foreground.

Overlapping
Talking too soon after any other sound or dialogue, or moving too quickly, leaving no room for cutting with scissors by the Editor. Even starting to speak or move too soon after "Action!" is overlapping.

Page Numbers
The numbers at the top right corner of script pages, usually followed by a period (to avoid confusion with *Scene* numbers that run down the side of script pages).

Panning
When camera frame moves from one actor or object to another or when action is filmed in moves from one point to another and the camera follows (pans) the move.

Per Diem
The meal allowance the actor receives when on location if not furnished meals by the production.

Pickup
The re-shooting of a part of a scene wherein something wasn't satisfactory.

Pilot
The usually two-hour series episode used to first obtain pickup of the series by a network. Pilots are often telecast as two-hour Movies of The Week by a network or as special two-hour programs prior to the series' starts. Pilots that don't achieve network pickup are often run as Movies Of The Week to recoup their production costs.

Pinks
The pink (usually second revision) pages of the script.

POV
This stands for "Point of View". The camera takes the actor's place; films what the actor is supposedly looking at.

Post Production
The work, such as editing, dubbing, printing, etc., remaining to be done after all of a film's shooting ends.

Powder Down!
The call for Makeup to come to the set and powder the actor's face to prevent or eliminate any perspiration or other shine on the face.

Print!
What the Director calls out when a shot has satisfied him, to direct that that shot be "printed" for probable cutting into the picture.

Process Stage (or just Process)
The two connected soundstages where a mockup car is filmed going along a street that is projected on a giant screen behind it, or actors cower before a tiger that's leaping down upon them but is actually on film projected behind them while they're being filmed in foreground by another camera.

Props
The person who handles hand props on the set is called "Props".

Recurring Role
A role which returns from time to time in a television series rather than being on a continuous contract basis. Actors in these roles are usually paid more than their usual salaries to encourage them to remain available when needed.

Regular (Series Regular)
A series starring or co-starring role that appears in all or most episodes of a series.

Ready
This means completely ready for filming, in makeup and wardrobe, at a designated spot.

Residuals
What the actor receives when motion pictures, telefilms and commercials are rerun.

Rest Period
On location filming projects, the number of hours the actor brought from Hollywood must be allowed for rest before or between work periods.

Retakes
Shooting of same scenes again, usually due to some problem.

Reverses (Reverse Shots)
Shots from totally reversed angles from angles shot earlier.

Revisions
Script change pages to be substituted for early versions of same.

Right Frame
To your left as you face the camera.

Right-to-Work State
Some States' Laws prevent an actor from losing a role simply because of not being a member of the Screen Actors Guild. In these states the law applies equally in all employments.

Roll 'Em!.. Speed!.. Scene Two, Take Six!
These are the usual last calls heard before the Director calls out **Action!** to begin a take. "Roll 'em!" means to roll Sound (or in some cases to roll Sound and Camera, interlocked). "Speed" (or an electronic beep) signals that both camera and sound are rolling together at the right speed for recording action and dialogue ideally. "Scene Two, Take What-ever" would be what "Slates" calls out hurriedly just before clapping the clapboards in front of the actor's face. All is then ready for the Director's "Action!"

Rough Cut
The first spliced-together version of the film which the Editor shows to the Producer and Director for their approval and suggestions.

SAG Eligible
This means an actor is eligible to join SAG at any time he chooses, having done a picture without joining, or being otherwise qualified under current SAG regulations for membership.

Scale
The minimum SAG-regulated salary for a daily, three-day (for TV only) or weekly for the actor's em-ployment.

Scene Numbers
The numbers running down the sides of the script pages.

Screening
Usually means the showing of a film with the producer, the director and department heads present for any suggestions or to simply show the film to guests.

Script Supervisor (or "Script")
This person times each shot, checks all details for matching with other shots of the same dialogue and action, corrects dialogue errors, records data, then at the end of all filming hands that script over to the Editor as the record of all footage of all scenes available for cutting into the picture.

Second Asst. Director (or "Second")
The staffmember who is in charge of the cast members at all times.

Second Team!
The call to bring the actors back to their start positions and to send the Stand-Ins off the set in preparation for a shot.

Separate Card
Actors' agents try to obtain billing for their starring players on *separate* card, with no other actor's name appearing in the frame at the same time.

Share Card
This means hat two or more leading cast members' names will appear in an opening credits frame at the same time.

Shooting Schedule
Production Department sheets showing scenes to be shot, locations where they're to be filmed, when they're planned, equipment needed, crews rand cast members.

Sides
Casting offices supply "sides" (a few pages of dialogue) to actors, for their preparing to read for roles, rather than complete scripts. SAG requires that "sides" be made available to actors to pick up at least 24 hours prior to their reading appointments.

Sighting
The most reliable manner of "hitting your marks" by finding intersecting points on both a nearby and a more distant object.

Slates
He or she holds the clapboards in front of the actor's face and claps them shut when a shot is ready to begin; also rides the camera dolly, continually adjusting focal depth.

Slopping
An actor is "slopping" when his role isn't finished on the day expected and he is to continue the next day or on another day.

Stand-Ins
The folks who literally "stand in" actors' positions while lighting is being set. They're called "Second Team", while the actor is a "First Team" member.

Station 12
That office at Screen Actors Guild

which must be checked with by the casting director to determine that an actor is a SAG member, is paid up in dues and can be set for the role.

Sticks
The tripod on which a camera may be mounted out on locations when camera dollies on laid tracks aren't practical.

Stills, Still Book, Still Department
Still photography shot by the Still Photographer on the set is printed into the film's Still Book and is available in the Still Department for actors to look at for the purpose of choosing some prints they'd like to order.

Stop Date
The date the production company promises a star they'll be finished with the actor so the actor can begin another film.

Stuntmen, Stuntwomen
They fight, fall from buildings, crash cars into barriers, etc., in hazardous sequences, while made up and wardrobed to look like the actors they're made to appear to be.

Taft-Hartley
The Law which allows actors to do their first film roles without having to join the Screen Actors Guild.

Take (or Shot)
What's filmed between the words "Action!" and "Cut!"

Three Day
The three day contract for a television role. (There is no three day contract for motion pictures.)

Time Sheet
What the Second Asst. Director has the actor sign on the set upon arrival and upon release at the end of

the day to verify length of time for pay purposes.

Top Of The Show
Television series announce there's a "Top of the Show" salary figure beyond which no actor will be paid.

Travel Time
The time during which an actor is required to travel to a remote location. A travel day is considered a work day.

Trims
Pieces of film clipped out of footage by the Editor for alternating actors' faces and dialogue in sequences during the cutting together of the picture. Actors' closeups ("heads") are filmed in single continuous takes, so in alternating two actors' closeups of dialogue and action into the picture clips of unused closeups of each actor are "trims".

Two Shot
A shot, medium or otherwise, which includes two characters.

Upgrading
When an actor has worked in less than a "principal" role in a commercial but is later "upgraded" into a recognizable face in the final version of the commercial and will therefore receive residuals.

Voice-Over
An actor's voice, when his face doesn't appear on screen.

Wardrobe
Either the person who handles all wardrobe for the film, or your character's wardrobe for the role you play. It's usually found hanging in the closet of your dressing room ready for you.

Weather Permitting
The phrase used in issuing actors' calls when the weather is questionable but shooting is planned at least tentatively.

Weaving
Drifting from side to side in a shot and causing problems for the cameraman trying to hold the actor in frame.

Weekly
The term for the contract of an actor who is hired for one or more weeks on a picture, rather than being employed on a "daily".

Whites
The original pages of the shooting script (the white pages).

Wild Lines
Lines said into a mike, on or off the set, as lines only (without picture). They're for adding to the track in a dubbing session.

Work Call
Usually the details of where, at what time and to whom the actor is to report for the next day's filming.

Wrangler
The horses' straw boss on western sets. Checks to see whether you know how to get on and off and what you're supposed to be able to do when riding. If you don't know enough, a "Riding Double" is immediately called for by the Wrangler.

Wrap
At the end of a day's shooting "**It's a wrap!**" is called out. At the end of a picture's final shots it's the signal for breaking out the Wrap Party champagne.

Wrap Party
Usually held on a soundstage with catering in Hollywood, or in a hotel suite for a location film. The occasion for everybody to breathe sighs of relief and forgive everybody.

130

INDEX

Personal Notes

Personal Notes

Personal Notes

Personal Notes